The Politics of Writing Islam

Suspensions: Contemporary Middle Eastern and Islamicate Thought
Series editors: Jason Bahbak Mohaghegh and Lucian Stone

This series interrupts standardized discourses involving the Islamicate world by introducing creative and emerging ideas. The incisive works included in this series provide a counterpoint to the reigning canons of theory, theology, philosophy, literature, and criticism through investigations of vast experiential typologies – such as violence, mourning, vulnerability, tension, and humour – in light of contemporary Islamicate thought.

On the Arab Revolts and the Iranian Revolution, Arshin Adib-Moghaddam
The Politics of Writing Islam, Mahmut Mutman
The Writing of Violence in the Middle East, Jason Bahbak Mohaghegh

The Politics of Writing Islam

Voicing Difference

Mahmut Mutman

Suspensions: Contemporary Middle Eastern and
Islamicate Thought

Bloomsbury Academic
An imprint of Bloomsbury Publishing Plc

B L O O M S B U R Y
LONDON • NEW DELHI • NEW YORK • SYDNEY

Bloomsbury Academic

An imprint of Bloomsbury Publishing Plc

50 Bedford Square	1385 Broadway
London	New York
WC1B 3DP	NY 10018
UK	USA

www.bloomsbury.com

BLOOMSBURY and the Diana logo are trademarks of Bloomsbury Publishing Plc

First published 2014
Paperback edition first published 2015

British Library Cataloguing-in-Publication Data
A catalogue record for this book is available from the British Library.

ISBN: HB: 978-1-44116-524-4
PB: 978-1-47423-761-1
ePDF: 978-1-44116-249-6
ePUB: 978-1-44116-470-4

Library of Congress Cataloging-in-Publication Data
Mutman, Mahmut.
Suspensions: contemporary Middle Eastern and Islamicate thought :
voicing difference/Mahmut Mutman.
pages cm
Summary: "Critical and theoretical essays on forms of studying, writing and representing
Islam in Western humanities and literature"– Provided by publisher.
Includes bibliographical references and index.
ISBN 978-1-4411-6524-4 (hardback) – ISBN 978-1-4411-6470-4 (epub) –
ISBN 978-1-4411-6249-6 (epdf) 1. Islam and literature. 2. Islam in literature.
3. Islam–Public opinion. 4. East and West in literature. 5. Reader-response criticism.
6. Discourse analysis. I. Title.
PN605.I8M88 2014
809'.9338297–dc23
2013033179

Series: Suspensions: Contemporary Middle Eastern and Islamicate Thought

Typeset by Newgen Knowledge Works (P) Ltd., Chennai, India

Contents

Series Foreword

Poets, artists, theologians, philosophers, and mystics in the Middle East and Islamicate world have been interrogating notions of desire, madness, sensuality, solitude, death, time, space, etc. for centuries, thus constituting an expansive and ever-mutating intellectual landscape. Like all theory and creative outpouring, then, theirs is its own vital constellation—a construction cobbled together from singular visceral experiences, intellectual ruins, novel aesthetic techniques, social-political-ideological detours, and premonitions of a future—built and torn down (partially or in toto), and rebuilt again with slight and severe variations. The horizons shift, and frequently leave those who dare traverse these lands bewildered and vulnerable.

Consequently, these thinkers and their visionary ideas largely remain unknown, or worse, mispronounced and misrepresented in the so-called Western world. In the hands of imperialistic frameworks, a select few are deemed worthy of notice and are spoken on behalf of, or rather about. Their ideas are simplified into mere social formulae and empirical scholarly categories. Whereas so-called Western philosophers and writers are given full leniency to contemplate the most incisive or abstract ideas, non-Western thinkers, especially those located in the imagined realms of the Middle East and Islamicate world, are reduced to speaking of purely political histories or monolithic cultural narratives. In other words, they are distorted and contorted to fit within hegemonic paradigms that steal away their more captivating potentials.

Contributors to this series provide a counterpoint to the reigning canons of theory, theology, philosophy, literature, and criticism through investigations of the vast experiential typologies of such regions. Each volume in the series acts as a "suspension" in the sense that the authors will position contemporary thought in an enigmatic new terrain of inquiry, where it will be compelled to confront unforeseen works of critical and creative imagination. These analyses will not only highlight the full range of current intellectual and artistic trends and their benefits for the citizens of these phantom spheres but also argue that the ideas themselves are borderless, and thus of great relevance to all citizens of the world.

Jason Bahbak Mohaghegh and Lucian Stone
Series editors

Acknowledgments

This book would be impossible without the support of many friends, colleagues, and institutions.

I am grateful to the Institute for Comparative Literature and Society at Columbia University for providing an intellectual home during the 2008–9 academic year when I developed some of the ideas in this book. I especially thank Gayatri Chakravorty Spivak. Like many others, I too consider myself lucky to have received her intellectual and instutional support, and I only hope to continue to learn from her in the future.

I am dearly thankful to Vicki Kirby for teaching me the criticism of ethnography I develop in the first chapter. If it were not for her careful reading of Blanchot and Bourdieu together, I would have never been able to pose the question of cultural difference in the way I do here. Although our research paths have somewhat diverged over the years, I owe my starting point to her reading of cultural difference in terms of embodied knowledge. I have shared many of the ideas in this book with Zafer Aracagök. I am grateful to him for reading some of the pieces here, for his useful feedback and suggestions, and above all, for his true intellectual friendship. Special thanks go to my good old students and friends for the class that is their gift: Burcu Yalım, Tuğba Ayas, Emre Koyuncu, Aykan Alemdaroğlu, Fırat Berksun, Evrim Engin, Ersan Ocak, and İrem Çağıl.

Many friends and colleagues gave support to my work in various ways. I am grateful to Donna Landry, Gerald MacLean, Hamid Dabashi, Nezih Erdoğan, and Andreas Treske for their feedback, insight, and encouragement. I have been lucky to be surrounded by inspiring and brilliant colleagues in the Program in Cultural Studies at Istanbul Sehir University. I thank them for the intellectually stimulating environment they have provided and for their unwavering support. I owe a great debt of gratitude to my editors Jason Bahbak Mohaghegh and Lucian Stone for their infinite patience and faith in me as much as for their invaluable reading, comments, and criticisms. I am honored to be published by the series they have courageously set out to edit in such a difficult and yet perhaps also strangely hopeful time. I also thank Chloë Shuttlewood and Dhara Patel for their help and supervision at different stages of the publication of this work and Srikanth Srinivasan for his careful copyediting.

I am profoundly indebted to my wife Meyda Yeğenoğlu. Without her untiring support, encouragement, and care, this book would simply have not happened. I dedicate it to her, for the love she taught me.

Slightly different versions of three chapters have previously appeared with different titles in the following publications: Chapter 1 "Writing Culture: The Name of Man" was published as "Writing Culture: Postmodernism and Ethnography" in *Anthropological Theory*, Vol. 6, No. 2 (June 2006), 153–78; Chapter 4 "Resonance of Light: Reading T. E. Lawrence" was published in *Parallax*, Vol. 18, No. 1 (2012), 74–86; a slightly different version of Chapter 7, "Reciting: the Voice of the Other," was published in *Sonic Interventions, Thamyris/Intersecting: Race, Sex, Place*, No. 18, edited by Sylvia Mieszkowski, Joy Smith, and Marijke de Valck (Amsterdam: Rodopi, 2007), 103–18. I thank the publishers for permission to reprint these articles.

Introduction

The purpose of *The Politics of Writing Islam: Voicing Difference* is to offer critical engagements with a number of texts on Islam. Some of these texts are directly about Islam or Islamic cultures, some of them are indirectly so; some are scholarly, some are fictional; and yet one has nothing to do with Islam, but it has a general relevance in terms of the context in which the issue of cultural identity or cultural difference is raised. My critical readings are deconstructively inspired and are guided by ethical and political as well as theoretical and methodological concerns about knowing, representing, criticizing, or liberating Islam. The question of how such an object of knowledge and writing came to exist in the first place is not easy to answer. No doubt Islam is a religion and culture of this world "out there." But the way in which it appears as an object of discourse—and as an object of discourse and writing of such a significance that there is a whole academic apparatus that is mobilized to produce knowledge of it—is an historical matter.

This has something to do with the political aspect of Islam. Islam is often described as a "political religion," a religion in which politics and religion are difficult to separate. This is no doubt a highly controversial and complicated issue. But since it is itself a modern claim, we can delimit ourselves here to modern history. And of course, insofar as Islam is concerned, such history begins with colonialism: with the Western colonization of the Muslim periphery (which thus became periphery). This is the first politicization of Islam. For a long time, until the formation of national identity appeared, Islam was the major, if not only, ground for resistance against colonial occupation, and it often played some role in the coding of national identity. This is the first politicization of Islam as we know it because it was an entirely new process in the sense that it now occurred under a condition in which the relationship between politics and religion radically changed. In the same colonial moment of modernity, Islam was also constructed as a traditional and backward religion (which, for instance, fails to separate itself from politics). This production of Islam must be considered in terms of Orientalist power-knowledge spacing (rather than mere stereotyping), in which the Orient is produced as the Other of the Western Man/Subject and Islam as part of the Orient.[1] Movements such as pan-Islamism also appeared during this period, but they soon gave way to nationalism, which proved to be more powerful in that particular conjuncture, and which approached Islam in terms of a secularism from above.

Speaking in very general (and necessarily generalizing) terms, we might say that, in many Muslim countries, following independence, Islam was not effective as an independent political movement with a strong mass base. Islamic element was certainly used as a banner for mobilization by nationalist regimes and various different political parties. It was also mobilized against communist and socialist movements by the United States in the cold war.[2] Political Islam or "Islamism" reappeared as a new political movement in the late 1970s, largely due to the failure and crisis of modernizing authoritarian nationalist elites and the defeat and crisis of socialist movements in the Muslim periphery. This is the second politicization of Islam. Political Islam or Islamism as we have it today is a product of the last four decades of this second wave of politicization. It is an entirely new movement that came out of particular historical and social conditions, and it bears their stamp. It is not a continuation of traditional society. This surely does not mean that any study of Islam should only be the study of this Islam because it is the only existing one, but it means that no study of Islam can be made in isolation from this singular condition.

As this brief historical account shows, Islam entered modernity under Western colonialism. An important aspect of Islam's historical trajectory in modernity is political economy and class. Although it would be impossible to make a full-fledged class analysis here, recent political Islamic movements can be described, in broad brushstrokes, as an alliance between emerging provincial bourgeoisie and the poor, disenfranchised working people, in opposition to the Westernizing nationalist elite, big capital, and the Westernized urban middle-class. When these two conditions are simultaneously considered, it becomes evident that secularism simplistically modeled on the European narrative cannot work—without severe consequences—for the people of the Muslim periphery. To quote Gayatri Spivak,

> those sanitized secularists who are hysterical at the mention of religion are
> quite out of touch with the world's peoples and have buried their heads in

the sand. Class-production has allowed them to rationalize and privatize the transcendental, and they see this as the welcome telos of everybody everywhere, without historical preparation for this particular class-episteme.[3]

We should therefore emphasize the newness of this recent political Islam: the singularity of its historical production cannot be understood in terms of the secularism of the grand European narrative.

In order to open up my methodological argument, I will go back to the beginning of the recent politicization of Islam and will choose a particular moment: the one that followed the oil crisis and the Iranian revolution, when a frightful image of Islam had become pervasive in the Western media in the late 1970s and early 1980s. Edward Said called attention to a specific aspect of these representations in his book *Covering Islam* published in 1981:

> [T]he image of Islam today, in every place that one encounters it, is an *unrestrained* and *immediate* one. There is an unstated assumption, first of all, that the proper name "Islam" denotes a simple thing to which one can refer immediately, as one refers to "democracy," or to a person, or to an institution like the Catholic Church. . . . If Islam's immediacy makes it seem directly available, then its divergence from our familiar reality and norms sets it against us directly, threateningly, drastically.[4]

Given that we live now in a world in which the White House observes Ramadan, is the situation improved? Surely there is a good deal of convincing analysis and argument to the contrary. I shall give an example that reconsiders Said's original point. In an interesting study on information warfare, Tiziana Terranova felt the necessity to return to Said's analysis and drew our attention to an important aspect of it: "All possibilities for sustained critique seemed here to Said to have been made impossible because of the decline of the narrative framework that allowed the critic to speak and be understood by an interpretive community."[5] For Terranova, Said's *Covering Islam* was a pioneering study in that it offered the first analysis of a new form of hegemony based on associating images and affects *without mediations*, while the earlier analysis in his *Orientalism* showed an older form of hegemony based on discursive articulation. The new hegemony formats events and constructs microframeworks that mobilize defensive passions and prejudices. The immediate or live image is then complemented by the appearance of the experts, who make objective and calm analysis that is instrumental to hegemonic politics.

The analysis of this real mutation nevertheless depends on an assumption that is not unproblematical: the presence of a proper narrative discourse that articulates the *truth* of Islam uncontaminated by Western power and discourse.[6] This was already the problem with Said's analysis in his *Orientalism*. By an eclectic though effective use of various theoretical references from Gramsci and Williams to Foucault, Said powerfully showed how the Orient was *produced* in and by Western hegemony. But he continued to see Orientalism as an *error of representation*, whose effects can be separated and undone in a discourse that is capable of representing the true, real Orient (or Islam in our case).[7] This conventional approach, which Said maintained in the background, tends to overlook the fact that Orientalism never simply consists of clichés and stereotypes; but indeed, as Said himself has demonstrated especially in the third part of his book, it is a practice of knowledge and is part of an apparatus of knowledge, from the universities to the research centers and think-tanks. Hence it is perfectly capable of producing factual, true knowledge as well as correcting and revising the knowledge it produced, while at the same time maintaining the unequal hegemonic structure. Revised factual knowledge would certainly not make the stereotype disappear, as psychoanalysis taught us that stereotypes and knowledge or facts can live well together in the same subjective structure, and the consistency in question is of a different kind than logical or empirical consistency. No doubt, to some extent we cannot but refer to knowledge and facts, and we cannot but correct them because we are always already within language that keeps us connected to the world of reference. But, as Said put it in a fine statement that is perhaps written and understood rather too quickly, "One never ought to assume that the structure of Orientalism is nothing more than a structure of lies or of myths which, were the truth about them to be told, would simply blow away."[8]

If the belief in a truthful narrative is constitutive of the social sciences and humanities, it seemed to take a new form in the "textual" pluralism of postmodern ethnography in the late 1980s. In disciplines such as anthropology and cultural studies in which this tendency became prevalent, it led to a questioning of the power and forms of textual representation, and this was intimately connected with the question of cultural difference. The problem now was how to include the authentic voice of the other *in* the text. The *immediacy* of the media image, which Said saw as an alarming new mutation of hegemonic ideology, was confronted by a new ethnographic and/or cultural narrative in which the other was supposed to be *present* in the text in his or her *own* voice.

I open this book with a reading of this paradigm in the first chapter, a paradigm that I believe is still with us in different forms. It depends on a powerful desire for hearing the voice of the other, for having him or her speak, especially in the face of a hegemonic politics that seems to block and suppress this speech in its image and information war. I would like to argue that, as powerful as the hegemonic condition that incites this desire might be, it actually maintains the conventional anthropological assumption and takes the risk of participating in an appropriation of difference. In the first chapter, I read James Clifford's programmatic texts in which the general framework of postmodern ethnography is established.[9] I critically examine his concepts of cultural information, writing, and plurality and argue that there is an older problematic working through this new set of concepts. This is the only chapter that is not directly about Islam, but the texts I read give the most elaborate articulation of a certain politics of writing that is also relevant in the case of Islam (and perhaps it will be increasingly more so in the future).

In the second chapter, I turn to Mehdi Abedi and Michael Fischer's well-known *Debating Muslims*, almost a classic work since its publication in 1990, in the fields of postmodern ethnography, anthropology of Islam, and Iranian studies.[10] In the same vein as Clifford's postmodern ethnography, Abedi and Fischer's politics of writing Islam is ethically guided by their concern to provide an access to the humanity of Muslims. Depending on a multiplicity of voices and genres of writing, and coauthored by an Iranian and an American, the ethics of this work is grounded on the concepts of face-to-face interaction and dialogue. In its performance, however, the ethnographic voice or genre gains the upper hand, while the concept of dialogue operates epistemologically as a means of authorizing knowledge by the interlocutor rather than providing an ethical opening. Abedi and Fischer's vibrant readings of the Qur'an, the hadith or Khomenei's discourse tend to privilege legitimation rather than disputation, as the epistemological concept of dialogue creates closure in the oral, face-to-face interaction and the processes of production of difference in language are lost in an aestheticization of religious language. The use of theory in postmodern ethnography remains highly problematic, since its most significant and constitutive claim of presenting an authentic, humane access to the other by giving voice to him or her ends up in a comforting miraculation of identity.

In the third chapter, I offer an extensive reading of Pierre Bourdieu's ethnographies in Algeria, together with his critics'.[11] Bourdieu's works and his overall intellectual trajectory participate in the Eurocentric problematic in the final analysis, but this is not because he has a bias against Islam. On the contrary, his politics of writing depends largely upon not writing the name of Islam. He avoids writing this name particularly in the sociological criticism he makes of peasant time. His studies are also conventional in comparison with the high theoretical claims of postmodern ethnography (though more philosophically supported than conventional ethnography). Nevertheless, I suggest that we return to his work, for it is much more interesting in terms of the way Bourdieu approached native knowledge as practical and improvizational embodied memory, which he called "habitus." There is something to learn from Bourdieu's healthy resistance to reducing the native's complex, embodied, and shifting practical world to the ethnographer's theoretical diagrams of kinship or the agricultural calendar constructed on the pages of his notebook.

Ethnographers of Islam, such as Gregory Starrett, Saba Mahmood, and Abdellah Hammoudi, were right in criticizing him for excluding the written culture of Islam from his ethnography.[12] I argue, however, that this is not because his concept of habitus is some wordless, unconscious bodily habit that excludes reflection (on the contrary it might indeed be useful in considering the embodied memory of Islamic subjectivity, its ethos, and its ethics); it is rather because, with the intellectual ambition of criticizing structuralism, Bourdieu carefully isolated the Kabyle society from all its written Islamic culture and constructed it as an ethnographically manageable and comparable mythico-ritual oral unit (while the above ethnographers had to assimilate the concept of discourse into consciousness rather than seeing its connection with the body). Bourdieu's criticism of structuralism depended on a phenomenological analysis of time, which only partially deconstructed the conventional concept of time. This confined him to the grand narrative of sociology and to the sociology of a practical, working body, which barely acknowledges desire and death, and eventually disallowed him from seeing the possibility of the link between aesthetics and ethics *in* the openness of embodied memory. Bourdieu's ethnography is a scientism, which paradoxically takes the risk of turning his declared intimacy with the native (informant) into a narcissistic attachment to his own rural European roots. In this chapter, I also elaborate on the concept of absolute past and the problematic of time that I have introduced in the previous chapters.

Given the enthusiasm that the Arab Spring has generated in the West, and the apparent new project of redrawing the borders of the Middle East, it might be timely to return to the good Orientalists, as they have sometimes been called, of the late nineteenth and the early twentieth century, which was perhaps a similar conjuncture. But I also have another ambition in reading the texts of T. E. Lawrence and Isabelle Eberhardt in the fourth and fifth chapters: to discuss a series of theoretical concepts, which are unfolded in their texts, such as landscape, desire, and nomadism, and the question of how we inhabit or occupy the earth, and how this is related to the concepts of sovereignty and writing.[13] Both crossdressers and sexually adventurous writers, one a homosexual British spy and the other an anarchist Sufi European woman, the texts of Lawrence and Eberhardt have been subject to close critical reading in postcolonial studies. In the case of Lawrence, Said offered a careful reading of his position as a new moment in Western colonialism and Orientalism, which signified a passage from a static to a dynamic or narrative point of view, one which was appreciative of the culture of the other while keeping the founding presupposition of its backwardness intact. In an almost completely opposite direction, and bypassing the question of colonialism, Gilles Deleuze read Lawrence as a great writer of landscapes and an inventor of revolutionary struggle in the desert.[14] I argue that, while Deleuze's reading is important in that it offers a fascinating insight into the desert of Lawrence's desire, his struggle of inhabiting it (both "landscaping" and "landscaped"), the place of colonialism cannot be easily dismissed in the production of this desire, and the resulting fabula is not the Arab's but the British man's.

The question becomes more intricate in the case of Isabelle Eberhardt, who, unlike the cunning Lawrence, had literally spent herself in the desert of her desire and whose short life ended with a tragic death in a flood. Deleuze and Guattari's concept of nomadism might indeed be useful in understanding her experience, when it is understood in terms of the problem of inhabiting the earth rather than as an abstract notion of displacement, or simply a reflection of their alleged colonialism. Going through Deborah Root's and Laura Rice's delicate readings of nomadism, travel, and colonialism in Bowles and Eberhardt, I demonstrate that the question of nomadism takes a singular turn in Eberhardt.[15] Eberhardt's writing is not independent of the sovereign imperial discourse of the West, but through it, she also develops a nomadic desire for an original intimate relationship with the earth, which Georges Bataille would have called sovereign in another sense, and which he related to religious experience, or as a search for it. While she remains a classical case of the intimacy of law and transgression, or of the axiomatics of imperialism and nineteenth-century feminism, her singular contribution to it seems to be her desire to reorder the order of love as a woman.

In Chapter 6, I critically examine the question of gender within the Islamic discourse. I follow the track of sexual difference in the psychoanalytical and fictional readings (and writings) of it by Fethi Benslama, Abdelkebir Khatibi, and Assia Djebar.[16] Fethi Benslama's work unfolds the Islamic narrative of sexual difference in various textual instances. Employing a Lacanian approach, Benslama judges that the Islamic claim of following an Abrahamic line of descent is problematic. Unlike Christianity and Judaism, Islam's God is not a father who is implicated in the geneaology that establishes and legitimizes the religion. This is also related with the absence of Hagar in the Qur'an. According to him, this lack has far-reaching implications, and it makes Islam suffer from a torment of origin. Benslama's approach is useful in the sense that it opens up the Abrahamic and Islamic texts for a comprehensive reading of sexual difference. But I argue that his mode of employment of psychoanalysis is dangerously essentializing. He completely isolates Islam from its history while pretending not to do so and making a judgment on its present condition. His insistence that Islam cannot belong to a modern political structure is simply dogmatic, and his failure to give a satisfactory account of the rise of political Islam is telling. Declaring that Islam suffers from a problem of origin, he frees himself of the burden of explaining the complex history of contemporary Islamic movements. Since Islam is a return of (the torment of) origin, we can safely return to the origin of Islam to understand what the "problem" is. This essentializing attitude not only repeats the same "Islamist" movement in reverse but also hides the failure and crisis of elitist authoritarian secularism as well as global political economy, which are two major historical causes of the rise of political Islam.

In the final chapter, I read Abdelkebir Khatibi's "Frontiers" and Assia Djebar's *Far from Madina*, and therein taking Gayatri Spivak's readings as a guide.[17] In a very different spirit than Benslama, Khatibi interprets the singularity of Islam as the prophet Muhammad's sacrifice of his signature. I connect this reading with the opening order of the Qur'an to "recite" and the practice of recitation in Islam, and suggest that what Khatibi calls the lost book or Spivak the encrypted signature must be considered as an uncanny past haunting and disrupting language in recitation. It is this past that returns in the social condition of exclusion, alienation, and oppression, but it is immediately sanctified in the letter. However, as the reciting of an absolute past rather than simply a present past, recitation is also open—it can be seen as spectralization in the sense that Gayatri Spivak finds in Assia Djebar's *Far from Madina*. This chapter ends with a discussion of what Spivak calls "radical counterfactual future past."

In conclusion, I make a few observations on Islamism or political Islam in our current context. While the new developments following the Arab Spring brought political Islam to power in many places, it also introduced this movement into a new context. Political Islam is now in a new relationship with capitalist, neoliberal techno-rationality, which it supplements with a moralizing identity politics. It is this new context that might lead to a more interesting and challenging result than the much-feared image of a fundamentalist regime of *sharia*. While the emerging Islamic governmentality is involved in neoliberal privatization and a new biopolitics, Islamic subjectivity enters into a new process of autoimmunization. I conclude by discussing the difficult task of detranscendentalizing religion while being able to respond to the oppressed within it.

Part I

Ethnographies: Writing Culture

Writing Culture: The Name of Man

Postmodernism is a strange object. On the one hand, it is often seen as a new opening and a new pluralistic method and outlook in the field of the humanities.[1] On the other hand, it is associated with the logic of commodification and is regarded as the most appropriate category for articulating "the cultural dominant" of our time.[2] When it is approached within the general purview of modernity, perhaps these two readings are not in contradiction since the apparent dynamic of modernity has always been the latest idea or commodity or technology in the market. On this level of generality, the argument for commodification is surely applicable for so-called postmodernism, as indeed it would be perfectly applicable for the last, most fervent liberal or Marxist criticism of it. Yet there is something disturbing in the discursive production of this object. What to do with the "post" of postmodernism, as it clearly promises a "beyond" of modernity? Further, there is the obvious fact that the French names associated with it (Barthes, Lacan, Lyotard, Baudrillard, Foucault, Derrida, and Deleuze) are all radical thinkers, most of whom are read as contributing to Marx's analysis as well as radical critics of its orthodox articulation. Is this "beyond" then only illusory and postmodernism another new commodity on the market, or is it an interruption of the grand narrative of commodification?[3] But the question might be rather uninteresting in this form, as if we have already decided what the term refers to. I would like to suggest that the transparency of the category of postmodernism might be suspect. Rather than modernity or its beyond, it might be advisable to focus on the limit that this notion of "post" or "beyond" promises to transcend or overcome. In this chapter, I will suggest that the limit in question as well as the question of the limit that it evokes are more intricate than they seem. I would further like to argue that, in order to see the convoluted nature of the limit or margin, we should perhaps look for a rather marginal site, the "ethnographic" postmodern, where the political unconscious or problematic of postmodernism might become readable in unexpected ways.

The ethnographic site

Indeed, what better site to test the homogeneity of the category of postmodernism than the border that distinguishes the West and the rest? And, what better site than anthropology, the science of man and of culture, watching precisely over this border? In the last two decades, anthropology as a characteristic form of knowledge of modernity has appeared to be one of the contested sites in the so-called postmodern debate. However marginal the anthropological or ethnographic debate might seem (especially when compared with the debates in literary criticism, philosophy, or psychoanalysis), it nevertheless witnessed the emergence of a challenging, new, "postmodern" ethnography or anthropology. The well-known collection, *Writing Culture*, by James Clifford and George E. Marcus,[4] served as a general statement. Another methodological work by George E. Marcus and Michael M. J. Fischer was also an attempt to articulate a similar sense of ethnographic work engaging questions of narrative and dialogue.[5] Johannes Fabian's theoretical critique of conventional ethnography and project of articulating a new ethnographic temporality in his *Time and the Other*[6] was already pointing in the same direction, as well as an important methodological article by Stephen Tyler.[7] Clifford further elaborated and developed the new ethnographic project in his later works,[8] while Fabian extended his reflections on time and anthropology[9] and Tyler his reflections on speech and writing.[10] Last but not least, Michael M. J. Fischer and Mehdi Abedi's *Debating Muslims* can be regarded as an exemplary fieldwork in postmodern ethnography.[11]

I am well aware that the legitimacy of this category might be open to debate, as the authors just mentioned have varying approaches to a critical and reflexive moment in anthropology and may not all agree on their appellation as "postmodern"—indeed perhaps none of them would, except Tyler. I use the term to refer to a specific articulation of this critical or reflexive moment: not just a new interpretive consciousness beyond positivist objectivism (such as we already have with the interpretive anthropology of Clifford Geertz[12]) but a particular tendency toward dialogue or communication with the anthropological other, a particular desire to bring this other into the text, to articulate his or her voice in a more plural anthropological representation. In summary, postmodern ethnography promises difference and otherness through and beyond a modern form of knowledge—anthropology—which, we must note, is itself established on a sense of culture as always belonging to an "other."

This is therefore a new moment in anthropology and in the humanities in general. It problematizes conventional anthropological representation of cultural others by placing its epistemological framework within a power structure including its colonial legacy and introduces a critical method in interdisciplinary spirit, that is, an entirely new set of concepts, issues, and problems such as power and representation, textuality and textualization, voice and narrative, which find their echo in other fields (such as philosophy and literature). I certainly do not think that the new critical or postmodern ethnography is simply a theoretical and methodological enterprise. It has articulated itself in a number of ethnographic studies that would require more detailed readings that I cannot undertake here.[13] Instead it seemed useful to me to focus on what appears to be a series of programmatic propositions, concepts, and arguments that are well expressed in a limited number of essays by James Clifford. My focus is intentionally narrow, and I do not aim to read Clifford's whole work. Although Clifford himself is a cultural historian, it would be inadvisable to deny his attempt to produce a more or less coherent set of concerns and formulations common to many ethnographies in the last two decades because he is an outsider or because he has not done fieldwork himself.[14] I approach his methodological essays as offering the most lucid theoretical elaboration of the general framework and theses of "postmodern ethnography."

Clifford himself now seems to regard his work as belonging to an earlier conjuncture in anthropology. This is how he describes his two important books in a recent interview:

> Books like *Writing Culture* and *The Predicament of Culture* have been part of a ferment, part of something already going on, that has, I think, significantly changed anthropological practices. Certainly those works did not introduce some new paradigm, the "postmodern anthropology" people sometimes love to hate. But the books, and the ferment that made them possible, did raise a set of critical questions that remain on the agenda of cross-cultural representation.[15]

As Clifford also emphasizes, his influence is obviously not a matter of following a number of methodological principles outlined in his programmatic texts. Clifford's work might be described as giving expression to a series of theoretical, methodological, and ideological transformations that were already occurring in the academic as well as the social and political world. But for exactly this reason, his theoretical texts produced programmatic effects in clearly outlining a new ethnographic project, if not a paradigmatic set of methodological principles having a transcendent status with regard to ethnographic practice. This is precisely why his theoretical arguments deserve a close reading. His critical questioning and problematizing of disciplinary borders (e.g. between anthropology and travel writing, hence literature) or of concepts (e.g. positivist notions of observation and writing) are productive challenges of a critical historian and interdisciplinary scholar.[16] But Clifford went further in formulating a number of methodological statements, which explicitly aimed to reconstruct and reform the ethnographic field. His singular reformulation of a new ethnographic project is surely not the only response to these ongoing phenomena, but it is a particularly significant one developed in the context of progressive Anglo-American academia, since it clearly brings together, in a theoretical and methodological fashion, a number of new issues and themes significant to many researchers and contributes to an emerging concept of culture in the humanities.[17] This is why I would like to examine some of the constitutive assumptions of the new ethnographic project as they are articulated in Clifford's seminal theoretical essays (and not his more historical work, for instance, on the relations between surrealism and ethnography, or the concept of travel).

I must also mention that I am not an anthropologist but a social theorist by training and I came to ethnographic arguments through my own theoretical, political, and cultural trajectory, which began with Edward Said's critique of Orientalism and its implications for the social sciences and humanities. If, however, I do not consider my disciplinary background (or lack of it) as an obstacle at all, this is not in the name of an abstract principle of interdisciplinarity as a merely rational academic aim. I follow the track/trace of a singular problem, the problem of (cultural) difference, which does not simply traverse manifold disciplines but retraces their margins/borders as well as reinscribing and reformulating itself on those margins. The purpose of this chapter is not to offer a new anthropological theoretical or methodological framework, nor to impose one on anthropology from outside, but to re-mark, in a deconstructive spirit, the singularity of a problem at the margin, the cut or angle of the discipline of anthropology, questioning its ethnographic protocols and methodologies while respecting its labor.[18]

Although this chapter will be critical of the new ethnography, it should be only too obvious that it is written in debt to the event its argument marked: the question of representing others, of who is speaking in a text or discourse in the name of whom and how, as a political and ethical problem. These questions are posed with great vehemence especially in James Clifford's seminal texts, which demonstrate that the disturbance one has with the "post" of postmodernism is ethico-political, implying a responsibility concerning representation. I would like to demonstrate in what follows that the ethico-political issue of representation proves to be more complicated than it appears, and while postmodern ethnography fails to come to terms with this complexity, we also need to ask what this failure means for the cultural description of the so-called postmodernism.

Because of the intimate relationship between representation and responsibility, Clifford opens his argument by drawing our attention to the textual aspect of ethnographic representation, ethnography as writing culture. In his introduction to *Writing Culture* to which several of the names mentioned earlier contributed, Clifford criticizes the narrow sense in which writing is understood in anthropology as "keeping good field notes."[19] For him, this notion of writing implies a concept of culture that is uncontaminated, transparent. It is necessary to examine rhetorical and textual aspects of ethnography, for not only does culture have a constructed and contested nature, but a series of exclusions—which characterized the modern Western notion of science—and is made possible by a number of rhetorical mechanisms. The scientific text can no longer be isolated, in positivist fashion, from the rhetorical devices that it employs, or the social and historical contexts of power in which it is produced.[20] In another article on the role of ethnographic allegory, Clifford powerfully demonstrates how ethnographic texts are made up of allegories, and how it would indeed be impossible for readers to make sense of these texts if our readings were not allegorical.[21] All ethnographic texts are constructions, fictions, "economies of truth" through which "power and history work."[22] The mapping of non-Western cultures positions the Western knowing subject as cultural and political authority. After arguing that ethnography has its own political economy of truth, Clifford reaches the conclusion that "ethnographic truths are thus inherently partial—committed and incomplete."[23]

In declaring ethnographic or cultural truth as partial, however, Clifford makes a universal claim on the truth of truth, and occupies a universal position from which he can say that all knowledge, including his own, is partial. Such an argument completes incompletion by appropriating it as truth.[24] A concern with questions of representation (i.e. questions of who is speaking in a text in the name of whom and how) would require that we ask who can actually make a statement in which the truth of culture is declared as incomplete. I suggest that we take the sense of "can-do-ness" seriously because Clifford's claim on the nature of truth assumes a position of power or *pouvoir* in Michel Foucault's original French sense, which implies a capacity to say or do things.[25] The play of universalism and relativism, which has characteristically been at the core of anthropology, is not overcome but rather reformulated in terms of a universally known and guaranteed partiality. Who is the subject of this epistemological guarantee? Where is its institutional, geographical, or political site? I will discuss this notion of partiality further later in this chapter.

According to Clifford, the meaning of a text is plural and polysemic, produced and multiplied by several levels of signification, interrupting the rhetoric of presence, questioning realism.[26] In fact the notion of ethnographic allegory is both fruitful and problematic. On the one hand, Clifford textualizes ethnography and shows the complexity of its representational practice. On the other hand, he desires to give this multilayered nature of ethnographic text a moral and political ideal by translating it into a notion of plurality. He opens his argument by referring to Marjorie Shostak's popular ethnographic work *Nisa: The Life and Words of a !Kung Woman*, and cites the passage where Nisa tells the story of her giving birth to a child. Although "the story has great immediacy" and "Nisa's voice is unmistakable," we do "more than register a unique event."[27] A long quotation is necessary here:

> The story's unfolding requires us, first, to imagine a cultural norm (!Kung birth, alone in the bush) and then to recognize a common human experience (the quiet heroism of childbirth, feelings of postpartum wonder and doubt). The story of an occurrence of birth somewhere in the Kalahari Desert cannot remain just that. It implies both local cultural meanings and a general story of birth. A difference is posited and transcended. Moreover Nisa's story tells us (how could it not?) something basic about woman's experience. Shostak's life of a !Kung individual inevitably becomes an allegory of (female) humanity.[28]

How to read this passage from the "cultural" to the "human"? Is this simply a question of mediating immediacy? Clifford wants to have both: the immediacy of Nisa's voice and the commonness of female humanity—even though he recognizes that actually the hearing of Nisa's voice corresponds to a certain conjuncture of US feminism. Although Clifford writes as if there is no hierarchy between these different levels of a text, in the very performance of his writing he cannot deny the hierarchical organization. There is nothing in Clifford's reading of Nisa that paralyzes the textual production of meaning. His claim is that the ethnographic narrative can represent the uniqueness of the event of birth. In this sense, Clifford's notion of allegory is what one of his references for the notion of allegory, Paul de Man, would call "symbol"—a sign that depends on the unity of subject and object—whereas allegory in Paul de Man's understanding "consists only in the repetition . . . of a previous sign with which it can never coincide, since it is of the essence of this previous sign to be of pure anteriority."[29] While symbol denies temporality and finitude, allegory highlights precisely temporal difference. Reminiscent of de Man's notion of symbol, Clifford argues that, in ethnographic allegory, "a difference is posited and transcended" and that "these kind of transcendent meanings are not abstractions or interpretations 'added' to the original 'simple' account. Rather they are conditions of its meaningfulness."[30]

While Clifford emphasizes transcendence of difference as a condition of meaningfulness, the text articulates a kind of abysmal limit where Nisa's narrative repeats itself in a strange (un)ending, a loss of meaning. Following the birth of her first child, Nisa experiences a strange feeling of wonder, which accompanies her physical exhaustion: "Then I thought, 'A big thing like that? How could it possibly have come from my genitals?' I sat there and looked at her, and looked and looked and looked."[31] The "look" repeats itself endlessly in the absence of words. Does this "look" not refer to Paul de Man's "pure anteriority," that is, "the essence of the previous sign" in the structure of allegory? Can the event of birth be signified or represented? At this unique moment, the immediate aftermath of birth, Nisa's self cannot form "an illusory unity with the non-self, which is now, fully, though painfully, recognized as non-self."[32] Although Paul de Man is writing about romantic poetry, we can still borrow his sense of the limits of making sense here and acknowledge the fact that there is no transcendence of difference in Nisa's look. The ethnographer, the so-called *participant* observer, cannot give voice to a speaking subject that is herself captured and ruptured in the *mis en abyme* of self-less organic life. The ethnographic allegorization is not merely a visualization, a *mis en scène*, but an avoidance of this abysmal scene where life is indissociable from the rupture of violence—the violence of birth. Shostak's ethnographic text is not maintained at all but is interrupted by the very look that she cannot help but articulate. This is not a new ethnography but the appearance, within the ethnographic text, of its limit. Such moments would be rare, if not nonexistent at all. They cannot be produced by an ethnographic program, which is a program of knowledge, of making sense of the other, and they will remain marginal and accidental to ethnographic text, produced unconsciously.

. . . or the scene of writing

Clifford's criticism of the visualism of ethnography takes the form of a distinction between textual levels, while the assumption of a scene is maintained: what appears other to the senses on the level of description is an underlying similitude by a coherent series of perceptions. Hence "ethnography's narrative of specific differences presupposes, and always refers to, an abstract plane of similarity."[33] This representational process is essentially the same in both evolutionary and relativist anthropologies. Strangely, for Clifford there is a way to avoid this explicitly hierarchical nature of ethnographic representation:

> Once all meaningful levels in a text, including theories and interpretations, are recognized as allegorical, it becomes difficult to view one of them as privileged, accounting for the rest. Once this anchor is dislodged, the staging and valuing of multiple allegorical registers or "voices," becomes an important area of concern for ethnographic writers.[34]

One may certainly read a text in ways that upset or undo its hierarchical organization, but how can one construct a nonhierarchical text by simply understanding the fact that a text is made up of several levels, that is to say, allegorical? This straightforward acceptance of plurality—what we must call a homogeneous and moralistic understanding of plurality—is a constitutive feature of Clifford's argument. Shostak's *Nisa* is offered as a text that illustrates this moral and epistemological ideal. Clifford's reading offers interesting insights into this widely read text, but his "three allegorical registers" (cultural subject, gendered subject, ethnographic production as dialogue) never encounter any limit to their meaning. Although Clifford finds scientific (generalizing) register in discrepancy with the others, which are more dialogically articulated, all three registers, all allegories return to the knowledge and meaning of an experience in his reading—indeed nothing quite remains irreducible. Generally speaking, his notion of plurality remains undeveloped, since, from a theoretical point of view, throughout his argument Clifford actually talked about only two levels: descriptive and allegorical (others are only mentioned). Indeed in other places too, wherever the notion of plurality is employed, there is always the ritual and ceremonial passage of a series of binarisms: recorded observation versus living voice, ethnographer versus native, descriptive versus allegorical, scientific versus poetic. But Clifford resolutely avoids dealing with this difficulty with the two, or binarism, always insisting on a sense or image of plurality that thus remains rather empty.

In a similar way, in the Introduction, Clifford proposes "a discursive rather than a visual paradigm," a shift away from the observing eye to the expressive, subjective speech and gesture.[35] New ethnography's discursive paradigm aims to include a plurality of voices in the text: poetic as well as scientific, allegorical as well as descriptive, and most important of all, the native's as well as the anthropologist's.[36] The native voice is strategic here: it is an original and authentic voice that is repressed in the visual paradigm. Postmodern ethnography's aim, its textual ideal, is to represent this voice in writing. In the Introduction, Clifford describes Stephen Tyler's formulation as "the crucial poetic problem for a discursive ethnography."[37] This is "how to achieve by written means what speech creates, and to do it without simply imitating speech."[38] How does Clifford understand the relationship between speech and writing? In "Ethnographic Allegory," he also offers a critique of "ethnographic pastoralism," that is, the fixing of societies in a tribal or traditional past. This allegory of cultural loss (of tradition) and textual rescue (in ethnography) is connected to the story of passage from the oral to the written cultures:

> Every ethnography enacts such a movement, and this is the source of peculiar authority that finds both rescue and irretrievable loss—a kind of death in life— in the making of texts from events and dialogues . . . The text embalms the event as it extends its "meaning." The fieldworker presides over, and controls in some degree, the making of a text out of life . . . The text is a record of something enunciated, in a past. The structure, if not the thematic content, of pastoral is repeated.[39]

Clifford argues at length why this can no longer be the case. This "no longer" here is undoubtedly one of the senses of the postmodern, its assumption of an external historical limit. Clifford gives a fine description of this set of conditions. First of all, the ethnographer is not the sole or primary bringer of culture into writing, hence the intertextual predicament; secondly, informants increasingly read and write; thirdly, tribal peoples become increasingly literate. And lastly, Clifford argues, Jacques Derrida has shown us that writing is not tied to alphabetic writing but must be considered as "the broad range of marks, spatial articulations, gestures and other inscriptions at work in human cultures" and has extended "the definition of the 'written,' in effect smudging its clear distinction from the 'spoken.'"[40] This "broad" description is closer to Leroi-Gourhan's concept of writing than Derrida's.[41] The latter offers no definition of writing and his concept of writing depends on the notion of "graphematicity"—markability. Clifford's confusion is not without reasons, as we will see in a moment. He rightly points out that, for Derrida, ethnographic writing cannot be seen as "an exterior imposition on a 'pure,' unwritten oral/aural universe."[42] We must therefore see ethnographic writing as "more complex"; the status of the ethnographer who brings the culture into writing is undercut. Clifford asks:

> Who, in fact, writes a myth that is recited into a tape recorder, or copied down to become part of field notes? Who writes (in a sense going beyond transcription) an interpretation of custom produced through intense conversations with knowledgeable native collaborators?[43]

This must also be the difficulty in a book such as Shostak's *Nisa*, in which Nisa's "own" voice is put into writing by Shostak as we have seen in the example given earlier. When Clifford asks "who writes," he means which of the two subjects, the anthropologist or the native? If anthropology is a knowledge predicated on the native, indeed the whole anthropological text is written by him or her—even though this writing is denied to the native. By assuming an opposition between transcription and interpretation while wishing to transform the native's status from object to subject, Clifford seems to move within a traditional concept of writing. In deconstruction, however, generalized writing is not just writing in the broad sense but also a concept that refers to a nonrecoverable loss. In other words, what is important in any text, including the ethnographic text, is not only what is inscribed but also what cannot be inscribed. Nisa's uncanny expression noticed and registered by Shostak (". . . looked and looked and looked") points to something without being able to signify it and thus opens the text into a generalized loss. Such a loss is also singular, and such a singularity is, in our case, the singularity of the event of birth. While such a singular affect can only be brought up in the text, there is also a sense in which no text can signify it (otherwise Clifford would not be speaking of the "immediacy" of this "unique event"). But Clifford's impulsive concern with "who speaks" in the text or "who writes" the text seems to have been guided by a moral anxiety of giving voice to the other rather than a careful marking of this singular moment; hence his translation of textual complexity into a moral ideal of plurality. This is a recuperative strategy of representation, which moves, in a single gesture, from suppressing the loss to the conjuring up of a textual plurality. Derrida's argument would be against precisely this gesture of attaching the loss to the pathos of the arrival of writing or representation. While Derrida generalizes the loss within the economy of writing, Clifford's theoretical gesture is redemptive, accommodating speech within ethnographic representation and thus transcending the limit in favor of a redemptive pluralism.[44]

In his more recent work, *Routes*, Clifford articulates the same ideal as follows:

> The staging of translated, edited "voices," to produce a "polyphonic" authority has never been an unproblematic exercise. But represented voices can be powerful indices of a living people—more so even than photographs, which however realistic and contemporary, always evoke a certain irreducible past tense. And to the extent that quotations are attributed to discrete individuals, they can communicate a sense of indigenous diversity.[45]

Clifford's aim is not to problematize the ethnographic text here, but to convince the anthropologist to adopt this supposedly postmodern invention, just as he said for the allegorical or multilayered structure of text. In a characteristic statement, he already formulated this in his introduction to *Writing Culture*:

> once accepted and built into ethnographic art, a rigorous sense of partiality can be a source of representational tact" and "once dialogism and polyphony are regarded as modes of textual production, monophonic authority is questioned, revealed to be characteristic of a science that has claimed to represent cultures.[46]

This moment marks an important shift in postmodern ethnography's argument. In arguing that ethnography is writing, Clifford emphasizes that it constructs, fabricates truth and knowledge rather than simply representing facts. In his attempt to include the native informant's voice, however, he offers a new "diplomatic" strategy of representation in which this voice is marked as such. Changing the strategy of representation from an exclusionary to an inclusionary one fails to interrogate the very place in which the other is included. Is this not the place from which Clifford announces that all truth is partial? New ethnography's appeal to notions of experience and voice depends on the assumption that an authentic expression of cultural diversity is possible. But this attempt to repair the exclusion fails to interrogate the very demand that the "other" should speak up—a conventional anthropological/ethnographic demand.[47] This inclusion of the "native voice" is postmodern ethnography's stronghold, the very stake of its claim to be different from conventional ethnography. As we again learn from Jacques Derrida's deconstruction, this problematic of voice assumes a conventional concept of human subject, according to which the human subject can bring his or her experience back in speech.[48] The postmodern graphing of culture is not beyond or outside what Derrida has called Western metaphysics.

At the threshold of knowledge

I would like to explore the thesis of incompleteness/partiality a little further. Although my earlier criticism of Clifford's notion of incompleteness is logical, perhaps he must be granted a concept of incompleteness in the sense of a processual incompleteness, hence maintaining a possibility of working out or elaboration understood in the Gramscian sense.[49] Although Clifford might agree with this, such an agreement should certainly require a recomposition of his argument for he uses the notions of partiality and incompleteness interchangeably. But the further difficulty is that Clifford's argument is ordered by an epistemological and methodological desire for a new, better, and inclusive discourse. If the course of knowledge and culture follows Clifford in his good intention, such a position should leave room for others to speak, include them, give them recognition, and recognize their "proper" selves. Can this project of reappropriation produce its desired effect? Such an effect is only possible on the condition that it remains blind to the other's resistance to anthropological subjectivation. This irreducibility of the otherness of the other, and of the relation to the other, is called ex-appropriation by Derrida.[50] By the concept of ex-appropriation, Derrida is not referring to excluding, disappropriating or expropriating others, to deprive them of the ownership of their selves or property, but the other's radical resistance to the knowing and speaking subject's self, discourse, or knowledge so that it becomes impossible for the subject to totalize and to appropriate. The question here is not a question of the other, nor a question of understanding the other or letting the other speak, but a question of the subject of knowledge. Focusing on such a moment of ex-appropriation or of the impossibility of appropriation is therefore not an irrelevant, irresponsible intellectual point at all; it is the ethico-political opening itself. Because it is at such a point that the discourse or text is ruptured, this is the moment of keeping it open to others and otherness. This point or moment (of deconstruction) happens, or better put, it is in the structure of our experience.[51]

I should begin by following Clifford's argument. If no individual member of a culture can fully retrieve cultural knowledge in his/her consciousness as postmodern ethnography insists, this does not necessarily mean that his/her knowledge is partial with respect to a universal "truth of culture." This is surely the old problem of relativism, which I have already pointed out in this chapter. But it is also more than that. Clifford offers a good example of his notion of the partiality of cultural truth/knowledge:

> Ethnographers are more and more like the Cree hunter who (the story goes) came to Montreal to testify in court concerning the fate of his hunting lands in the new James Bay hydroelectric scheme. He would describe his way of life. But when administered the oath he hesitated: "I am not sure I can tell the truth . . . I can only tell what I know."[52]

The new ethnographer wishes to see himself in the position of the Cree hunter. His model of partial knowledge is rooted in the very partiality and incompleteness of cultural knowledge itself. However, what is at stake in the Cree hunter's admission is not simply the partiality or incompleteness of his knowledge in the quasi-philosophical, general, and universal sense Clifford means when he writes that "all knowledge is partial." Troubled and distressed by the pressure of a system based on an appropriative relationship to a finalistic truth, the Cree hunter can but react to what the legal procedure demands from him ("truth, nothing but the truth"). It is this particular confrontation that compels him to admit the limited and particular nature of his knowledge, a strategic move in a particular context of power. But since Clifford offers this example as an instance of cultural knowledge in general, he must be responded to on this level. The hunter's position may not be as transparent as it seems. For, in necessarily admitting the limit, he is now in performative possession of it: he knows that he does not know. This is an inevitable entanglement that emerges as a result of being inserted into the interrogative abstract syntax of law and language.[53] This is why, rather than simply accepting the limited nature of knowledge (which might be a hidden acceptance of the law of culture), it might be more advisable to ask what this limit of knowledge is. But the query of the being (the "is") of the limit of knowledge delivers no straightforward answer. Maurice Blanchot draws our attention to how knowledge is bound to miss its limit:

> There is an "I do not know" that is at the limit of knowledge but that belongs to knowledge. We always pronounce it too early, still knowing all—or too late, when I no longer know that I do not know.[54]

In order to see the relevance of Blanchot's deconstruction of the (non)knowledge of the limit of knowledge, I need to return to a well-known definition of collective knowledge. Cultural or social, that is, collective/communal knowledge, is often seen as inscribed in body, words, and actions, constituting a level of language that is not readily available to consciousness but is perhaps "known" in a different, a sort of intuitive, way. This is what is often meant by the tacit character of such knowledge—which also implies the paradoxical sense of a nativity outside consciousness. Although Pierre Bourdieu would appear a rather conventional figure from a postmodern ethnographic perspective—as he has, for instance, no manifest desire to articulate a native voice in his text—he is attentive to precisely such a complexity. In an important methodological criticism and a kind of warning to the ethnographer, he complicates the widely accepted definition of collective knowledge by introducing into it the very subject who is supposed to know it and can therefore appropriate it. I am referring to his definition of "class habitus." In Bourdieu's text, this appears as a criticism of American symbolic interactionism and ethnomethodology:

> interpersonal relations are never, except in appearance, individual-to-individual relationships and the truth of an interaction is never entirely contained in the interaction.[55]

Surely no ethnography can overlook this careful warning. But what is at stake here may not be transparent either. For Bourdieu's useful critical warning about an outsider's accessibility to cultural or social space is made possible by the conventional epistemological figure of "appearance vs. truth." Does this philosophical language not assume that there is some kind of access to the truth of a collectivity, that there is a "first interaction" in which this truth is present? Bourdieu's philosophically learned, sophisticated, and vigilant text would not easily yield to this interpretation. The French sociologist produced his concept of "habitus" by introducing philosophical elaborations (especially on time and body) that he borrowed from a strange mixture of seventeenth-century rationalism and modern phenomenology (Leibniz, Spinoza, Hegel, Husserl, Heidegger, and Merleau-Ponty) and used to rewrite classical social theories (Marx, Weber, and Durkheim). This singular theoretical operation has the great merit of drawing our attention to the embodied, inscribed, and fluctuating nature of sociality. But Bourdieu's endless and circular redefinitions and elaborations of habitus, which is marked by his desire to offer a methodologically more refined understanding of sociality beyond binarisms of "subject vs. object" or "structure vs. agency," can also be read as instances of a symptomatic, though often productive, failure. A founding cognitive desire, consistent with the phenomenological tradition he follows, marks Bourdieu's notion of past as an originary past that was once present. This becomes clear in the definition of the past as a present past, when, for instance, Bourdieu agrees with Durkheim that "it is yesterday's man who inevitably predominates in us."[56] The belief in knowledge stored in a (present) past makes it difficult to think the necessary failure of (non)knowledge and to attend to the radical impossibility articulated in Blanchot's uncanny statement. If only the past were a radical or absolute past, that is to say if only it were a past that has never been present (as we learn, for instance, from Gilles Deleuze's reading of Bergson[57]), then we would have a chance to take note of such a limit. Bourdieu's cautionary remark must therefore be supplemented by the deconstruction of the philosophical tradition he follows. Especially Jacques Derrida's deconstruction has demonstrated the impossibility of an originary experience present to itself.[58] If collective/communal or cultural knowledge is one that comes in experience, then it must be kept in mind that there is an aspect to all experience that remains irreducible to presence, but is related to absence and loss. Following Derrida then, I suggest that we approach collective/communal knowledge as always subjected to an absolute past: a past that has never been present—yet a past that is always here without being present. This absolute past or *différance* produces differences, spacing them, while withdrawing "itself" from the differences it produces. In Derrida's own words, "if différance is (and I also cross out the is) what makes possible the presentation of the being-present, it is never presented as such."[59] This loss is also what I have lost at the limit of knowledge in Blanchot's attentive thinking: the limit whose movement I necessarily miss when I admit my ignorance while still remaining within knowledge. One does not have to regard this limit experience as negative at all, since the limit is always already on the move. It is an opening where the knowing subject (or the subject of discourse) is exposed to an infinite questioning, and not to a transcendental signified (the meaning of birth, of what the "other" says or desires and so on).

Postmodern ethnography's attempt at appropriating plurality and otherness in an ethnographic text is therefore necessarily mistaken, for the subject of such a project is constituted in an imaginary appropriation of the limit of knowledge. This is a failure to remark the limit rather than an opening up of the text to that limit. As a result, postmodern ethnography's pluralist and relativist rhetoric is the discursive articulation of a (reappropriative) project of information retrieval.[60] Not unsurprisingly, this apparently pluralist project turns out to depend on a moralistic dichotomy between a "bad" (unfair, excluding) representation and a "good" (fair, inclusive) one. It is not for nothing that, in his critical reading of Edward Said's *Orientalism*, Clifford dismisses Said's definition of Orientalism as a discourse of power/knowledge and redefines it in terms of an Orientalist "tradition."[61] This neutralization enables him to claim that there is a good, well-intended, and sympathetic Orientalism as well as a bad, racist one. However, this is unavoidably giving intention priority and purity, thus paradoxically willing (as unintended as such a will is) a reduction of the material production and placing of one's own intentionality and subjectivity in and by a textual network. Would it not be more meaningful for the scholar to admit and fight the necessary possibility of complicity, instead of finding relief in good intention?[62] This humanist strategy does not question the subject of knowledge and the place of representation. While apparently withdrawing him/herself in order to leave room for the other to speak his/her truth, does the subject of postmodern ethnography not protect his/her position of authority in terms of a manager of partial truths, the diplomatic proprietor of the universal truth of culture as "partial"?

The inscription of man

Jacques Derrida's vigilant reading reveals the double meaning of the old Greek word *problema*: it might be "the projection of a project" but also "the protection created by a substitute, a prosthesis that we put forth in order to represent, replace, shelter or dissimulate ourselves, or so as to hide something unavowable—like a shield."[63] Is the postmodern ethnographic project, that is, "the problem of 'how to achieve by written means what speech creates, and to do it without simply imitating speech'" in the above formulation, also a shield, protecting the oldest anthropological desire? And if so, what is unavowable here? What is it that the anthropological profession of faith cannot profess? I would like to argue that it is an infrastructural textual or inscriptive economy as well as a certain economy of desire that are at work in the postmodern ethnographic demand for authentic voice.

In *A Critique of Postcolonial Reason*, Gayatri Spivak makes the astonishing suggestion that we read "the encrypting of the name of the native informant as the name of Man—a name that carries the inaugurating affect of being human."[64] Spivak's formulation supports and further complicates my earlier description of postmodern ethnography as information retrieval. How to read the new ethnographer's desire to make the native voice heard in the text, to make the native one of the signatories of the anthropological text? Following Spivak, we may consider the possibility that this desire is itself the dissembling of an unacknowledged loss. As a knowledge predicated on the native informant, anthropology is Western Subject's/Man's coding of the untranslatability of his origin. This untranslatability remarks the very limit that the transcription or transliteration of the native voice is supposed to overcome.

Although information retrieval is conventionally defined as "the tracing of information stored in books, computers, or other collections of reference material" (Oxford English Dictionary), such a tracing or graphing is not only the following of a predetermined route or the copying of a pre-existing figure, but leaving your own trace as well. The computer expert encodes information in order to be able to retrieve the previously lost information. Perhaps the inscription of the native voice must be regarded as transliteration rather than transcription. Simultaneously "foreclosed and needed" in Spivak's words,[65] the retrieved (reappropriated) voice of the native other is only a further encrypting of the name of Man, maintaining the untranslatability of his origin. I should immediately add: in the postmodern, the name of Man as displaced subject (and no longer the subject of evolution). The sense of "displacement" here is both theoretical (an apparently "nonessentialist" humanism: a reversal of essentialism that defines the essence of Man/Subject as displaced) and cultural or geographical—hence the popularity of the notion of hybridity that brings these two senses together. This last point, however, would require further reading, which goes beyond the scope and limit of my present argument.

This sense of geographical and cultural "displacement" is emphatically articulated in Clifford's more recent work, *Routes*.[66] In his prologue, Clifford repeats the same methodological argument for the partiality of knowledge from a different angle. In a characteristic statement, he writes that "full accountability, of course, like the dream of self-knowledge, is elusive."[67] As I have already argued in this chapter, the methodological binary opposition between fullness and partiality hides the presupposition of a knowing subject, whether fully or partially knowing. But more importantly, Clifford introduces a new term, "translation," in the context of what he calls "comparative cultural studies."[68] In arguing for the located nature of thinking in both space and time, he describes a location as "an itinerary rather than a bounded site—a series of encounters and translations"—and he suggests a "situated analysis" that is "inherently partial." This kind of analysis "assumes that all broadly meaningful concepts, terms such as travel, are translations built from imperfect equivalences," and comparative or translation terms are "approximations."[69] In an effort to provide a balanced account, Clifford writes that "in successful translation . . . something different is brought over, made available for understanding, appreciation, consumption. At the same time . . . the moment of failure is inevitable."[70] The idea of translation as an imperfect equivalence or approximation, or the idea of "partial translatability,"[71] seems to indicate an approach that takes cultural difference into account, since it accepts that perfect or full translation is impossible. But it also assumes that there is a native speaker who can fully express him/herself in his/her native language. This assumption of a homogeneous original language translatable to itself is a conventional idea of translation and, by implication, of linguistic and cultural difference.

Although Clifford wants to see himself "in the tradition of Walter Benjamin's cultural criticism"[72] and "in a lineage of Brechtian or Benjaminian modernism,"[73] it was precisely this apparently simple yet rather confused idea of "imperfect translation" that Walter Benjamin criticized in his well-known essay, "The Task of the Translator."[74] Indeed Benjamin begins by criticizing the very idea that translation is meant for the readers who do not understand, in other words, foreigners. For Benjamin, translation is a literary "mode" and the law governing it is "translatability."[75] The complex notion of translatability is not the same as translation: the former is what makes the latter possible and impossible at the same time. Translatability presumes the difference of languages as already contained within a single language, and refers to a movement in the original language that is most aptly described by Blanchot in his own essay on Benjamin as "a gesture toward another language or . . . the possibilities of being different from itself and foreign to itself."[76] It is in this sense that, for Benjamin, translation involves "the foreignness of languages."[77] When Clifford refers to a necessarily imperfect translation, this seems to him to be a natural fact of cultural or linguistic difference. For Benjamin, however, if translation is impossible, it is not that a language is necessarily incompletely translated, but rather that there is never one language in a language; in other words, every language is, in a sense, a translation from another, unknown language. I should go so far as to say that this kind of approach opens language to a cryptic reading in the sense that the psychoanalysts Nicolas Abraham and Maria Torok understand.[78] Elaborating the psychoanalytic notions of shell and kernel, Abraham and Torok argue that, although the cryptic nature of unconscious language implies a kernel (an unknown language) for which the known or manifest language should stand as an external shell, the relationship between the shell and the kernel is not so simple. There is a dynamic, "cryptonymic" movement between the shell and the kernel on the very border where they touch and separate from each other. This can be described as a movement involving alterity (rather than pure identity or pure virginity). Is it not precisely this that Benjamin calls the "sacred" character of language, its idiomatic nature that makes translation both necessary and impossible? If, as Benjamin argues, the original text is like the sacred text, absolutely original and absolutely untranslatable (because the two flows of the letter and the meaning are indissociable), there is also, as Derrida shows in his reading of Benjamin, "an 'intralineal' translation into one's own language of the sacred text" and a movement of "pure translatability" makes it possible to "read between the lines."[79]

Moreover, for Benjamin, this movement has to do with the life of language, what Derrida calls its "surviving structure." Translating is responding to this demand for survival, which, as Derrida shows, is the very structure of the original text. Once more, translation has nothing to do with communication, reception, or information, whether full or partial. Rather it "augments and modifies the original, which, insofar as it is living on, never ceases to be transformed and to grow."[80] It is in this way that translation reveals what Benjamin called "the kinship of languages." It is not a question of constituting a whole that is already given as a unity of its parts, but rather constituting a whole as itself a fragment in a series of fragments that remain separate. This is not quite Clifford's redemptive polyphony that aims to restore the immediacy of an original and authentic native voice, since, in Benjamin, linguistic difference is articulated immanently by the notion of a linguistic original that, in its movement, is always already foreign to its own sentences, and forever remaining out of the reach of its very own production.

Interestingly, by the concept of an "imperfect translation," Clifford undermines his own powerful criticism of "salvage ethnography"—the benevolent anthropologist's project of saving the vanishing primitive.[81] Salvage ethnography fixes a society in an ethnographic present that is a past (an operation that depends on the "post-Darwinian bourgeois experience of time—a linear, relentless progress"). Clifford questions "the assumption that with rapid change something essential ('culture'), a coherent differential identity, vanishes."[82] He follows Raymond Williams' *The Country and the City* in locating this structure within the Western tradition of the "pastoral": "a relentless placement of others in a present becoming-past."[83] As he shows, this benevolent ethnographic desire for an authentic other is a hegemonic desire. By the same token, the native's adoption of European culture is regarded as contamination or disappearance of authentic culture. When approached in terms of translation, however, such an adoption can also be seen as survival, that is, an adaptation.[84] Ethnography as salvage paradigm appears to be a resistance to the native's translation of the other's culture. But does Clifford's notion of imperfect translation not share the same assumption of a "coherent, differential identity" of language that he identifies in the salvage paradigm? One of the senses of salvage is retrieval.

This salvaging or retrieval is the core methodological problem of postmodern ethnography as formulated by Tyler: "achieving by written means what speech creates, and to do it without simply imitating speech."[85] If the idea of creating the effect of speech in writing were not indeed imitating speech in writing, Tyler would not have said that it should be done "without simply imitating speech." Since the distinction between "creating the effect of speech" and "simply imitating speech" seems to hide a denial, we need to ask: is imitation simple? For Derrida, who seems to be the source of inspiration for such complex desires and formulations, imitation is by definition nonsimple: "imitation does not correspond to its essence, is not what it is— imitation—unless it is in some way at fault or rather in default."[86] Tyler's and Clifford's desire to create an effect of speech in writing by "following" Derrida implies a concept of self-present speech, which is precisely what Derrida's deconstruction deconstructs.

A lesson of writing?

It is not simply that postmodern ethnography maintains the same anthropological presupposition in another form, but it is only deconstruction (supposedly a moment or variety of so-called postmodernism) that can demonstrate that this is so. Postmodern ethnography wishes to represent a self-present voice, the native other's living speech, in writing, whereas deconstruction points to a singular moment or event that undoes representation and ex-appropriates the knowing, speaking, or writing subject. We are surely reminded of the question of whether the "post" of postmodernism is an instance of commodity logic, or in a cultural register, modernity's new. If there is not much difference between the commodity logic and modernity's new, this does not mean that resistance is impossible. Although no academic text can be exempt from commodification today, precisely for this reason, the question of how one can resist the consumptive mode is of strategic significance. Rather than delivering a "new" method, deconstruction insists on the generalization of loss and the absolutization of past that cannot simply be brought back in an authentic, native speech and that should therefore always be remarked in speech and writing.[87] The "post" or "beyond" of postmodernism is precisely the promise or assurance that a limit is finally overcome and whatever is left behind is no longer (i.e. the old anthropology where the native is not one of the signatories of the text and writing is reduced to keeping good field notes). The sense of accomplishment here might indeed give in to the consumptive mode. Such a radically nondeconstructive stance is a salvaging of the limit and its appropriation as the universal certainty of partial knowledge. Against this incorporation and swallowing of the limit in and as the speech of the other, I suggest, following deconstruction, that the ethnographic representation, the graphing or writing the ethnos should not fail to remark the limit.[88] This is not a merely external limit that one can cross over in the model of the displaced migrant, but the limit of knowledge we have encountered in Blanchot's uncanny formulation. The experience of this limit is rather the experience (or passing) of a nonpassage, or the experience of an absence or loss rather than simply of presence. It is only by re-marking this undecidable and moving limit that the ethnographic text can open itself up to an otherness beyond its account and can thus keep the promise as promise. But, following Blanchot carefully, this re-marking is not a mere acknowledgement of ignorance that can be the object of a new reflection or reflexivity. It is not, in other words, the question of a new epistemology, more poetic and less scientific, more native and less Western. Such a new epistemology would claim to transcend the ethnographic by preserving it. As I have argued earlier, this is an incorporation of the limit. The re-marking is not a dialectical surmounting or Hegelian *aufheben* but a writing of the ethnos otherwise.

How to write "otherwise"? There can be no easy answer. And more importantly, what follows this question cannot be in the order of an answer. What must be kept in mind is that the limit, the margin, or the mark that the re-mark re-marks, is also the one that distinguishes the "West" from the "rest." Following Spivak's formulation (the encrypting of the name of the native informant as the name of Man), we might say that it is structurally the "rest" (for instance, the "Orient" in Orientalism) that is marked in Western discourse (as the "Other," as object of knowledge or subject of speech in demand). Such an inscription or marking confirms the law of spacing, which Derrida describes as "a movement, a displacement that indicates an irreducible alterity."[89] It is at this very limit of ethnographic knowledge, at the margin of writing the ethnos, where no reflexivity and no return to self is possible, at the moment of ex-appropriation, that the ethnographic writing is given a chance of altering itself, and it is there that the re-mark re-marks incommensurable and irreducible alterity.

Since this kind of practice of re-marking can only occur in a strategic field, it can offer no model to be followed. Without forgetting the most important lesson of deconstruction—that the field of writing is a strategic force field—I should nevertheless give a unique "example": Smadar Lavie's ethnography of a Bedouin community under Israeli and Egyptian rule, *The Poetics of Military Occupation*. Lavie's work focuses on the production of a resistant identity in theatrical performance and allegory rather than celebrating a plurality of voices. Toward the end of her narrative, one of her native informants describes Lavie herself as "the one who writes us."[90] In accepting this as a cultural description of herself and making it the title of her last chapter, Lavie has acknowledged the problematic nature of ethnographic writing as an allegory of allegory. This is a way of re-marking the limit, of writing the ethnos otherwise, and giving further strength to a resistance that is not content with depending on the certainty or transparency of its representative authority. It is also a singular and limited re-marking, which is focused on the ethnographer's drama. Lavie's narrative maintains the anthropological dream of an intimate mutuality between the anthropologist and the native in the form of a paradox of self and other, that is to say the nonsynchronous nature of the mutual exchange of these positions, the impossibility of the "at the same time."[91] Perhaps it should be supplemented by a question: While it is the native informant's description of the anthropologist that makes her (and us) aware of the paradoxical nature of mutuality in the nonsynchrony of self and other, the moment we have read this description ("the one who writes us") and have understood and have interpreted it (anthropologist as both inside and outside, both self and other, but never both at the same time), have we not already forgotten that it is said in a different language, in a singular accent of the Bedouin Arabic, which performs and mimics itself as resistant allegory rather than native information?

The postmodern as a foreclosure of the native informant

The postmodern ethnographic project itself may turn out to be an allegory of Anglo-American academic culture. Derrida's deconstruction of metaphysics, Deleuze's project of a philosophy of event as what comes before the subject,

Foucault's genealogical critique of human sciences are all radical critiques of the humanist subject or cogito, despite their absolutely significant differences. The case of ethnography shows that a privileged moment of the Anglo-American "postmodern" translation of these genealogies and deconstructions is to insert them back into the epistemological field of a knowing subject, through a certain notion of limit that is, as I have argued here, external, simple, and stable, a boundary that one can simply cross over. New ethnography as "writing culture" plays a special role in the translation of deconstruction of metaphysics into cultural constructionism, which takes the risk of reconstructing rather than deconstructing the West's cultural other(ing). This is surely not a question of blaming the theoretical backwardness of anthropologists (compared with literary critics, for instance) so much as examining how the production of an academic and cultural object such as postmodernism is necessarily marked by a reworking of ethnography's conventional displacement of humanism, of the "Western Subject/Man." I do not mean that postmodern ethnography is not authentic postmodernism but rather an American misreading, an "imperfect" translation. Nor is it merely a subspecies of a general postmodernism. On the contrary, I would like to argue that this general and totalizing notion of the postmodern itself is a translation in which the ethnographic postmodern plays a particular role as the site where a certain political unconscious becomes readable.[92] Where to find this singular political unconscious but in Fredric Jameson's grand historical account, *Postmodernism, or the Cultural Logic of Late Capitalism*? The sheer absence of any discussion of such an ethically and politically loaded methodological argument as postmodern ethnography in Jameson's fascinating theoretical appropriation of the postmodern is symptomatic. Depending on the passage from the modern to the postmodern, a change the direction of which is already given, Jameson's narrativization could only have been a self-contained history of the modern capitalist West.[93] Having been produced in the same force field where Jameson collects his own articulating terms such as "the death of the author" or "intertextuality,"[94] does the postmodern ethnographic text not constitute a kind of political unconscious for his work? The ethnographic postmodern is a significant site of what I would describe as a prior translative inscription of the so-called postmodern language and vocabulary (a genealogical layer of concepts, terms, phrases, and so on, which constitute the postmodern as the translation of a radical moment in postwar French philosophy). Indeed, literary criticism and art history seemingly play a more important role in this genealogical inscription. But perhaps ethnography's role is more difficult to articulate since, in its encrypting of the name of the native informant as the name of Man, it ineluctably brings up a certain untranslatability into play, like a trace disclosing itself in its erasure. If Jameson's historical account cannot come to terms with this prior translative inscription of, precisely, terms such as "the death of the author" and "intertextuality" but rather registers and theorizes it as cognitive mapping, this is not only because it acts on a level of generality that is produced by it but also because, in the suppressed case of ethnography, this inscription threatens to open Jameson's narrative to an otherness that may disturb the self-contained nature of his postmodern object. Is it not the (un)naming of the native informant that is at stake in all these discourses on "postmodernism"?

Native Speaker, Master Audience

Published in 1990, Mehdi Abedi and Michael M. J. Fischer's *Debating Muslims: Cultural Dialogues in Postmodernity and Tradition* is often regarded as an exemplary and classic work of postmodern ethnography. Ambitious in its scope, Abedi and Fischer's book engages ethnographic, autobiographical, hermeneutic, cultural, and literary discourses, while offering a wide range of subjects, analyses, and methods of study within the scope of the same work. It begins with an autobiographical account of Abedi's own socialization in Iran (interjected with ethnographic observations and analyses), goes through hermeneutically inspired readings of the Qur'an, hadiths, and the hajj, offers ethnographies of the minority Baha'i community in Iran and minority Iranian community in Houston in the United States, makes a semiotic analysis of Islamic posters in revolutionary Iran, and ends with a fascinating reading of Salman Rushdie's *Satanic Verses*. In this chapter, I will focus on certain parts of this important work on Islam. What follows is not a comprehensive critical review of the book, but a critical focus on its singular theoretical framework.

Knowledge, ethics, dialogue

Abedi and Fischer's depth of knowledge of Islamic texts, culture, and history, especially of Iranian Shi'ite Islam, as well as their familiarity with theory, is admirable. But it is also not unquestionable. Rich in cultural and historical facts, well informed in high theory, and shrewd in interpretation, is this an example of the kind of academic work that Sande Cohen heavily criticized some years ago for its all-inclusive fantasy? As he states: "The Good Object is that which demonstrates our interpretive cleverness (where nothing of the object remains outside of language), and the Good Academic is legitimized by the saturation of the object in our interpretive language."[1] For Cohen, the good object is also related with the "book" as object. A book's convenience is always mistaken for its benevolence, as he put it; it "comes forward as a 'resolution' or an 'answer' or model or norm."[2] The fact that *Debating Muslims* is a collaborative work produced by two anthropologists, an American *and* an Iranian, is an essential aspect of its reading. This enfolding or framing of the reading is also the very call and calling of the text. As the opening passage reads:

> There are times, increasingly, when we need touchstones, reminders and access to the humanism of others. The opening essay is a response to requests for reading material on lives of people in the Middle East, lives that can reach through the numbing opaqueness of news accounts of confrontation, ideological war and endless killing; through the reifying opaqueness of histories of political regimes, kings, dictators, coups, and revolutionary masses; through the idealizing opaqueness of theologies of Islam or symbolic analyses of ritual.[3]

While the ethical stake is high, the organization of the argument depends on the epistemological *access* to the other's world, which is obstructed by media, politics, and religion. Is there a straight path from knowledge to ethics in acts of writing and reading? Although knowledges have all kinds of uses (depending also on who made the request), a project of knowledge establishes a hierarchical relationship of determination and appropriation of a (known) object by a (knowing) subject. Following Gayatri Spivak's reading of ethical singularity in Mahasweta Devi's literature, Dawn Rae Davis argued that ethics involves a kind of "not-knowing."[4] Ethics interrupts the identity intrinsic to the act of knowing by keeping the *difference* of the other outside of knowledge (as in love, ethical singularity is the sharing of a secret that is carried in acts of language but that cannot be put in words). This surely does not mean that we give up any project of knowledge; but it suggests that we develop means of interrupting the totalizing hegemonic effect of knowledge by paying attention to "what knowledge cannot make available."[5]

While Abedi and Fischer maintain the presupposition that knowledge or truth provides the appropriate moral response to the humanity or "humanism of others," the ethical import of their argument, and the promise of its unity, is specifically weighed by a concept of *dialogue* that is rationally determinable, that is, one which is seen in terms of questions of authorization, legitimation, and disputation. Following a postmodern ethnographic principle, the authors offer a pluralistic text, with many voices, genres of writing, and different levels of meaning, and present a good, fair, inclusive, and plural representation, which attempts to go beyond the narrow and reductive representations of media, politics, and religion. But further and more importantly, *Debating Muslims* carries what Clifford calls "representational tact" over to an entirely new epistemological and methodological level by the central, organizing role it gives to the concept of dialogue conceptualized as a conversation between rational, linguistically capable partners following a set of rules. In their captivating chapter on the Qur'an, the authors explain that they use this concept in three different senses:

> . . . dialogue in the colloquial sense of oral communication between two face-to-face persons; dia-logue in the Greek etymological sense of cross-play between arguments; and dialogue in the sense of juxtaposition of points of view in a political struggle for hegemonic control of interpretation . . .

> These also translate into three ethical registers: the ethnographic effort to understand other people(s) in their own terms, the political effort to establish a public world where the rights and interests of all can be protected and negotiated, and the self-evaluative and the self-reflective effort to break out of ethnocentrism and to place one's own perspectives into dialogical relation to others.[6]

Abedi and Fischer's concept of dialogue is quite specific indeed in their strong emphasis in its face-to-face and oral nature, which becomes clear in their analysis of the reading and teaching of the Qur'an. We are of course reminded of Pierre Bourdieu's important methodological caution that I have already emphasized in the first chapter: "interpersonal relations are never, except in appearance, individual-to-individual relationships and the truth of an interaction is never entirely contained in the interaction."[7] But Abedi and Fischer also want to think the concept of dialogue in a hermeneutic sense. They frequently refer to Gadamer in the context of the concept of dialogue[8] and in the context of hermeneutics.[9] Yet these references do not necessarily indicate a strict following of Gadamer's concept of dialogue or hermeneutic concept of understanding.[10] Abedi and Fischer develop their own reading of Platonic dialogue, which privileges its rational, pedagogical, and maieutic aspect. They set up an opposition between *the prescriptive* and *the dialogical-hermeneutic* aspects: "Western audiences, out of ignorance, yield too easily to fundamentalist Muslim claims that Islam is prescriptive in simple ways. To argue otherwise requires knowledge of Islamic hermeneutics, dialectics and dialogics."[11] Western ignorance is based not only on the "opaqueness" propagated by media, politics, and religion, but also on the fact that Westerners have lost touch with their own hermeneutic and dialogical Christian, Judaic, and Greek traditions. But Abedi and Fischer's purpose is not limited to informing the Western audiences about Islam. Their wish and struggle is also to give priority to the tradition of disputation, *bahth*, over the concept of *tawhid* (unity), which became the support for a fundamentalist and totalitarian tendency in Islam, as they see the *bahth* in the same nature as Gadamer's hermeneutics or Habermas' communicative ethics and as capable of providing a democratic public ethos.[12] Abedi and Fischer do not develop a specific discussion of how Habermas and Gadamer (whose debate is well-known) can be put together, especially in conjunction with the Islamic concept of *bahth* without any further theoretical elaboration.

Native autobiography and the return of the ethnographic authority

I would like to begin with an instance of the concept of "dialogue" or the "dialogical" in the text. I put the word in quotation marks now, because it is not clear if it is applicable for the first part of *Debating Muslims*, "Oral Life Worlds,"[13] yet we are made to feel its relevance. Abedi and Fischer described the book as "written in two 'I's and a bifocal and stereoscopic 'we' . . . a better device than hyperreal, but false omniscience."[14] But this does not apply to each and every chapter:

> There are obvious places where the "I"s mark perspective [Abedi's eye in Chapter 1, Fischer's in Chapter 2], and other places where they mark rather a difference in text(u)ral voice; elsewhere, such markers fade (we hope) into unnoticed stereoscopic coordination.[15]

As the first chapter is *also* titled "Shi'ite Socialization in Pahlavi Iran: Autobiographical Sondages in a Postmodern World" and described as a "Bildungsroman of transition from a fundamentalist to a cosmopolitan consciousness," crossing "class as well as cultural boundaries" and accessing "multiple worlds of interpretive nuance,"[16] we read it as written by Mehdi Abedi. But who is "Mehdi Abedi"? We know that he used to be the anthropologist Michael M. J. Fischer's native informant in his previous research (this is how he met him and came to the United States to obtain a PhD degree in anthropology).[17]

Since he is writing his life story in which this part of his life is also narrated, he is now a native autobiographer. But there is another aspect of this chapter that should not escape our attention: the autobiographical discourse is occasionally interrupted by "bracketed annotations" that are "meant to highlight analytic themes, especially those which will be taken up in subsequent chapters."[18] Abedi's autobiography fulfills an initiatory and originating function. While this sentence is part of the autobiographical chapter, its subject is clearly an anthropologist, and more importantly someone who has *already* read what is written. Questions abound here in terms of the textual ideal of the new ethnography. Are the bracketed parts written by *both* Abedi and Fischer (forming a three-dimensional image in "stereoscopic coordination")? The question is legitimate because they are not marked by the "I" but by an authoritative, explanatory, objective, anthropological voice. Or, are they written by Abedi himself? But this is not simply a matter of which empirical person (Abedi or Fischer) wrote the bracketed annotations. For, given their *explanatory* function, the signature is clearly that of an anthropologist, that is to say the native information is constantly *interrupted* and *explained* by an anthropological voice, or indeed over-voice. But then, the native voice of autobiography loses its singular value as a particular kind of knowledge and writing, as it is in need of explanation by a superior form of knowledge and writing. Which means that the text is no longer plural, dialogical, or stereoscopic but inevitably hierarchical. Since Abedi himself is also an anthropologist, and is likely to be the writer (or one of the writers) of these bracketed annotations, is this auto-ethno-bio-graphy (cultural self writing itself) not a fantasy of appropriating one's own cultural origin? As strange and paradoxical as it may sound, how do we distinguish this from a quasi-nationalistic fantasy?

In a later text, Fischer gives the following account of their collaboration:

> In these dual-voiced biographies, I am fascinated by the mirroring relationships between the life history of the author and the life history of the subject (mirrors can be set at varying angles; the reflections are not simple repetitions) and the ways in which the life histories of sometimes long-dead individuals provoke reflections on clarification and self-reconstruction in contemporary lives and reinterpretations of moral traditions. I am also interested in the fluidity of the line between autobiography and biography, or life history as narrative procedures.
>
> *Debating Muslims: Cultural Dialogues in Postmodernity and Tradition* (written with Mehdi Abedi) explores this fluidity a bit further and is partly

structured around seven life histories of people standing in different relations to the Islamic revolution in Iran.. . . The longest of these life histories is an autobiography that the two of us reconstructed out of stories from Mehdi Abedi's life. Shorter life histories of two provincial religious leaders are constructed similarly out of stories from participants in their lives; life histories of two national religious leaders are constructed out of orally circulating parabolic stories about them, and their own writings.[19]

"Life story," or "life history," is a method used in social sciences. It is a form of biography, often constructed by the researcher depending on the interviews with the subject. The first chapter is an *auto*biography, not just a biography or life story, so "the life history of the author and the life history of the subject" coincide. Indeed, if, as we learn from Benveniste,[20] the distinction between the subject of enunciation and the subject of the statement is constitutive of language, then autobiography should imply an imaginary identity of the two. For instance, when the "I" of the first chapter appears on page 6 by giving a *description* of the village in which he was born and grew up ("Dareh [valley] is the name of the village I was born"), we have a classic case of imaginary identity: the author as the main character in a narrative of the imagined real. But, as I have argued above, when the autobiographical voice is interrupted by an ethnographic, scholarly, and authoritative voice in brackets, we clearly have a hierarchical relationship between the two discourses:

> Near the mosque in the upper neighborhood there was an ancient plane tree that was even more venerable. Someone on an Ashura day had said he had seen it bleeding in sympathy with the martyrdom of Hussain. And so people believed that if you attempted to cut its branches, especially on Ashura, something terrible would befall you.
>
> [Such folklore provides the weft in the rich anectodal tapesty of the village's sense of itself: both its sense of place and its social composition through the lives of its highly individualistic characters. It is a humane tapestry viewed with much humor, as well as suspended judgement: only God knows what is possible; and in a materially hard world, folkloric elaboration provides humane comfort and endless material for storytelling sociability. A few characters may serve to illustrate.]
>
> At the top of the upper village lived a wealthy hajji and usurer (nozulkhor), who had connections with both the police and the clergy. . . .[21]

This is a highly regulated and hierarchical interruption (and maybe quite rightly so, from an analytic point of view), which, in turn, makes other "life stories" *its illustrations* ("A few characters may serve to illustrate . . ."), rather than treating them as separate stories, which would thus be allowed to mirror or exchange with others. As for the mirrorings and reflections between life histories and moral traditions that Fischer brings up above, as fascinating as these might sometimes be (for instance, when producing new angles on the already known material), is this not rather routine work for an anthropologist?[22] Are we in the presence of a genuinely new approach, or the justification of an old practice with new "theoretical" discourse and with a new textual, formal arrangement?[23]

This textual aspect must have something to do with the literary. What is the status of the latter in *Debating Muslims*, especially if we remember that autobiography is a literary genre? Immediately after describing the function of the chapter as "an ethnographic document of worlds that are barely, if at all, accesible in books," the authors tell "a joke from the field":

> Indeed as the folklorist, historian, and librarian Iraj Afshar one day in Yazd jokingly but quite seriously commented to an American geography student for whom Abedi was translating a local history, collecting marketing data, and serving as translator, cultural broker, and protector from mishap: the real book is found in such bright boys, not in texts.[24]

But the wit itself can also be taken as the proof that an oral life world cannot present itself *except* in the book form. In reading the joke literally and taking it as wit, I draw on the romantic concept of wit as it is understood by Philippe Lacoue-Labarthe and Jean-Luc Nancy.[25] A wit is often seen as keenness of perception or intelligence, and the humorous expression of a relationship between seemingly disparate things (for instance, book and life). A perfect example of the romantic concept of fragment as we learn from Lacoue-Labarthe and Nancy, the *Witz* is "dialogical and dialectical," "knowledge that is other than the knowledge of analytic and predicative discursivity," "the preferred genre of conversation, of sociality," "the living and free exchange of opinions," "immediate, absolute knowing-seeing," and "absolute social spirit."[26] Yet there is also a romantic suspicion of the wit: "its absolute combinative quality is always threatened from below by its inferior, fleeting, almost formless character."[27] This is why "genuine *Witz* is still conceivable only in the written form" and "it must be put to work in the work."[28] Although Abedi and Fischer's concept of dialogue is rationalistic, it is possible to argue that their work repeats the same movement that romanticism had already conceptualized in terms of fragment and wit. This is demonstrated in their writing of the above wit, that is, in the putting of the wit to work in the work, which itself characterizes the real book as wit. As we shall see below, Abedi and Fischer's rational concept of dialogue is constantly haunted by poetry and music that they cannot not hear, a haunting that we should also read as "what knowledge cannot make available" in Davis' formulation.[29]

Are Abedi and Fischer romantics without knowing that they are, as there is also an affinity between the romantic ideal of "the self-adequate auto-production of the Work-Subject, of the Work-Self-knowledge"[30] and what I have called above the "auto-ethno-bio-graphy"? Abedi and Fischer's aspiration for a comprehensive account, a kind of total work, is nevertheless determined by an epistemological (anthropological) program, the working of which is supposed to deliver an ethical result. What remains debatable is if authentic life story has the power to unmask or counterbalance the discourses of media, religion, or politics. Perhaps what is urgently needed, though much less found in academia, is a little bit more attention to precisely those *languages in circulation* (media, politics, religion), so as not to allow them to demonstrate their ([un]motivated) power. For instance, the authors use the metaphor of *sondage* in the title ("autobiographical sondage") and write that the task "is to provide one life as an archeological sondage back into the strata of the life worlds of the provincial Iran of the 1950s, '60s and '70s."[31] The autobiographical sondage must be understood in analogy with the archeological sondage, that is to say *an extraction of knowledge from a stratified native other*. But if so, then why is the chapter called autobiography, especially when clearly this would very well pass as the native informant's life story on the pages of the anthropologist's notebook? Literary theory taught us that the graphing of the life of self by the self requires a fantasy of the wholeness of self-life (auto-bio) in its representation/graphing. In *Discerning the Subject*, Paul Smith has argued that autobiography "cannot be underestimated as a privileged form of ideological text wherein the demand that we should consist as coherent and recognizable 'subjects' *in relation to a particular knowledge* appears to be rationalized."[32] Smith's formulation can be rewritten in our case: the demand that we should consist as coherent and recognizable native "subjects" ("reading material" in times of "opaqueness") *in relation to ethnographic knowledge* appears to be rationalized.[33]

The Qur'anic dialogics: The passion of the Other

Abedi and Fischer's fascinating reading of the Qur'an and hadith (the prophet's sayings) develops a highly unique approach to Islamic texts. I have no particular objection to their readings of specific passages in the Qur'an or in Khomenei's discourse, but I would like to show that their supposed theoretical framework is characterized by a shift or displacement, which enables them to set up a highly questionable opposition between the oral and the textual. To put it in a nutshell, while Abedi and Fischer argue that Islam insists on the oral, dialogical, and recitative nature of the Qur'an and warns against its writing, they also constantly refer to its allusive nature, its allegorical aspect, its poetry, its rhythm, its fragmentary structure, its levels of meaning, its musicality (in a manner that can be described as romantic). This other, poetic and musical aspect of the Qur'an is also collapsed into the notion of orality, via an ambiguous use of the notions of sound and vocality.[34] However, while the notion of oral, face-to-face interaction refers to a rationally controlled dialogue between linguistically competent partners, poetic and musical aspects have nothing to do with such a concept of dialogue.

In this context, Abedi and Fischer emphasize the art of *tajwid*, that is, cantillation, chanting, or recitation. Reminding us that the angel Gabriel recites from the mother book in the seventh heaven according to Islam, they refer to the ideal of "preserving the original celestial music."[35] They emphasize that such recitation or cantillation is *both singing and reading* and is conceived in contrast to the pure texts (*hadith* or the *mus-haf*, the written Qur'an).[36] This is why the passage from the oral to the textual was not unproblematic. Abedi and Fischer offer a suggestive analysis of the problem of the compilation of the Qur'an and various historical disputes over giving priority to the oral or the textual. Although their own discussion does not necessarily show any absolute or definitive decision on the priority given to the oral recitation, they draw a highly specific conclusion: in the history of Islam, many Muslim scholars demonstrate a "distrust of texts" and argue that the Qur'an should be stored in the knowledgeable scholar's memory and should be transmitted in a face-to-face context. According to this widespread scholastic attitude, the student needs guidance, for the sacred text is not self-explanatory and those who are not pious can be misled. Thus the Qur'an comes in various dialogic forms: teacher versus student, imam versus follower, student versus student. Most importantly, its teaching is characterized by the "debating of argument and counterargument to clarify the basis for decision-making"; although dialogue does not exclude the inscription of authority, still it demonstrates a "resistance to taking authority out of the dialogic, face-to-face context."[37]

Keeping the authority in a dialogic, face-to-face context might well be a pedagogical requirement; but is there really such a strong emphasis on the oral nature of the Qur'an that is specifically different than what we already find in the metaphysical tradition in general? The singularity of the Qur'an is that it is regarded as the voice of God, and not a report written by the prophet. This is, after all, the privilege of Arabic as a *language* (not just speech but also writing). In an erudite study of the Islamic art of writing, *The Splendor of Islamic Calligraphy*, Abdelkebir Khatibi and Mohammed Sijelmassi remind that "Allah speaks Arabic first: so the Qur'an is not seen as a gospel to be revealed in any language."[38] This miraculous status of the Arabic language produces a series of problems (linguistic, philosophical, theological) for Muslims rather than a simple rejection of writing.

> How can a miraculous language be transcribed without giving the lie to its implicit perfection? And since all revelation enjoins silence as well as hushed voices, the scribe's sublime task is beset with grave problems. From the inception of Islam conflicts broke out over different recensions of the Qur'an, which did not acquire its definitive form until the death of the Prophet. The recensions themselves were transcribed in an orthographically incomplete form of writing: the system of vowel and diacritical signs—so important in calligraphy—was deficient. This is a major (but not only) reason for the custom of chanting and reciting the text. It was not until the third Caliph, Uthman (23/644–35/655) that an "authorized" version is produced. Calligraphy, though not yet codified, was born at that moment, to establish the miraculous nature of the Qur'an's origin.[39]

While Abedi and Fischer demonstrate the continuity and similarity between the Platonic and Islamic paradigms, Khatibi and Sijelmassi describe a singularity:

> In Islam, writing is an absolute, *the* Absolute, the *Sanctum Sanctorum*. True, there may also be discerned in it the Greek theory of writing, formulated differently, that writing is the fine garment which clothes meaning, but the status of writing is nevertheless given a sacred character, and in a fundamental way. When writing is seen as an aspect of the Absolute, then scientific thought itself partakes of, and prolongs the nature of revelation.[40]

Khatibi and Sijelmassi's study shows that the voice is not simply opposed to writing in Islam, as the latter is not a mere transcription, not a "dead body of symbol without name or feature,"[41] but "the letter recreated as image."[42] Calligraphy is not mere decoration and it implies "a theory of language and writing."[43] It is a unique form in which the agency of the written sign is configured entirely differently than in our universal Latinity: "reading is not a matter of following a single line of text . . . it can in fact be recognized by any permutation of its letters."[44] Because Fischer and Abedi operate by the classic opposition between voice as living (face-to-face, dialogical) and writing as dead letter (unchanging and monological) in the name of emphasizing Islam's similarity to the European tradition, they foreclose the possibility of thinking a different reading and visual activity that is outside Latin grammar and linear reading habits. Latinity remains the universal norm. The word "calligraphy" (a major Islamic art) does not appear on the pages of such a comprehensive work as *Debating Muslims*.

Abedi and Fischer's concept of the "graphics of absence" begins by making reference to Jacques Derrida's concept of the "trace": "Writing is one of the representatives of the trace in general, it is not the trace itself. *The trace itself does not exist*";[45] but there is no discussion of the concept of absence or loss, nor of Derrida's concept of the trace. So we remain in the dark about the place of this reference to Derrida in Abedi and Fischer's analysis. If Abedi and Fischer wanted to make a reference to the concept of the trace in a religious context, they could have found this discussion toward the end of the first part of *Of Grammatology*.[46] If they wanted to make a discussion of the concept of the trace in the context of Islam, should they have not referred to the Islamic concept of *ghayb* (which is usually translated as the "unseen"—but it also means "absence" or "absent"), especially in the context of the affinity of the trace and *différance* with the absolute past?[47] We have instead a semiological and hermeneutic discussion of the levels of meaning in the Qur'an and the hadith: *muhkam* (literal or established) and *mutashabih* (allegorical or metaphorical) as well as *zahir* (exoteric) and *batin* (esoteric) meanings. As the allegorical level renders the text open to interpretation, moral struggle, and access to techniques of interpretation such as *tafsir* (exegesis), *tawil* (prolepsis), and *bahth* (disputation), their focus turns to struggle for interpreting and controlling the text. The significance of this view is obvious, as it replaces the image of a monolithic, prescriptive, and authoritarian religion with one that foregrounds a passionate scene of debate and counter-debate, a plurality of interpretations, exercises of reasoning and rhetorical skill, and constant disputation. But what does this have to with Derrida's notion of the trace?

Although Abedi and Fischer acknowledge the "ultimate unknowability" (or unreadability) of the Qur'an as a kind of negative basis for this historical, cultural, and interpretive plurality, their view falls short of the theoretical signs they give off by a series of quotes from theorists and writers such as Derrida, Levinas, Jabes, or Joyce. Indeed the realistic acceptance of this pluralistic scene is questionable for it leads to the repression of a problematic of the trace. What is at stake in several historical references as well as in readings of Khomenei's contemporary discourse is the figure of the Muslim scholar, a subject knowledgeable and competent in reasoning and rhetoric. The problem is not simply elitism (which is the obvious risk Abedi and Fischer take); rather it is a concept of speech and dialogue, which, depending on the structure of question and answer, reproduces a certain concept of language or text as speech under the rational and rhetorical command of a linguistically and hermeneutically competent subject. When they write that the Islamic privileging of the oral over the textual does not exclude the literate; on the contrary "the literate is problematized and kept from being a tyrannical authority,"[48] it is the little word "tyrannical" that does the work of absolving the authority. But does the Socratic dialogue they take as model not push them in the direction of *legitimation rather than disputation*? For although this model begins from the Socratic knowledge of not-knowing (*docta ignorantia*), its opposition to the given knowledge of doxa is already in the name of a higher truth, that is to say it is *epistemologically* motivated.[49] When Abedi and Fischer suggest that "the play of dialogue, dialectic and hermeneutic prevents the closure that Khomenei seeks,"[50] they overlook the fact that, in each and every demonstration, a certain authority and closure are established, even though this cannot end all interpretation, let alone disputation. Further, however free the dialogue is, in the particular case that Abedi and Fischer read it is important to keep in mind that Khomenei is not entirely devoid of authority and the occasion is one of the passage from religious to political authority (of course this has been repeated several times before). From the point of view of the ultimate unknowability of the Qur'an (which might be seen as a kind of guarantee of a democratic ethos), all nonknowledge is guaranteed in reference to God who holds in check what we cannot know, while the "rest" is known and commanded, granted we follow the right interpreter. If this is a game that is constantly played by religious and political actors, who keep replacing each other, it is the game of the established religion, of religion as always-already established. Nothing is lost (*ghayb*) therefore; all loss is already under the command of the sacred text whose words are regarded as subject to interpretation and control in practice. In Abedi and Fischer's problematic, the text or language are thought entirely within the domain of reason, of rational and rhetorical competence, an instance of what Derrida would have called "writing in the narrow sense," and certainly not the trace.[51]

More interestingly, this is only one aspect of the Islamic text according to Abedi and Fischer. Having engaged in a reading of the Qur'an and the hadith,

Abedi and Fischer inevitably develop an intimacy with the Muslim text and language. (Surely Abedi is already intimate with the text.) It is the literary aspect of their intellectual project that makes the textual intimacy possible. Their emphasis on the literary and musical aspect of the Qur'an is not simply a question of taste. Abedi and Fischer particularly emphasize that cantillation is not mere vocalization, but that different intonations and articulations produce different meanings.[52] There is a particular sensitivity to and control over the process of cantillation ordered by special manuals: "Cantillation manuals include explanations of phonology: the points of articulation in the vocal tract, allophones, rules of assimilation, nasality, duration."[53] What is at stake in the manual? Clearly aesthetic construction as well as pedagogical and political control. The cantillation manual is witness to the work of *Bildung* as giving-form and culture: sectioning the text, constructing rhythms, repetition as refrain and echo as well as the necessity of guidance in dialogic forms (teacher-student, imam-follower). Abedi and Fischer conclude that, from Peter Abelard to Renaissance philosophy, various European dialogic forms were actually borrowings from the Islamic and Jewish style of unveiling the truth, especially through Muslim Spain.[54]

This matter of marking the throat and the ear, of governing the sound and its flow, is and must be considered, according to Abedi and Fischer, as *a means* of dialogical interpretation and contestation. Islam is thus brought closer to a democratic public ethos (understood as communicative ethics of the Habermasian kind[55]), and is taken farther away from the unitary interpretations (such as the one fundamentalism offered). But meanwhile something else happened. Abedi and Fischer have reduced the literary to the status of rhetorical technique and play in the unity of speech or address (also controlling the implications of textual intimacy). In their desire to demonstrate the presence of a rational, rhetorical, and dialogical tradition in Islam, Abedi and Fischer never pose the question of *what it is that is controlled and governed* by reason and rhetoric. For instance, how is disputation, that is, difference, produced as different from legitimation? Disputation cannot be the same as legitimation. But this moment can have no particular significance for Abedi and Fischer. It is immediately legitimation or turns into it. Although the very logic of the cantillation manual (a logic they follow) admits a differential force field of intonation, timbre, resonance, and rhythm that needs to be controlled, this heterogeneity or differentiation itself, that is to say something like *the becoming-language of language*, is never taken into account outside the control of speech and dialogue (except containing it in a rhetoric of "divine, celestial beauty," reproducing the religious gesture itself). Does the very desire to control not show that this process remains beyond the powers of the cognitive-hermeneutic subject of dialogue?

In classifying "several distinctive features of the Qur'an," Abedi and Fischer's second category defines an unusual principle: "the narrative unit is the fragment, not the sura."[56] They never explain what they mean by fragment. In the above discussion of a joke from the field, I have already argued that the joke must be read as wit, that is, fragment in the romantic sense, which is put to work in the work. We have now another instance of the same romantic concept of the fragment. As the next distinctive feature of the Qur'an, Abedi and Fischer emphasize that "meaning is conveyed by the sound, and would be much more difficult to establish by the text alone."[57] Despite their constant reference to a line from James Joyce's *Finnegans Wake* ("In the buginning is the woid, in the muddle is the sounddance and thereinofter you're in the unbewised again"), the inscriptive role of the "sound" (what Saussure called "psychic imprint" and what Derrida deconstructed in terms of "trace") is never taken into account. Abedi and Fischer constantly evoke these references (woid, sounddance, trace), but they continue to regard *sound simply as the vehicle of meaning* (hence rhetoric for instance can only have an instrumental value). The same happens now with the concept of the "fragment." What is a fragment? Why is it the narrative unit? How could something fragmentary (as a fragment should be) constitute a "unit," that is, something unitary (as a unit should be)? What are the consequences of considering the fragment as a "unit"? We remain in the dark again with regard to the status of this concept. I am also reminded here of Khatibi and Sijelmassi's reason for the difficulty of the scribe's sublime task: "all revelation enjoins silence as well as hushed voices."[58] What is the status of *discontinuity* brought to our attention by these concepts of fragment and silence?

It is here that Derrida's deconstruction is most useful. Since Abedi and Fischer refer to Derrida's concept of "trace" without any explanation or articulation in the beginning of their chapter as if it already explains their subsequent reading of the Qur'an, we emphasize that the trace cannot be controlled at all. It is another name for that which remains beyond the control of speaking (or chanting) subject, as it has to do with the play of differences within a system (such as the system of the Qur'an):

> *Whether in the order of spoken or written discourse*, no element can function as a sign without referring to another element which itself is not simply present. This interweaving results in each "element"—*phoneme or grapheme*—being constituted on the basis of the trace within it of other elements of the chain or system.[59]

We must note here that it does not matter whether the "element" is phoneme or grapheme. It is in the zone of the trace that signs (differences) appear, whether they are spoken or written signs.[60] The unity of the sign is *always-already* broken or compromised in its reference to the other sign, in its trace as well as in its spacing.[61] If the trace is thus the origin of the sign(s), it is at the same time the origin as nonorigin, for it withdraws itself from the differences it produces (all these sentences remain highly problematic, as if the trace were a subject). As a (non)origin of difference, the trace is "the opening of the first exteriority in general, the enigmatic relationship of the living to its other and of an inside to an outside."[62]

Perhaps it is their commitment to the concept of the fragment as an incomplete piece (therefore a piece in the process of completion), which disallows Abedi and Fischer to understand a ceaseless internal fragmentation that is at work in the sign. While they point to the fragmentary, discontinuous, rythmic nature of the text of the Qur'an (or the hadith), they can only consider this in terms of already constituted discrete elements and/or units, that is to say as a pedagogical object of teaching and memorization, or as an object of rhetorical play and discursive manipulation, and *never* in terms of the trace, that is, the unheard difference between the appearing and the appearance of the sound.[63] And while they point to the "poeticity" or "musicality" in an appreciative manner, the radically nontransitive aspect of the text, which is experienced in the chanting or recitation of the Qur'an, is never approached as a certain kind of *exposure* of language. This "poeticity" is not merely an aesthetic matter of beauty. Its exposure of language, which produces the aesthetic effect, does not take language as an object; it is a radical passivity and a failure of transitivity that cannot be reduced to a technique of memorization or chanting. In Maurice Blanchot's words, the work (the very process of the formation of the form, the articulation of the units) is also an "unworking."[64] The closest Islamic concept here is *ghayb* (which again must be translated as "absence" or "absent"). The religious text is thus opened to a general economy, or generalized writing. What Abedi and Fischer call "oral" is already *textual* in the sense of trace, which is the unheard difference, and in the sense of spacing, which "designates nothing . . . no presence at a distance; it is the index of an irreducible exterior, and at the same time of a movement, a displacement that indicates an irreducible alterity."[65] It is the *constitutively discontinuous* (rather than merely incomplete) nature of the fragment that gives the text its openness, its drifting, and its diversion. The ceaseless separation of the sign from "itself" constitutes *the necessary possibility of disputation*. Indeed Abedi and Fischer present a case of disputation when they demonstrate by a careful reading of the *Satanic Verses* that Salman Rushdie's satire depends on his close reading of the Qur'an rather than merely dismissing its narrative knowledge and moral tension.[66] In Chapter 7, I will read Gayatri Spivak's reading of Asja Djebar's narration (or re-citation) of female figures in her *Far from Madina* as an instance of disputation.

While Abedi and Fischer provide a highly interesting reading of the ritual of hajj alongside the critical discourses of two important figures of the Iranian revolution, Mutahhari and Shariati, their claim of employing Benjamin's method of representing modernity as well as their reference to Derrida's concept of *différance* in the context of these readings is again very debatable.[67] Benjamin's discontinuous, fragmentary style of writing in the essay on nineteenth-century Paris is motivated by his singular aim of finding an effective political and cultural resistance to the perception in a state of distraction as well as what he calls the empty phrase prevalent in journalism.[68] It is not clear in what sense and how Abedi and Fischer employ this method in their otherwise quite interesting, lively, and absolutely relevant readings of Mutahhari and Shariati, which are presented in a rather straightforward way (especially when compared with Benjamin's radical form of presentation in the Arcades project).[69] The same applies for Derrida's concept of *différance*, Lacan's psychoanalysis, or feminist theory. The chapter on the hajj is opened by a presentation of *différance*, which is read in continuity with the psychoanalytic project interpreted by the authors as an "ethics of deferral," and with Irigaray and French feminist theorists who use "a similar notion of inherent plurality and multiplicity of female sexual body"![70] Treating all these theories as simply versions of each other without further elaboration of their relations and differences only leads to confusion. Abedi and Fischer infer a striking conclusion from this "theoretical" framework:

> The point here, in any case, is that the rhetorics of contemporary politicized Islam both simply fear difference and blocks access to the ethics of *différance*. They are defensively anxious about manhood and insistent on subordinating women.[71]

By Derrida's account, any culture is characterized by a fear of *différance*, not just Islamic or American conservative academic cultures, for *différance* is "a sameness that is not identical," "never presents itself as such," and cannot be made manifest.[72] More importantly, in their generalizing perspective, Abedi and Fischer tend to take *différance* as feminine; but *différance* is what produces the difference between man and woman.

Despite these hasty inferences and generalizations, a positive achievement of Abedi and Fischer's reading of hajj is to draw the attention to the role of Hagar in the primal scene of Islam. As is well-known, Abraham's maid Hagar was exiled to Mecca and gave birth to Ishmael, Abraham's son and the future father of the Arab nation. Abedi and Fischer call Hagar "the alternative female body at the core of Islamic ethics," indicating the inherent contradictions and anxieties of the Islamic text.[73] Although this formulation is radical, their reading is not as rich and strong as Ali Shariati's reading in his moving account of the hajj.[74] Shariati draws the attention to the "wall of Hagar," which is in the shape of a skirt and is placed toward the West of the Ka'ba. Since Shariati reads the Ka'ba as the house of Allah, he asks his reader to consider why Allah gave a special place to an *oppressed* figure ("woman, maid, black," he specifies) nearby the Ka'ba. Shariati's pro-socialist position is well-known; he calls the Ka'ba the house of people. The consequences of inscribing the oppressed other into the place of the One may be problematical insofar as the oppressed other is homogenized (this remains undecided in Shariati's discourse). Of course there is also no explicitly feminist argument in his text (and it certainly remains open to a male hegemonic appropriation).[75] With these reservations in mind, it is nevertheless difficult to overlook Shariati's strong emphasis on Hagar's gender as paradigmatic of the oppressed. If "Islam is defensively anxious about manhood and insistent on subordinating women" as Abedi and Fischer underline, there is at least a slightly different egalitarian tendency from within its political discourse, however problematic it may be.

Native speaker, master audience: A postcolonial scene

I have argued that Abedi and Fischer's rationalist concept of dialogue privileges knowledge rather than ethics, maintains a hierarchical relationship between autobiographical narrative and ethnographic explanation while keeping an appearance of plurality of discourses, and privileges orality via an intentional conflation of the Qur'anic oral recitation with the face-to-face nature of oral communication and dialogue. The overall privileging of dialogue implies in fact a dialogical concept of culture as face-to-face interaction. This is an old, mainstream American social scientific belief and tradition, which Abedi and Fischer reinforce with Gadamer's concept of dialogue while evoking, at the same time, an array of theoretical vocabularies from Derrida and Joyce to Habermas. Despite the contrary claim, this remains a sophisticated form of essentialism, which reduces cultural diversity to a dialogical essence and creates the possibility of mastering cultural productivity on the basis of a dialogical model of reading. But the "other" discourse that is interpreted and responded to here is first of all listened to. This listening, which the authors once described as "archeological sondage," is entirely *epistemologically* guided. It is geared toward "understanding" the other and producing a thorough, complete cultural knowledge of her world, a knowledge that aims to detect similarities as well as differences with this other culture, and perhaps even infer lessons for its own (we read, throughout the book, various references to "us" in relation to "Muslims" or "Islam"). The fundamental assumption of this liberal humanist model is that the production of an inclusive or dialogical knowledge of the other, that is to say an epistemological program, delivers a moral, that is, nonexclusionary, nonoppressive relationship in which the other is recognized. I have criticized this assumption above as well as in the first chapter. I must nevertheless emphasize that what is at stake here is not merely a false idea or method, which can simply be replaced with another, but a politics of writing. What makes Abedi and Fischer's work so unique is the way in which it actually performs and exhibits a certain kind of determination in the global order and formation of knowledge today. This determination is a result of global historical struggles and transformations. It constructs a stage or scene, which *produces* not only Abedi and Fischer themselves but the author of these lines as well as you the reader. I would like to make clear in this sense that when I write the names "Abedi" and "Fischer" below I read them as signs, which bind us all.

A picture at the back cover of *Debating Muslims* gives a fine illustration of this stage. The photograph shows the two authors in dialogue: Abedi holds the Qur'an in his one hand, his other hand open, talking to Fischer; while his interlocutor is attentively listening and taking notes. What is striking is of course the similarity of this scene to the conventional ethnographic setting. Is it a mere coincidence that the Iranian Muslim is speaking, while the American ethnographer is listening and recording? We know that logically a reversal of roles is perfectly possible; but something tells us that this is a much more effective and more alluring image. If the picture reproduces the conventional scene, it nevertheless presents a number of visible changes that make it more complicated. First of all, their body postures and gestures position them equally as two intellectuals in a conversation. As Abedi holds the Qur'an and speaks comfortably, Fischer listens to him carefully, just before taking a note. But secondly, the division between speech and writing, which interrupts the presumed equality and symmetry, can only articulate itself as a relationship in which the Iranian speaks and the American records. This is the return of the ethnographic authority I have already highlighted in my above reading of the autobiographical chapter. This return seems impossible without the native participation and requires it as a constitutive moment or dimension of its production. Abedi holds the Qur'an with his one hand and presses it on his chest, his other hand is put on a pillow, open in the manner of explaining a concept, a gesture of unfolding (as Clifford already said, "gesture or speech"). But this gesture of unfolding does not so much unfold the word as the hermeneutics of the Qur'an as it unfolds the unfolding itself: delivering the word with one hand but keeping it with the other (the Qur'an held tight and pressed on his chest), Abedi cannot deliver the truth unless he is at the same time attempting to possess it: what he delivers is made his own in the same act. He has to own his own identity. The gesture admits the differential movement of desire, which miraculates an origin. It is important to realize therefore that here Abedi is not simply talking about himself, his experience, his life-world, his culture in a transparent way. But he is, to quote Deleuze and Guattari somewhat freely, "appropriating for himself all surplus production and arrogating to himself both the whole and the parts of the process, which now seem to emanate from him as a quasi-cause."[76] In giving while keeping, in giving what it keeps, and keeping what it gives, he is producing himself as the origin of his own speech. We are also reminded here of the *originating* function of Abedi's autobiography, in which "bracketed annotations" are "meant to highlight analytic themes, especially those which will be taken up in subsequent chapters."[77]

It would be preposterous to say that the scene is simply manipulated by the Western anthropologist. On the contrary, it is the movement of hands, the differential movement of desire, that frames it: a mode of production of cultural origin, identity, or authenticity. By the time such a miraculation is effected, however, a lot had already taken place: manifold inscriptions of affective as well as economic value—gender, class, ethnicity, religion, geography—interrupting and maintaining, enabling and disabling each other. Is such complexity accessible by a science, a book, a decision?[78] This is certainly no reason not to write books or make decisions. A decision is not simply an act of will, but also an experience of its heterogeneity. Precisely in its effort to bring the Muslims "closer" to the West, *Debating Muslims* might have missed the otherness that is already close and familiar.

What is "culture"? What is an "object" of research? Can one make, for instance, a genealogy of "Islam" as a recent and popular object of research? Such questions, usually confined to the methodology part of the works of social science, cannot be left behind once the research begins. Indeed, the "research" should perhaps never begin, or should ever begin, always interrupting itself, never letting itself go as if what is researched were not already an interruption, or the effect of an interruption. Is it this that makes the researcher to fictionalize an origin? When Abedi tells of his journey from a small Iranian village to a prestigious American university, "from a fundamentalist to a cosmopolitan consciousness,"[79] this narrative of upward mobility is presented as the story of an oral life-world. But this is not simply a literary, authentic, or micrological perspective; the narrative of individual change is isolated from the history and political economy of the region, and of the relations between the United States and Iran. If, as the authors argue, such a story is open to digression, elaboration, multiple references to other stories, why do we have a linear narrative that is occasionally "interrupted" by the authoritative, explanatory discourse of ethnography alone? The narrative is designed in a classical linear fashion "for outsiders who do not share the experiential background listeners in other contexts might have."[80] But is the distance between the United States and Iran natural, however different their cultural worlds might be? While cultural difference is surely irreducible, has "culture" ever been a pure and simple object, out there? There is a *very close* relationship between Americans and Iranians despite the geographical or cultural distance that separates them. Would contemporary American "culture" with its massive auto industry, its consumerist middle-class lifestyle, its highways—not to mention a variety of products dependent on oil industry—be possible without oil, some significant part of which came from Iran for a long time in the twentieth century? And would Iranians and Muslims have the history they had without this structural politico-economic link with the United States? It is certainly an important task to tell Americans who the Iranians or Muslims are—their culture, morals, thoughts, and values. But is it not an equally important and perhaps even more urgent task to explain to them that Iranians or "Muslims" *have been here* in their "culture," in the middle of what they consider to be the closest to themselves, despite their physical absence or geographical distance? Rather than relegating this past, this history, to "other" disciplines, we need to recognize the way it has contributed to the complexity of what cannot be observed or heard in our cultural interactions and dialogues. It is the *culturally unreadable* trace of the Iranian or Muslim other in American cultural identity and sameness that challenges the conventional concept of culture as a territorially bound and shared set of values and norms. While the authors value the postmodern as a "multilinguistic and multicultural inter-reference that throws into question the utility of the notion of bounded cultures," they themselves reproduce this very boundedness by their exclusion of what cannot be read in a dialogical, face-to-face interaction: the text of political economy.[81] The fashionable sense of postmodernism as "intertextuality" is seen as a kind of objective cultural scene produced by the global economy, carefully described as follows:

> the global economy deeply structures local events, so that *cultural understandings are saturated with borrowings, comparisons, and references to others*, drawing partly upon traditionally evolved stereotypes and partly upon the contemporary experiences of the media, of labor migration, of mass politicization, and of internationally organized social stratification.[82]

This is more a celebration of "borrowings, comparisons and references to others" than a criticism of global economy. And this is why the references to Derrida, Gadamer, Levinas, or Joyce are often merely redolent: reference itself is meant to evoke the general, given culture of multi- or inter-referentiality, otherness, borrowings, which these theories are simply supposed to reflect or express. Certainly we cannot deny the fact that today we are living in a world in which cultural exchanges are much more intense due to the abstract logic of global capitalism, technological changes, and mass migration. It would be rather naïve, however, to assume that this constitutes sufficient ground for access to plurality via a concept of dialogue conceived as the essence of culture.[83] Despite Abedi and Fischer's sincere criticism of media stereotypes, one wonders if their dialogical perspective, especially in its emphasis on the face-to-face, oral nature of dialogue, shares something of what it criticizes: the widespread modern technological presupposition of bringing the distant closer and making the world accessible. If, as various modern critics of modernity, from Segalen to Heidegger, have pointed out that the reductions in real distance do not necessarily lead to a smaller, more interactive, or smoother world but the erection of new barriers and the production of new distances, one should perhaps consider discontinuing identity rather than miraculating it, and interrupting knowledge and truth rather than legitimizing and authorizing it.

3

Exchange Past and Future

Anthropology and sociology have allowed me to reconcile myself with my primary experiences and to take them upon myself, to assume them without losing anything I subsequently acquired.

An Invitation to Reflexive Sociology (204)

I have indeed the feeling that, particularly on account of the scale of my path through social space and the practical incompatibility of the social worlds that it links without reconciling them, I cannot wager—being far from sure of achieving it myself with the instruments of sociology—that the reader will be able to bring to bear on the experience that I shall be led to evoke, the gaze that, in my view, is the appropriate one.

Sketch for a Self-Analysis (1)

Pierre Bourdieu's fascinating sociological and ethnographic work continues to provoke criticism and commentary in contemporary humanities and social sciences. In the first chapter, I have already argued that his strong criticism of interactionism should be taken as a warning against all forms of ethnographic pluralism based on an unquestioned inclusion of native voice. I have also underscored the limits of Bourdieu's criticism, his dependence on a conventional epistemological distinction between appearance and truth, and his notion of past, which is a constitutive aspect of his major contribution to social theory, the concept of *habitus*. In this chapter, I would like to further investigate this concept, especially in the context of Bourdieu's own ethnographic works in colonized Algeria.

Native difference

Bourdieu's choice of the ethnography of Kabylia as the major case or illustration of his theory of practice[1] has recently been questioned in a collection of essays titled *Bourdieu in Algeria* (2009). As the editors Jane E. Goodman and Paul A. Silverstein argue in their introduction, although the Kabylia society is taken as an ethnographic exemplar, "the colonial location of Bourdieu's work is nearly impossible to discern from the *Outline*, the primary ethnographic study in which the notion of *habitus* is brought to maturity."[2] Silverstein and Goodman do not question Bourdieu's commitment to anticolonialism and his unwavering support for Algerian independence (nor do I), yet they are critical of the dualistic picture of Algerian society that emerges in his work as well as his failure to recognize the colonial conditions of his ethnographic research. In his later work, *Sketch for a Self-Analysis*, Bourdieu brings up the issue of the colonial context of his ethnography, yet his account relates how the colonial military authorities, which put him on a red list, produced numerous difficulties and obstacles.[3] However, in his theoretical texts such as the *Outline of a Theory of Practice*, *The Logic of Practice*, *Pascalian Meditations*, and *Masculine Domination*, while having engaged in sophisticated epistemological discussions of structure and agency, or structuralism and phenomenology, which are discussions "incarnated" in Kabylian examples, Bourdieu never takes into account a simple fact: it is colonialism that made it possible for him to *be there* as a researcher. Accordingly, the status of such "ethnographic data" itself should be put under interrogation before it is allegorized into theory.

Why and how does the ethnographic data come to occupy such a privileged, exemplary place in a theory of practice? What makes it different than other kinds of data? Although Bourdieu fails to consider the epistemic violence of colonialism as an immanent aspect of his research, he is not simply unaware of the nature of his scientific enterprise. In fact, he is highly conscious of the fact that, as native knowledge or "habitus" never reaches the level of full consciousness, it cannot be known in the way it is experienced or practiced by the native. Further, ethnographic or sociological knowledge of habitus changes the nature of this tacit, practical, and embodied knowledge. This is not a question of cultural difference as such; it is an epistemological problem, perhaps even the very problem of epistemology, that must be given careful attention. Scholarly habitus is disposed to forget that practical, bodily knowledge is not the same as theoretical or speculative knowledge produced from a sovereign, scientific position. Hence Bourdieu's ethnography argues for the *difference* of the native, embodied knowledge. Although habitus involves language, it is in the nature of this kind of embodied knowledge to escape from full and clear articulation (whether this native knowledge or habitus be cultural, classed, or gendered). Never explicitly articulated, though constantly adjusted and improvised, the kind of embodied knowledge that characterizes habitus is not necessarily what is told by the native informant. Bourdieu mistrusts what he calls "official knowledge"; for instance, one must be aware of the difference between "official" and "practical" kinship.[4]

But all is not limited to this constitutive distinction between appearance and truth of practice. Indeed, the truth of practice is not like any other truth: it does not authorize uninterrupted access to itself. There is no direct route from the data to the truth that underlies it. There is a sort of uncontrollable *variation* inherent to the difference of native, practical knowledge, similar to the latitude of the rules of a game (Bourdieu often speaks of a "feel for the game"). The information gathered suggests *equivalence* rather than identity of practice even in the same habitus. It is always a play of contrasts, of analogies, and of homologies.[5] The ethnographer is expected to perform a particular vigilance with respect to this variation and lacunae. As we observe in the famous example of the Kabylia calendar, the ethnographer's immediate desire is the "lacuna-free, contradiction-free whole, a sort of *unwritten score* of which all the calendars derived from informants are then regarded as imperfect, impoverished *performances*."[6] Once put on paper, however,

> a calendar substitutes a linear, homogeneous, continuous time for a practical time, which is made up of incommensurable islands of duration, each with its own rhythm, the time that flies by or drags, depending on what one is *doing*, i.e. on the *functions* conferred on it by the activity in progress.[7]

That Bourdieu brings up this kind of paradox should certainly not mislead us about his firm belief in a scientific (or sociological) theory of practice. Bourdieu's aim is refinement of knowledge rather than setting merely external limits to it. The task of the sociologist is to reveal the *truth* of a social relationship, practice, or institution. The difference between appearance and truth maintains its strategic significance, for, based on an arbitrary principle, every group or society "conceals from itself its own truth."[8] In a good faith economy such as the Kabylian society,

> the operation of gift exchange presupposes (individual and collective) misrecognition of the reality of the objective "mechanism" of the exchange, a

reality which an immediate response brutally exposes: the interval between gift and counter-gift is what allows a pattern of exchange that is always liable to strike the observer and also the participants as reversible, i.e. both forced and interested, to be experienced as irreversible.[9]

By the interval of time they introduce into the process of exchange, the agents deny the interests involved in it and transform it into reciprocity. Bourdieu's theory is supposed to "remove the conditions making possible the *institutionally organized and guaranteed misrecognition*, which is the basis of gift exchange."[10]

In epistemologically correcting theoretical knowledge by taking the point of view of real practice,[11] Bourdieu's scholarly gesture is one of demystification in the tradition of the Enlightenment.[12] If sociology based on ethnographic data is a "political science," then the native is invited to understand the nature of his or her practical knowledge and change his or her relationship to it and to the world.[13] But *who* is the native? Or, how is the native produced? In theoretical books such as the *Outline*, *The Logic of Practice*, *Pascalian Meditations*, and the *Masculine Domination*, Bourdieu isolates the Kabylia society from its social, political, and historical context and identifies it in terms of a closed, traditional gift economy. In the only place where he comes close to acknowledging something like *the presence of colonial power as a condition of his research*, he refers to the high quality of a photograph he took in the Collo region because the roof of a house had been destroyed by the French army so that the occupants would not be able to return to it. The light of such photographic record, of scientific and technological *Aufklärung*, is aptly called "colonial light" by a critic,[14] as it is the result of a clearing of habitus by the colonizer's military destruction. Looking at the photograph years later, Bourdieu is reminded of "questioning the determinants of a so obviously 'misplaced' *libido sciendi*."[15] But this self-criticism never goes as far as questioning the very *place* of the ethnographer. On the contrary, he writes in the sentence immediately following this statement: "my disquiet was relieved to some extent by the *interest* my informants always manifested in my research when it became theirs too, in other words a striving to recover a meaning that was both their own and alien to them."[16] Such a meaning, which the native knows without knowing, is the authentic, true meaning, which can only be delivered by the sociologist (on the condition that he keeps a distance from his own academic habitus). Goodman and Silverstein rightly describe Bourdieu's project as a version of "salvage ethnography."[17] It also needs to be emphasized that in Bourdieu's research the place of the ethnographer is both necessary and impossible; for, if the native ever reaches such true knowledge of his/her practice, there will be no ethnographer left, as everyone will now be their own ethnographers.

Habit versus consciousness?

We have so far seen that, in spite of his political opposition to colonialism, Bourdieu cannot read colonialism's epistemic violence as an immanent, enabling dimension of his own research. There is another, no less serious charge directed at Bourdieu by anthropologists of Islam: his emphasis on habitus as an unconscious, embodied, practical knowledge involves the exclusion of the intellectual, discursive, and interpretive traditions of Islam. This can be connected to two further criticisms. First of all, Bourdieu's exclusion of the discursive dimension enables him to isolate and fashion a kind of "native" information and a kind of ethnographic "data" that is convenient for the conventional anthropological object (tribal, ritualistic, oral culture), by means of which he can then produce a theoretical criticism of Levi-Strauss' structuralism (through a demonstration of the role played by time in the gift exchange). Jane Goodman stresses, for instance, how Bourdieu's narrow focus on the oral culture completely leaves out the written aspects of Kabyle culture in his theoretical texts.[18] Secondly, Bourdieu's exclusion of the discursive aspects of Islam is connected with (and reinforces) the widespread criticism of his work as a strong version of objectivism, which is often attributed to his privileging of the unconscious, embodied, and repetitive aspects of practice in the concept of habitus. I should now go through these criticisms.

Gregory Starrett's refreshing work on Islamic education in Egypt makes use of the concept of "hexis," which is also used by Bourdieu.[19] This ancient Greek notion means "having" or "state" in the sense of an active state or disposition that is acquired by training or habituation rather than a natural property. Aristotle uses it in his *Metaphysics* (5.1022b). Its Latin translation is "habitus." In English translation, the usual choices are "disposition" (which is also one of the meanings of the term according to Aristotle: *diathesis*) or "habit." Focusing on the Muslim hexis, Starrett develops his own conceptual framework in a critical dialogue with Bourdieu. When Bourdieu uses the word "hexis" it is always "body hexis" (e.g. manner of walking or speaking). If it is not the same thing as habitus, they are nevertheless very close for Bourdieu.[20] For Starrett however, there seems to be some distance between the two. Starrett's main criticism is that Bourdieu offers a "*narrow* reading of hexis as habitus-formation" and

> rather than conceiving of hexis primarily as a wordless, unconscious, and practical transmission of bodily habit, we might instead read "the embodiment of ideology in habit" as a set of processes through which individuals and groups *consciously ascribe meaning* to—or learn to perceive meaning in— bodily disposition, and to establish, maintain, and contest publicly its political valence.[21]

These statements imply that hexis is *more* than habitus taken as habit, as Starrett argues that we make the process of conscious ascription of meaning and/or the meaning ascribed to bodily disposition a *part* of hexis (which could only be conscious meaning). However, in the same place Starrett also uses the concept of hexis in the sense of bodily disposition that receives signification and interpretation from the outside: ". . . bodily habit is inherently ambigious, so that *hexis is always subject to multiple interpretations*. More significant than the implicit meanings of *bodily hexis*, then, are its public mediation and uses."[22] Hexis is then *both* the bodily disposition subject to conscious signification and interpretation *and* the very process of conscious ascription of meaning to bodily disposition.

As Starrett's purpose is to make self-conscious signifying activity a part of habitus or hexis, perhaps this almost imperceptible paradox is forgivable. In his illuminating research, he observes such self-conscious discursive activity in the pedagogical discourses of colonialism and nationalism. The European travelers and colonial administrators read the Egyptian Muslim body as a sign of cultural inferiority, an instance of primitive religion and fanaticism: repetitive physical motion in performances such as the Qur'an recitation in schools and in the prayer or energetic, intoxicating whirling in Sufi *dervish* dances are opposed to an idealized, steady, composed body, which expressed the more spiritual and mature European approach to the sacred.[23] Hence, following the European pedagogical model of an upright, still, and disciplined body, national educational establishment eliminated certain aspects of traditional teaching that were seen as overemphasized (such as memorization or repetitive bodily movement) and replaced them with a new educational discourse that emphasized hygiene and medical aspects. Currently educators "use Islamic principles to legitimize new technologies like in vitro fertilization, as well as corroborating Islamic concepts and practices with scientific and medical vocabulary."[24] National pedagogy overturned the colonial discourse, first of all by constructing Islam as a sign of cultural advancement, social order, and progress (as it establishes an internal link between health and cleanliness, the very signs of civilization, *and* the precepts of Islamic faith), and secondly by fitting Muslim ritual prayer into a disciplinary space.[25] According to Starrett,

> What is important in both these shifts is their illustration of the essential ambiguity in attributions of ideology to hexis. This is due both to contestations over the significance of specific habits (what does repetitive prostration mean?) and to the fact that in any ritual there are a number of features that can be made to signify.[26]

In other words, the same bodily hexis is interpreted in opposite ways and is ascribed opposite meanings by colonial and national discourses. Predicting the trap of falling into the assumption of a zero point of meaning, that is, a meaningless ritual, Starrett gives a warning:

> Pointing out that the school operates to fix bodily disposition with explicit meaning is *not just* to say that the historical development of formal educational systems involves the articulation and explication by intellectuals of *a formerly mute habitus*, the creation of a hegemonic orthodoxy out of the ineffable background of doxa.[27]

When Starrett rightly cautions us that there is no "mute habitus," he is in contradiction with his previous description of habitus as "wordless, unconscious bodily habit."[28] These turns and paradoxes of his argument, the different and opposed meanings attributed to both habitus and hexis throughout the text, are the textual effects of his unquestioned faith in an old binary opposition: body versus mind, or as it appears here, body versus discourse, in which body is always either inert and passive or a lifeless mechanism. In either case, it is consciousness that gives it meaning from outside. Accordingly, Starrett seems to have no doubt about the sites of production and reception of meaning, what produces and what receives it. He is confident for instance that "'meaning does not lie in the body' [Cowan 1990], and by themselves, of course, neither stillness nor motion means anything at all,"[29] or "bodily meaning is inherently ambiguous, so that hexis is always subject to multiple interpretations."[30] But why is ambiguity an inherent feature *of the body* only? How would it be possible for the Egyptian nationalist to overturn the colonial discourse if language or discourse were not inherently ambiguous too?[31] When Starret attributes an inherent ambiguity to body alone, it is in order to reinforce a prior decision he made without stating: it is the body that must receive meaning from outside, as it is obviously passive, inert, dead matter.

Bourdieu's constant reference to speech (as opposed to the abstract structure of language)[32] and especially to the *manner* of speaking as a constitutive disposition of habitus, as well as his numerous references to the proverbs, make clear that he does *not* see habitus as wordless or mute at all. Indeed, although Bourdieu strongly emphasizes that the practical knowledge embodied in habitus is below the level of consciousness, the issue of cognition is not simply resolved in his text (which is rich in contradictions). The kind of "unconscious" he has in mind refers to a practical sense, which is itself constantly changing and is constantly adjusted, rather than simply excluding all cognition.[33] Bourdieu's is a criticism of the transcendent consciousness, and not a dismissal of all cognitive acitivity. He never rules out for instance that "the responses of the habitus may be accompanied by a strategic calculation tending to carry on quasi-consciously the operation the habitus carries on in a quite different way."[34] Similarly he refers to the habitus as "a cognitive and motivating" structure.[35] In his declared fight against the dichotomy of structure versus agency, if it is a kind of objectivism that has the upper hand in the final analysis,[36] this is an objectivism of a very singular kind that becomes interesting in its failure of turning "generative schemes" and "improvisations" of habitus into occasions of reproduction rather than of change and transformation.

I now turn to Saba Mahmood's criticism of Bourdieu in her stimulating research on the women's mosque movement in Egypt.[37] It is through a critical reading of Bourdieu that Mahmood introduces her own concept of habitus, based on Aristotle's concept habitus or hexis as well as a certain reading of Foucault's concept of ethics as the cultivation of self.[38]

Mahmood's work is a fascinating ethnographic study of the women's mosque movement in Egypt—a movement in which voluntary women teachers teach religious piety to women audiences. Developing spontaneously in various neighborhood mosques in Cairo, the women's mosque movement is a singular instance of Islamic revival in Egypt. Its proponents argue that, since Islam is folklorized and its pious essence is destroyed by nationalist establishment, Muslim women must be taught Islamic virtues in order to enable them to maintain genuine piety in everyday life under modern conditions. It is important to emphasize that the movement does not have an intellectual aim; their whole purpose is to educate and prepare Muslim women for a pious life. It is this particular orientation of articulating piety and virtue embodied in Islamic precepts and rituals with the routine practice of everyday life that Mahmood finds singularly significant in the women's mosque movement. By focusing on the discourses and techniques of cultivating an ethical, pious Muslim self and on how such an instruction is effected by a strong emphasis on the everyday lives of women, she draws the map of a complex and intriguing instance of women's agency. Her argument is opened with a powerful criticism of Western, liberal, and feminist concepts of freedom, agency, and resistance: the problematic underlying the liberal discourse is the Kantian universal concept of autonomous will and reason, which excludes collective forms of agency emerging from local and particular conditions. Further, such an approach identifies agency with resistance to power and fails to see that it is power that often enables agency and gives birth to resistance in its practice. It is at this point of Mahmood's argument that ritual plays a significant role as performative repetition. While Mahmood's concept of agency largely depends on Butler's well-known theory of performative iteration or repetition of hegemonic norms,[39] she is also critical of Butler's "agonistic" framework in which the norms are either reproduced or subverted, without any sense of the role they might play beyond this duality within the constitution of the subject.[40] Mahmood's work is also inspired to some extent by Foucault's concept of the technologies of self-care or self-making, which she reads mostly through Claire Colebrook's reading of Foucault with Aristotle.[41] Utilizing Foucault's distinction between morals (norms and interdictions) and ethics (practices, techniques, and discourses), Mahmood focuses on the ways "through which a subject transforms herself in order to achieve a particular state of being."[42] This framework enables her to distinguish and analyze various techniques and discourses employed by women in the mosque movement to transform themselves into ethical, pious subjects.

Critical of the universalizing and rationalizing tendency of the Kantian approach, Mahmood is interested in the local texture and morphology of moral actions. This is why she turns her focus on Bourdieu's concept of habitus. According to Mahmood, although Bourdieu acknowledges that the habitus is learned, his approach remains limited because his primary concern is the unconscious and mimetic ways of learning at the expense of an attention to *the pedagogical process* by which a habitus is learned. The mosque participants approach *the body as a site* of moral training and cultivation. Of course, the aim of conscious training in the habituation of virtues is to make consciousness redundant to the practice of virtues. And yet, "insofar as the point is not simply that one acts virtuously but also how one enacts a virtue (with what intent, emotion, commitment, etc.), constant vigilance and monitoring of one's practices is a critical element in this model of ethical formation."[43] The significance of the discursive aspect comes from its reflective nature for Mahmood. This is certainly not totally alien to Foucault's readings of technologies of self-care, but Mahmood's position is somewhat closer to Aristotle than Foucault. She stresses that, although the concept of habitus (or hexis) comes from Aristotle, Bourdieu completely ignores the degree to which the so-called durable, embodied dispositions might have been the product of conscious vigilance and self-reflection, acquired as moral and practical craft. In the *Metaphysics* and the *Nicomachean Ethics*, Aristotle develops a concept of habitus according to which moral virtue takes root in one's character in a process of learning by doing.[44] Mahmood also points out that Foucault's concept of ethics is "Aristotelian in that it conceives of ethics not as an Idea, or as a set of regulatory norms, but as a set of practical activities that are germane to a certain way of life."[45] This is an immanent ethics that is particular and local rather than universal and transcendent.[46] Mahmood further shows that the same Aristotelian concept can be found in various Islamic thinkers such as Al-Ghazali, Ibn Rushd, and Ibn Khaldun: the Arabic term *malaka* is a virtue, quality, or capacity learned through repeated practice until it leaves a permanent mark on one's character.[47] In every respect, she finds Aristotle's concept theoretically richer and more convenient for her purpose than Bourdieu's "model of unconscious imbibing."[48]

Without any objection to the relevance of Mahmood's research, I would nevertheless like to question her criticism of Bourdieu for overlooking and excluding what seems to be the most interesting and useful aspect of Bourdieu's theory of practice. I would not like to say that Starrett's and Mahmood's criticisms are "wrong" in any simple sense. It is true that Bourdieu's theory of practice underestimates the discursive aspect (in the intellectual sense that these critics intend it). This is largely because of his sociological objectivism and realism. Although this sociological objectivism must definitely be criticized, the criticism should not be directed at the "unconscious" aspect of habitus, which is Bourdieu's distinctive contribution as a concept opening up *a new way* of thinking the relations between body *and* language. The kind of criticism that targets the unconscious aspect of habitus in a manner that opposes it to discourse only takes the concept of discourse back into the old problematic of constitutive consciousness and thus reproduce the same series of binarisms (consciousness vs real determination, structure vs agency, body vs mind) rather than keeping the field of research open. Often despite himself, Bourdieu makes a significant potential contribution to a theory of practice that should not be reduced to mechanical, habitual reproduction of given or hegemonic norms and that might be taken in the direction of Foucault's ethics. I should offer one interesting example from Mahmood's own work, which shows us how the remarkable positivity of Bourdieu's concept of habitus as embodied past might have been missed by these critics.

A significant example of Mahmood's detailed and informative analyses of various disciplinary discourses and techniques is the pious approach to the daily prayer. If the pious Muslim must fight the ever-threatening possibility of the daily prayer's turning into routine, formal, habitually performed duty, devoid of religious content, it is of utmost importance that she prays with *hushu*, which is the virtuous state of humility and submission. Hence the problem of acquiring this disposition is a veritable instance of Aristotelian hexis. It is important to emphasize here what cannot be registered in a binary framework of "reflective discourse vs. unconscious habit": the pious Muslim has to gain a new habit (the good, virtuous disposition of *hushu*) in order to fight another (the bad habit of empty formalism). Ancient ethics seems to have a homeopathic surprise for the reflective opponents of unconscious, wordless imitation: *habit, the most habitual thing in the world, cannot be separated from change.*[49] As Mahmood relates, a widely circulated booklet on this subject mentions a particular technique, which is supposed to produce the state of *hushu*: "weeping during the course of prayer, especially at the time of supplications, as a means for the expression and realization of a fearful and reverential attitude (*khashya*) toward God."[50] The act of weeping must be induced, if the desired affect of pious tenderness is to emerge. Mahmood specifies that this has nothing to do with grief: rather than a cathartic release of stressful emotions, it must express one's awe for God. She describes it as "rehearsed spontaneity" (which is also the title of her article). She mentions a few common exercises women use in order to produce the intended affect:

> envisioning that one was being physically held between the hands of God during prayer; visualizing crossing the legendary bridge (*al-sarat*), narrow as a sharp blade, that all Muslims will be required to walk in the Hereafter but that only the pious will be able to traverse successfully; or avoiding the fires of hell that lie underneath . . . imagining the immensity of God's power and their own insignificance.[51]

While Mahmood's argument is focused on the *reorientation* of one's motivations by the effort of imagination, she may be underestimating the role played by the simplest aspect of this exercise. How do the women bring themselves to weeping? How can the "repeated invocation" guarantee the reorientation of affects and the cultivation of ethical virtue? Bourdieu's emphasis on the embodied aspect of mimesis could have been only helpful in understanding this practice. Indeed Mahmood quoted an interesting passage in which Bourdieu gives weeping as an example of bodily mimesis.[52] Bourdieu writes:

> . . . more importantly, the process of acquisition—a practical mimesis (or mimeticism) which implies an overall relation of identification and has nothing in common with an imitation that would presuppose a conscious effort to reproduce a gesture, an utterance or an object explicitly constituted as a model—and the process of reproduction—a practical reactivation which is opposed to both memory and knowledge—tend to take place below the level of consciousness, expression and the reflexive distance which these presuppose. *The body believes in what it plays at: it weeps if it mimes grief. It does not represent what it performs, it does not memorize the past, it enacts the past, bringing it back to life. What is "learned by body" is not something that one has, like knowledge that can be brandished, but something that one is.*[53]

While making this quote in her own text, Mahmood omitted the part on weeping because she has probably read it as an illustration of Bourdieu's theory of unconscious, unreflective, mechanical imitation. As Mahmood rightly specifies, *Bourdieu does not deny that the habitus is learned*, but the fact that dispositions come from the outside does not mean for him that the body is passive, inert matter, or a "tool" that can be used by the mind.[54] On the contrary, we read in Bourdieu's sentences an active body. It seems as if, since Bourdieu's example is grief, it cannot apply for Mahmood's case of the ritual prayer that is not a cathartic experience but awe for God. Without disrespect for the singularity of this religious affect, we must nevertheless keep in mind that it would be impossible for an act such as weeping not to produce its own affect, not to come with its own affect *as* it is performed. Bourdieu does not say, "you must weep in order to look like you are in grief, since the latter is the cause of weeping." He says, "weeping is *what a body can perform* whether in grief or not." It is not a question of representing or memorizing but one of *enacting* past. This is the enigma of *what is brought back* in this performance, what is *learned by the body*, by its unique mimetic power, as different from "knowledge that can be brandished."

Surely the women must make themselves cry, must produce the affect of weeping. But it is never sufficient to think of weeping or something associated with it in order to cry: the effort of thinking or feeling must at the same time experience a limit, that which it cannot think or imagine, an "other" side women can never cross, as pious as they might be. Therefore it is true that they bring "something" back, but the past that is enacted has never existed as a past present. It is what thinkers as varied as Bergson, Merleau-Ponty, Deleuze, and Derrida call "absolute past": a past that has never been present but that is always here, *in* the present. It is not that the women try to remember how they have wept the last time they did; for Bourdieu, the body *is* the absolute memory of weeping that only it can enact. It would not be wrong to say that the religious stories in these women's imaginative exercises are allegories of absolute past.

This is not an insignificant point, given the association of woman with body and nature in the series of binarisms that inform the data of social and cultural theory (man vs woman, sign vs referent, culture vs nature, body vs mind, west vs rest). A perspective that conceives of the body as inert, passive matter on which signs are inscribed will have unintended effects on feminist as well as postcolonial thought, ethics, and politics, as these "others" are always associated with body and nature conceived as passive, primitive, etc. This is why Mahmood's study would have certainly benefited from including Bourdieu's insight articulated in his concept of habitus rather than dismissing it as unconscious assimilation, for what is at stake in this concept are the relations between body and time, memory and inscription. I wonder if her own argument, despite its unique contribution to the debates on agency, is guided by a certain fantasy of going beyond the binarism of structure versus agency—similar to Bourdieu's. Mahmood's research reveals that, although the women's mosque movement reproduces submission to male authority on a thematic level, it has nevertheless produced a veritable instance of women's agency in the middle of a strong male hegemony (it would be sufficient to think that the mosque is a space effectively hegemonized and physically occupied by male religious authority and men). It is surprising however to read that Mahmood is not sure if such agency must be attributed to the women themselves! In a theoretical elaboration, she emphasizes:

> Even though I focus on the practices of the mosque participants, this does not mean that their activities and the operations they perform on themselves are products of their independent wills; rather, my argument is that these activities are the products of authoritative discursive traditions whose logic and power far exceeds the consciousness of the subjects they enable. The kind of agency I am exploring here does not belong to the women themselves, but is a product of the historically contingent discursive traditions in which they are located.[55]

In arguing that "their activity is not a product of their independent will," has Mahmood not taken the liberal feminist argument from the back door (an argument that depends on the notion of independent will)? Moreover, what exactly are those other "historically contingent" discourses (i.e. other than the authoritative tradition of religion) that produce the agency that "does not belong to women" and that is beyond their consciousness? After all, whose agency is this, if not the women's, *an agency embodied in their practices and experiences and enacted by their bodies*? This is surely *an agency that no other body, experience, or knowledge* would have been able to enact. It is one of the oldest, the most ancient, yet one that seldom gets recognition *as agency*.

I must immediately add, however, that Bourdieu's attention to a unique concept of practical bodily knowledge and action does not make him an exemplary theorist for feminism. Despite the fact that his own progressive, well-intended work on women's oppression, *Masculine Domination* (2001), is particularly instructive in its singular attention to the minutiae of everyday life (bodily gestures, words, and behavior) as the time and space of production of women's subordinate position in society, Bourdieu approaches this system in typically objectivist terms. As he uses the same already highly problematical Kabylian examples (examples in which women—in sharp contradistinction to what the theory of practice declares—only walk and talk the way the rules prescribe, their bodies being a surface where not only masculine domination is established but also all domination is modeled), his treatment of the literary texts of Virginia Woolf as mere illustrations of his theory does not pay sufficient attention to the critical literary power of their author's language.

The problem with Bourdieu's approach is not the concept of habitus, which is indeed his unique contribution to social theory, but his objectivist and economic-structuralist reductionism. I should now move on to the question of body and memory.

"A torsion of habitus"

As Butler recognizes, Bourdieu's approach is influenced by Merleau-Ponty's phenomenology.[56] In her illuminating reading of Bourdieu, Butler also points out how Bourdieu's understanding of the body's action as "incorporated memory" resonates with Bergson's philosophy.[57] If we employ Bergson's distinction between "habit memory" and "pure memory," Bourdieu's perspective is limited to the first one. Coinciding with the acquisition of the sensory-motor mechanism, *habit memory* has to do with automatic behavior by means of repetition, hence with perception and present action, serving a practical purpose only, whereas *pure memory* has to do with a kind of "unconscious" survival of memories, that is to say memory as such.[58] Although Merleau-Ponty's phenomenological approach to the body chooses to focus on present, useful, and habitual perception (like Bourdieu's), interestingly this concept is not alien to Merleau-Ponty who refers to it as "a kind of original past, a past which has never been present."[59] Having made the decision that nothing can surpass or subvert social determination (except sociological knowledge, the very knowledge of this determination), Bourdieu reduces all action to the present and practical action, and all memory to the practical, useful memory: the result is the endless reproduction of a given order of habitus, with necessary improvisations or adjustments depending on the nature of the task. This is why for instance "virtue made of necessity" is an expression that is frequently found in Bourdieu's ethnographies of working-class taste or peasant society. The body in Bourdieu's concept of habitus is a *body of work or labor*. It seems as if Bourdieu's agents never fall in love, never think of death, never like to read poetry, are never curious about the origins of the universe, or sing at night for no reason. Remembering his most well-known example of Kabylian Muslim habitus, men and women walk and talk only the way the rules prescribe, and even though they play with the rules of kinship, they never seem to secretly meet at the far end of the fields.[60]

Nevertheless, Bourdieu's text is also full of contradictions, ambiguities, and shifts. For instance, when he contrasts the "linear, homogeneous and continuous" calendarical time produced by the ethnographer with the peasant's practical time, which is "made up of *incommensurable islands of duration, each with its own rhythm*, the time that flies by or drags, depending on what one is *doing*, i.e. on the *functions* conferred on it by the activity in progress,"[61] he distinguishes a heterogeneous duration and rhythm that remains irreducible and outside quantitative measure.[62] In the same sentence, however, such heterogeneity is immediately connected with a "doing" conceived as "function." A more intriguing example is directly related with the concept of habitus: Bourdieu writes that dispositions and operational schemes are "analogous to *the rhythm of a line of verse whose words have been forgotten*."[63] This allusion to literature for understanding such a strictly and modestly practical sense is supposed to work analogically, like practical sense itself (even though the agent of such sense is not always credited with literary competence). Bourdieu's text performs what it says: which means that it also works in analogy with the rhythm of a line of verse whose words are forgotten by its author. If we follow Bourdieu's analogy, then in each case an agent employs his/her practical sense he/she brings the words back by their rhythm. That is to say, rather than remembering the words, they are enacted by the "rhythm" that is left in the place of their composition. The agent does not necessarily bring the same words back; there is always analogy, improvisation, transference, transposition, and so on by the very logic of this formulation.[64] Should a different word not change the rhythm? An analogy, it seems from a practical point of view, is only an analogy. One also suspects, naturally, if this rhythm is preserved in and as body. But it would be too fast a decision to infer from this the conclusion that the body is therefore "wordless," for the moment we make such a decision we have forgotten that the rhythm *belongs to* the line of verse that is already composed of words. Most significantly, rhythm, tempo, and especially improvisation—not to mention the virtuoso— are frequently used *musical* concepts in Bourdieu. Such a literary and musical set of allusions implies Bergson's pure memory and Merleau-Ponty's original past. What Bergson calls memory as such welcomes and registers everything, whether useful or not.[65] Since Bourdieu's philosophical background and his intellectual affinity with phenomenological arguments and debates on time enabled him to introduce a radically new perspective into social issues he is often very close to the concept of absolute past, as we have seen in the instance of weeping. Indeed this example itself suggests an original theory of body as incorporated past, that is, a past or memory that is heterogeneous to consciousness yet always existing in the present in and as bodily capacity. But his *sociological objectivism* never allows this pure or absolute memory to demonstrate its excess, its play of difference, always bringing it back to its practical sense or keeping it within the limits of need, use, and function.[66] Practical sense ("social necessity turned into nature, converted into motor schemes and body automatisms") is destined to be blind to its own principle, which can *only* be grasped *from a sociological point of view, a point of view which holds fast to the strategic difference between appearence and truth.* In a silent passage, supported by the real determinations of class and domination, all difference and heterogeneity of practice is collapsed into the strategic difference between appearance and truth. An epistemological and sociological discourse gains the upper hand as the sole arbiter of the ethico-political.[67] Because, if the difference of practice is something else than a failure of reason, this can only mean that those incommensurable durations and rhythms affirm themselves and begin to have another life, produce other signs, which begin to circulate without market, without interest, indifferent to their capitalization, that is to say, indifferent to the truth that can only be articulated by *sociology, and no other discourse.* This is why, for Bourdieu, misrecognition is an integral part of practical social sense, which could be known only by the sociologist on the condition that he is himself not misled by his own theoretical practice as a theorist of practice.[68]

In his lectures on Kant, Gilles Deleuze refers precisely to such incommensurable durations and rhythms as constructed by the ethnologist: schemata, manners, blocks of space-time and spatio-temporal rhythms specific to a civilization. He also finds such blocks of space-time or spatio-temporal rhythms in *art*, as created by the artist who is a "rhythmicist."[69] As is well-known, while in the *Critique of Pure Reason* Kant treats the imaginative act of synthesis unproblematically as the successive apprehension of the parts of an object, in the *Critique of Judgment* what counts as part becomes a problem for him. He takes body as the sensible, qualitative unit of measure in aesthetic comprehension and demonstrates that this measure is determined subjectively, rather than objectively.[70] If a Kabylian peasant were to describe a tree "as tall as five men" and a mountain "as high as twenty trees," I doubt whether Kant or Bourdieu would have granted him any aesthetic capacity, but his perception is based on the kind of measure Kant called aesthetic. Going a step further, Deleuze argues that aesthetic comprehension of units can only be grasped as *rhythm*. Although Kant does not use this concept, rhythm refers to the *heterogeneous* nature of aesthetic measure for Deleuze. "To restore to practice its practical truth" Bourdieu writes, "we must reintroduce time into the theoretical representation of practice, which being temporally structured, is intrinsically defined by its tempo."[71] If both time and tempo (rhythm) share the same structure revealed by the regular beat of the latter, that is, if both are *homogeneously divided*, what do we make of those "incommensurable islands of duration, each with its own rhythm"?[72] As expected, Deleuze distinguishes rhythm from tempo with respect to the concept: "A concept, at best, will give you the beat or the tempo. Which is to say a homogeneous beat, but rhythmicity is something entirely different from a homogeneous beat, something entirely different from a tempo."[73] This is because for Deleuze rhythm communicates with chaos. It seems difficult to avoid a logic of priority here, whether it is the form or the unformed that comes first; in any case, Deleuze's effort suggests that the regularity and composition that make a habitus or ethos are characterized by internal discontinuity and heterogeneity. I am referring to the radical openness of habitus as bodily memory rather than opposing artistic creativity to practical sense (from this point of view, habit memory is already pure memory, which should problematize any tendency of opposing them to each other). When Jacques Rancière criticizes Bourdieu for essentializing the class distinction by his dismissal of the working class taste as virtue made of necessity, he brings up the interesting example of the carpenter Gauny, who "offers the gaze of an aesthete on the décor of his servitude."[74] He describes Gauny's singular acquisition of aesthetic gaze as a "*torsion of habitus* that he imposes upon himself."[75] Bourdieu never seems to allow a habitus to have such twists and turns, even though literary references and allusions abound in his texts. As Fanny Colona writes,

> the sophistication of the Kabyle poetic tradition, the genuinely sapiential role of the poets in this culture . . . and the known horizontality of cultural practice in this culture . . . all went counter to any depiction of culture as something merely incorporated in reproducing itself mechanically through practice.[76]

In fact, no cultural practice can be homogenized in the habit memory of practical time, and no poetry and no art would be possible without pure memory or pure past. We will have to examine Bourdieu's problematic of time more closely.

Time of the other: Absolute past

I need to sum up my argument. First of all, although Bourdieu is politically critical of colonialism, he cannot think of the way in which colonialism is an internal condition of the possibility of his research. Secondly, the form in which social determination appears inevitable in Bourdieu's theory is problematic. Although he makes a unique contribution to the way in which we think of the relationship between body, time, and practice, and helps us see the heterogeneity or excess of native difference to some extent, his position is characterized by a privileging of scientific knowledge that depends on a classical distinction between appearance and truth. The heterogeneous nature of native difference is therefore always held within the limits of a strictly determining instance and of practical adjustment that makes virtue of necessity.

I would now like to read more closely the interesting problematic of time in the first part of Bourdieu's *Algeria 1960*: "The Disenchantment of the World."[77] As the Weberian title already suggests, Bourdieu's analysis is guided by the *sociological grand narrative* of change from traditional to modern economy (with quasi-Marxian overtones). He gives an entirely new twist to the grand narrative by introducing into it *a problematic of time and body* that he learned from Merleau-Ponty. I would like to demonstrate how Bourdieu's problematic of time turns out to be a denial of time in support of a completely binary model. "The Disenchantment of the World" is certainly not as refined as the later theoretical texts such the *Outline*, *The Logic of Practice*, or *Pascalian Meditations*. Although one imagines that Bourdieu must have later given up his overly dichotomous tone here, the text strikes the reader with its strictly evolutionist framework, despite its genuine opposition to colonialism. I must warn in the beginning that I do not criticize various analytic aspects of Bourdieu's economic sociology, which is indeed as fascinating as it is informative, but the way in which he sees the Algerian peasants and workers, especially with regard to the issue of time.

Bourdieu's sociological narrative begins with a criticism of mainstream sociology's cultural bias and the abstract nature of its analyses of development. It is "only a sociology of temporal dispositions" that enables us to go beyond this conventional approach.[78] As a constitutive aspect of habitus, this concept of "temporal disposition" is located at the intersection of the economic and the cultural. It is a cultural attitude toward time that cannot be distinguished from the economic position of the agent.[79] As a veritable contribution to the Weberian theory of the structure of social and economic action, Bourdieu's approach conceptualizes the Algerian process of transformation in terms of *rationalization* and *differentiation of fields*. His analysis distributes two major "temporal dispositions" on an evolutionary line of rationalization of economic action and positive differentiation of economic and cultural fields. As expected, what appears is indeed an entirely *binary* view. The traditional, closed, agrarian, gift economy of Algerian society depends on a concept of time Bourdieu calls "forthcoming time" (à *venir*) as opposed to the concept of future (*futur*), which belongs to the rationally managed, calculative, modern "cash economy." Determined by the need for immediate consumption rather than production-oriented to make profit, the traditional peasant "spends in relation to the income derived from the last harvest, and not the income expected on the next."[80] Accordingly, the Algerian peasant's temporal disposition is "foresight" (*prévoyance*), which is the grasping of "the forthcoming reality inherent in the situation itself," whereas the modern temporal disposition is forecasting (*prévoir*), which depends on "a goal explicitly posited as future established by calculation within the framework of a plan."[81] In an agrarian economy, the peasant's time is a cyclical time determined by the organic unity of the present time of the labor with its forthcoming product. This unity is broken in the capitalist economy where the long production cycle presupposes the constitution of a mediated, abstract future, replacing rational calculation for the intuitive grasp of the whole process. The problem is precisely that in Algeria capitalism is not nascent, but imported by colonialism. Hence it is not guided by internal logic but by an exogenenous, imposed, and accelerated change. Customary dispositions of the old habitus outlast the disappearance of their social foundation on the one hand; they turn out to be obsolete under entirely new conditions, on the other.[82] How to creatively reinvent a new system of dispositions, especially when the discrepancy between habitus and structure is wide? Bourdieu's answer is negative: the peasant "cannot discover himself as a historical agent."[83] Traditionalism makes chronological order dependent on a mythic-ritual eternal order. But the modern temporal disposition, that is, forecasting, can conceive of future involving the unforeseen. It is built upon mastering the future and the contingent event, whereas traditionalism can neither recognize nor master future.

Similarly Bourdieu contrasts two social categories in the cities: on the one hand, the unformed mass of subproletariat (the unemployed, the small shopkeeper, the itinerant seller, the uprooted, proletarianized peasant, the army of unskilled laborers), and on the other the regular factory worker, who is a minority. The same problem of time is repeated in a different way. Depending on patronage and connections, having no secure and stable employment, the old sense of forthcoming reality is lost for the subproletariat in the face of severe objective limits without any chance of exit (improvisation is limited and illusory). Since nothing has replaced the old disposition under the condition of external imposition except an "affective quasi-systematization," the colonial system is grasped only in its manifestations. Bourdieu specifically argues that the subproletariat is not a revolutionary force, as they can produce neither the analysis of the objective truth of their position nor the concept of abstract future required by the revolutionary consciousness. Occupying a position in the rationalized part of the economy, the regular workers are the force who can accomplish this forward projection and revolutionary transformation.[84] As this answer is tailor-made by the sociological grand narrative, it is in fact inconsistent with Bourdieu's own suggestion that the change must be initiated by a creative *reinvention* of new dispositions.[85]

In Bourdieu's binary and linear problematic of time, modern temporal disposition is also the very measure of the comparison between itself and the other temporal disposition—the rather well-known case of the judge who is also the prosecutor. Insofar as the political implications are concerned, Bourdieu's reductionist objectivism reaches its peak in this essay. Bourdieu's own student Fanny Colona offered an apt criticism of this pessimistic and disturbing view of the Algerian. Based on her own ethnographies of Algeria, she succinctly argues that Bourdieu's deprivation model "left the peasants' own cultural resources entirely out of the picture"[86] and their "different, though not totally different" culture and temporality is represented by Bourdieu in terms of "lack, loss, and discrepancy, as an atemporal, non-culture."[87] He also completely underestimated the written aspect of the Kabylian culture, especially the role played by poets, and created the fiction of a purely oral culture—and this despite his own targeted criticism of interactionism.[88]

What is it that makes such a view possible? I have already argued that the problem is more Bourdieu's reductionist objectivism than his concept of habitus as such, in opposition to a number of critics who criticized Bourdieu for his underestimation of the reflective aspect of subjectivity. As I have also indicated above, this issue is one of time and body, especially the status of the past in Bourdieu's text. A number of writers have underlined Merleau-Ponty's influence on Bourdieu. In a superb essay on "Phenomenology and Ethnography," Abdellah Hammoudi emphasized the continuities and discontinuties between Merleau-Ponty's phenomenology of body and Bourdieu's concept of habitus.[89] Since Bourdieu took the concept of the "forthcoming" time (à *venir*) as a positive aspect of habitus in his later theoretical texts, Hammoudi punctuates this "coming future, proximate and preformed by shared past."[90] The analogical transfer of schemata that enable the agent to solve practical problems, the semiformalized wisdom at work, is made up of "tested formulae that respond in the immediacy of the moment."[91] Improvisation, that is, the openness of rules and the differential play, is made possible by time. I must add that the forthcoming, proximate future has to do with the movement of retention and expectation, which forms habits.[92] Hammoudi indicates that "this process escapes the consciousness of agents, for, due to its practical character, it cannot be perceived through reflexive distance."[93] This was in fact Bourdieu's reworking of Merleau-Ponty's theory of "the primacy of one's *pre-reflexive* and *corporeal* relationship to the world" and of his idea of "an embodied, practical intentionality that is *anterior* to the construction of things as pure objects of knowledge."[94] Hammoudi is of the opinion that Bourdieu's way of developing Merleau-Ponty's approach reveals the limits of "the pertinence of phenomenology for ethnography" as the habitus appears as rigid, static, and fixed in Bourdieu.[95] As we observe in the example of the football player in action, while

> Merleau Ponty describes a game that ceaselessly modifies itself according to the maneuvers that change the perceived dimension of the playing field, Bourdieu posits that a limit is marked by social utility, which outlines a

tradition that remains more or less intact . . . (and Merleau-Ponty) evokes action as an unfolding event. Such an approach is nowhere to be found in Bourdieu's Kabyle ethnography.[96]

What is at stake is not merely a requirement of translating phenomenology into sociology, for Hammoudi: "what is missing . . . are the relations of tension and accommodation between prereflexive and *reflexive* consciousness, the latter being ▉▉ cally *absent from Bourdieu's theory* and ethnography of tradition."[97] This is the case if, although Hammoudi himself has told above that there is a prereflexive and practical level that necessarily escapes the consciousness of the agents, his own return to reflexivity implies logically that there must be *some special kind of agent* who is in reflexive command of his or her practice. Bourdieu would not accept the presence of such an agent, except as an ideal one might and should approximate. Hammoudi turns to the phenomenal field of Kabylia and gives various examples of such reflexivity by introducing the concept of *tradition*: the multiplicity of languages, the Sufi habitus often in tension with the everyday habitus, various other mystical brotherhoods through which certain customs may be questioned, and the significance of the written aspect of the Kabyle culture. These multiple and contesting levels and layers of cultural fabric reveal a complex picture, which is definitely lacking in Bourdieu's restricted account of a mythical-ritual oral culture.

This criticism of Bourdieu is applicable for the empirical case of Kabyle culture, and I have nothing against including these levels and layers in the analysis, but I remain puzzled by the fact that Bourdieu often describes his own effort as *reflexive sociology*. How do we explain this? What exactly is the problem here? As Bourdieu is always interested in what a society or group does not know about itself, this is in no way limited to the natives or workers. It also involves those subjects of knowledge who are supposed to know their practice for social unconscious does not stop at the border of practice before entering the world of theory, and involves the scholarly thinking as well as all those intellectual or reflective instances Hammoudi introduces. *Practice is everywhere and it always hides domination*—which basically means that the unthought categories of social unconscious, those categories in which domination slips through the games of time, are embedded everywhere including the scholarly, intellectual, and reflective worlds, though in different forms.[98] I am not necessarily in defense of Bourdieu here, but only follow his thinking. I wonder if Bourdieu were to include all those aspects that his ethnography is said to be missing whether the resulting picture would have been different. In a way, perhaps Bourdieu wants to say that every true society is a primitive, traditional society *in the first place*! Certainly not an unproblematic statement. On the other hand, if the sociologist must also turn the objectifying gaze upon himself, who will objectify the sociologist who objectifies himself? How and who can we trust *in practice*? Bourdieu's sociological text endlessly repeats and revises itself in ceaseless, circular descriptions and definitions of habitus, domination, or determination, *without being able to* make the tension between structure and agency disappear (even though it is refined), as Hammoudi himself carefully observes. But this also implies that, contrary to what the critics claim, there is an implicit (in addition to the explicit) demand for *permanent vigilance*, since there is no end to hiding, games, and error *in practice*. This is why Colona's apparently similar, though nuanced criticism is much more to the point: rather than lacking reflexivity, Bourdieu's perspective overlooks the native's cultural resources and reduces the value of their temporality in a binary hegemonic framework.

What is, then, this other time? We need to go back to the problematic of time in a phenomenological and postphenomenological context. Merleau-Ponty's idea of an embodied, practical intentionality anterior to the construction of objects of knowledge might have presupposed the *more radical anteriority* of "a kind of original past, a past which has never been present" rather than taking it into account in the *Phenomenology of Perception*.[99] The difficulty of coming to terms with this impossible past has unfolded itself in Merleau-Ponty's later work interrupted by his early death.[100] Merleau-Ponty's singular unsealing of phenomenology thus remained limited to the practical, everyday body, even though his many examples and discussions went far beyond it. As for Bourdieu, although the sense of an absolute past is readable in some examples he brings up, and although the habitus clearly presupposes it, he continues to think the past as *present* past, in terms of a rigid social determination. Nevertheless his uses of the past are ambiguous and constantly shifting: on the one hand, this past is unconscious; on the other, practically operating. On the one hand, ". . . the anticipations of the habitus . . . give disproportionate weight to early experiences";[101] on the other, it is incorporated history, "forgotten as history" and at the same time, "the active presence of the whole past of which it is the product."[102] According to Bourdieu, then, although the body might be passive with regard to its social inscription, its being-inscribed is *always already* active in the present.

This "active-ness," which is the meaning of practice in Bourdieu, is also the very movement of time that is forthcoming. What is then the forthcoming time of the tradition, which becomes the forthcoming time of practice in Bourdieu's later theoretical texts? It takes us back to Husserl's passive synthesis of time and Derrida's deconstruction of Husserl's phenomenology, as well as Deleuze's reading of Bergson. As is well known, in the *Phenomenology of the Consciousness of Internal Time*, Husserl demonstrated that the present necessarily includes the phases of past and future, which he called retention and protention, and that time is a continual movement of retentional and protential *traces*.[103] There can be no isolated and simple present moment according to this demonstration. Derrida showed however that Husserl still maintained a certain notion of actual living-now in its self-same identity.[104] In fact, it is the finite *trace* that constitutes the pure present *and* disturbs the boundary that separates it at the same time. The originary, living now or present can only be constituted *after* the trace or the nonoriginary.[105] If the synthesis of time is passive, then this is an irreducible passivity, which refers to an absolute past, *a past that has never been present*. The past cannot be seen simply as a present that is past in a linear series of homogenous and successive nows. What is on target in Derrida's deconstruction is the privilege of the present, which still gives the past and future its form in the conventional understanding of time. Deleuze also refers to the "past in general," a pure or virtual past, in his work on Bergson as well as in his other works: a past that is *contemporaneous* with the present.[106] No present would ever pass without being past *at the same time*.

Should the same not apply for protention as well? We need to pay attention to Paola Marrati's cautionary remark:

> Doubtless this is true. Yet *any privilege accorded to anticipation* inevitably runs the risk of *effacing the passivity of time*, its always-already-thereness. Now, the always-already-thereness of time does not of course mean that everything has already taken place; rather it means that what has taken place cannot be mastered . . .[107]

As there is no simple present that is free of the past, something about the past remains irretrievable. This is not because I cannot remember what happened in the past, not because my memory is weak. Rather it is because what happened has never come full circle; it has never happened in an originary instant present to itself. Marrati clarifies the consequence of the concept of absolute past:

> The passivity of the past that is not a past-present is *also* the relation to a future that is not a future-present. Were this not so, the future would not truly be a future; it would remain within a horizon of anticipation; it could be anticipated

and calculated, hostile to anything that might arrive: first and foremost, to the coming or the event of the other.[108]

What is at stake here is a radical difference in the nature of future, of that which is to come. While Bourdieu's forthcoming time is limited to a socially programmed practical anticipation with a margin left for improvisation, in the case of Derrida's deconstruction we have a radical time of the event and an opening of the future (which is neither anticipation, nor conscious project). It is because, in privileging anticipation in the name of practice, Bourdieu runs the risk of effacing the passivity of time, its always-already-thereness, which opens up the *unanticipable* future. This is directly related to the question of colonialism, as we shall see. Before this, however, I need to specify that Bourdieu's concept of forthcoming time is a version of Husserl's protention as anticipation. Already in Merleau-Ponty this took a unique form: as Merleau-Ponty's well-known clinical examples show, *anticipation* is what an abled body brings to a situation.[109] It is more or less the same (practical, working) body and the same anticipation of forthcoming reality in Bourdieu. In his later work, Bourdieu makes a clear, positive reference to Husserl's concept of "the future that he calls protention, or preperceptive anticipation, a relationship to a future that is not a future, to a future that is almost present."[110] This is distinguished from the concept of future seen as project. But in privileging anticipation (hence privileging a presence determined by a *present* past), this approach has already missed the alterity of the past, or experience of the past as to come, and therefore the *possibility* of transformation.[111]

Bourdieu's problem is not overlooking the reflexive in favor of the prereflexive, as he never leaves language outside the habitus. The question is indeed one of time. While Bourdieu claims to demonstrate the superiority of sociology over philosophy, he keeps the latter's classical metaphysics of time in its Husserlian form. The passive synthesis cannot be conceived as identical to social determination. All social and cultural inscription involves this synthesis and inscribes time and futurality as it inscribes its cultural marks, "those infinity of traces, without an inventory" that Gramsci mentions.[112] Body is never *tabula rasa*, and never the colonizer's *terra incognito*, but its contractions and tensions, its passive syntheses are always already involved in its own inscription. It is symptomatic that, in the very last paragraph of the chapter on habitus in the *Outline*, Bourdieu refers to the habitus' "endless capacity to engender products,"[113] but never explains how, and ends his chapter by describing a middle way between the two extremes: "as remote from a creation of unpredictable novelty as it is from simple mechanical reproduction of the initial conditionings."[114] In order for him to be able to actually demonstrate the habitus' endless creative capacity, those "initial conditionings" themselves must have been preceded by a more radical past that has never been present, which thus opens the very possibility of future, of the to-come.

In fact, despite Bourdieu's brilliant criticisms of the sociology of modernization, the same linear problematic of time also applies for his narrative of rationalization, as we have seen. But this has a further consequence in view of the deconstruction of time. The colonial world was not simply divided into two, putting the Algerian on this side with their traditionalism and lost sense of time, and the French on the other with their imposed rational time, and the passage from the one to the other being in the direction of rationalization (however impeded). This division is already experienced as a *displacement* in the time and body of the Algerian. It means that *the present is out of tune with itself.* The colonized does not suffer from being stuck with a traditional sense of time that they can no longer experience vis-à-vis a future that is external and imposed on them.[115] The distinction Bourdieu makes between the subproletariat and the proletariat is his way of maintaining this linear, homogenenous, static, and oppositional view of time. But the colonial antagonism is not just an objective structure external to the Algerian, for the implantation of its "Manichean" morality is *experienced* by the colonized as the force of a crisis (the crisis of the intentionality or anticipation given in the old habitus[116]), hence as a dramatic change, a dislocation, that is, the emergence of another future, the "to-come." What is actually grafted in the opposition is a body and time "out-of-joint," the time of the event.[117] It is this disjointed time that Frantz Fanon was able to read in the contractions, tensions, and dreams of the Algerian body, in the very transformation of its corporeal schema.[118]

In his other published ethnography, *Algerians*, Bourdieu gives a more positive account of the Algerian anticolonial struggle.[119] This is partly because, rather than isolating the concept of habitus in the native tradition, Bourdieu could not avoid attending to the colonial system in this early work originally published in the middle of the war in 1958:

> when carried along by its own internal logic, the colonial system tends to develop all the consequences implied at the time of its founding—the complete separation of the social castes . . . Thus it must be granted that the primary and indeed the sole radical challenge to the system was the one that the system itself engendered; the revolt against the principles on which it is founded.[120]

Although Bourdieu never used the concept of habitus in this book, there is the implication that it is the habitus itself that underwent a change. For instance, while the veil was a mere vestimentary detail and a simple, unconsciously devised symbol in the traditional society, in "colonial traditionalism" it took the function of a sign of resistance.[121] At the same time, "the traditional patterns for the relations between sexes have also been altered . . . the Algerian woman has acquired a greater independence and . . . a keener pride at her tasks and responsibilities."[122] *Algerians* is a solid, conventional, ethnographic account of various ethnicities and groups in Algeria in a process of "social change," supplemented by an account of the revolutionary war. Bourdieu's typically Weberian discussion of the case of Mozabites, "the Protestants and the Puritans of Islam," praises their work ethic and discipline.[123] In fact, the case of the Mozabites turns out to be the confession of *an implicit sociological ideal*: "never perhaps has the interaction between permanence and change been presented so clearly and distinctly. The maintenance of stability, far from excluding change, presupposes the capacity to modify oneself to adapt to new situations."[124] In *Algeria 1960*, the regular wage earner seemed to be the ideal agent of change in opposition to the miserable "subproletarian" who was trapped between the surviving old habitus and the imposed change. In the earlier *Algerians*, the imposed nature of the change was not a strong emphasis and the truth of rationalization was found in puritanism, that is, solid work ethic, as the royal road to real change, the ideal habitus in which stability is maintained by "*adapting* to new situations."

Exchange past and present

Bourdieu's analysis of gift exchange is the other important area where he introduces the concept of time. Bourdieu demonstrates how Mauss (phenomenological, internal, subjective) and Levi-Strauss (structural, external, objective) might be offering one-sided views of the same reality of the gift: the gift as experienced and the gift as seen from the outside.[125] His own perspective then aims to transcend this dualism, which is inherent in the nature of the social practice of gift exchange, and which Bourdieu calls the double truth of the gift. As Ilana Silber clarifies, for Bourdieu, the gift exchange is an instance of collective denial and sincere fiction, paradigmatic of symbolic violence and of social practice as orchestrated improvisation and sense of the game.[126] In terms of the analysis of the gift, Bourdieu focuses on the agents' *use* of time in the process of gift and counter-gift. The double truth of the gift exchange is made possible by *time*: "the *interval* between gift and counter-gift is what allows a pattern of exchange that is always liable to strike the observer and also the participants as *reversible*, i.e. both forced and interested, to be experienced as irreversible."[127] The "interval," the passing of time or duration, is what makes it possible to experience an exchange (which potentially involves inequality and force) as if it is gift. Since an immediate response may expose the reality of the gift as exchange, it is through a distinct art of *kairos*, which involves creating an interval, letting the time pass, that the truth of the gift is repressed. Further, it is through this manipulation of time that the interests are played out and that gentle and hidden form of violence called "symbolic" violence is exercised.[128]

Bourdieu's analysis has no specific reference to Islam, but his precursor Mauss mentioned Islam and the monotheistic tradition as constitutive of the concept of gift, claiming also that the Arabic *sadaqah* and the Hebrew *zedaka* originally meant "justice."[129] In a careful reading of the Qur'an, Thierry Kochuyt demonstrates that the official Islamic concept of *zakat* (obligatory alms), which is one of the five pillars of Islam, is in conformity with the double truth of gift in Bourdieu's sense.[130] As the Qur'an says, it is the duty of the Muslim to give to the poor and the needy (107.2, 3). The donor must simply say without any expectation of return: "We feed you for the sake of Allah alone: no reward do we desire from you, nor thanks" (76.9). Although the donee has no obligation to return (otherwise it is not a gift), he or she must actually return the gift *by praying for their donors* so that the latter will feel safe and secure: "Of their goods, take alms so though mightest purify and sanctify them; and pray on their behalf. Verily thy prayers are a source of security for them: and Allah is One who heareth and knoweth" (9.103).[131] This ambivalence is further complicated by the fact that the Qur'an uses the *zakat* (obligatory alms) and the *sadaqah* (voluntary alms) *interchangeably* (9.60, 103). Kochuyt exposes the significance of this with regard to the double truth: "the objective commandment to give also requires the subjective input of some free will" (*niyya*, that is, sincere intention is a requirement of *zakat*).[132] As she argues, considered as legal enforcement (from the outside), one can always fake solidarity, whereas the religious (inner) point of view requires the good intention (*niyya*) of selfless giving. It is because there are two sides that "the Qur'an should mix up the compulsory and the free."[133] The working of the system depends on the *textual performance* of a confusion between the compulsory *zakat* and the voluntary *sadaqah*. Although Kochuyt's analysis actually depends on a reading of the Qur'an, she does not see the double truth of gift as the effect of a textual performance.[134]

That Bourdieu does not pay any attention to the Qur'an is certainly criticizable, but again it remains debatable whether his resulting picture of the Kabyle economy would be different. The interval of time Bourdieu emphasizes can be considered as another form of supplementing the obligatory with the voluntary. The receiver voluntarily delays the gift so that it will not be exposed as exchange, which is obligatory.[135] In an actual Muslim context, the symbolic return would be immediate as a rule of politeness as well as a requirement of faith: "may Allah be pleased with you." It is *this essential aspect of the habitus, the immediate expression of thankfulness in religious idiom*, which Bourdieu might have overlooked. This verbal return is one of the instances of Derrida's well-known argument that the gift is impossible: "a gift must never appear in a present, given the risk of its being annulled in thanks, in the symbolic, in exchange or economy, indeed of its becoming a benefit."[136]

In his later work, Bourdieu criticizes Derrida's deconstruction of the gift.[137] While the *Outline* concentrated upon the symbolic violence and domination hidden by the manipulation of time in the exchange of gifts, in *Practical Reason* Bourdieu elaborates a theory of "interest in the *disinterestedness*," raising the possibility of a generous giving without the calculation of profit, based on collective self-deception inculcated by socialization[138] (Islamic *niyya* would be an instance of such a disposition). For Bourdieu, Derrida's argument is blind to a socially inculcated belief in disinterestedness (which might be mystified yet real in its effect), for it depends on the implicit assumption of a freely acting subject, independent of social determination. In *Given Time*, however, Derrida emphasizes that, from the point of view of the "compound structure" of the gift ("A gives B to C") it does not matter if the giving or receiving subject is individual or collective.[139] Nor does it matter "whether the restitution is immediate or whether it is programmed by a complex calculation of a long-term differal or difference."[140] Because once a gift enters into the circuit of exchange, reciprocity, or restitution, it is annulled as gift (whether the donor is individual or collective). If it is recognized as a gift by the donor or the donee, it will have to be reciprocated: hence the expectation of repayment, indebtedness, thankfulness, etc.[141] As soon as the other receives, we cannot speak of the gift but as exchange and economy. The gift is absolute, unconditional; once given it is no longer a gift. The double bind is the *impossibility* of the gift.[142] Better put, the gift is "aporetic": it is present only when it is destroyed. This process of destruction, Derrida argues, is set in motion by *time, before* it is "manipulated" by any agent: "it suffices that the movement of acceptance . . . lasts a little, however little that may be, more than an instant, an instant already caught up in the temporalizing synthesis . . . there is no more gift as soon as the other receives."[143] For Derrida, the gift and time have the same structure. As Pheng Cheah nicely puts it, both are characterized by "nonphenomenality":

> The gift is aporetic because it can appear, preserve and be present to itself only by being destroyed. In Derrida's words, the giving of time is "a giving that gives without giving anything and without anyone giving anything." The gift is thus an apposite figure of the experience of time under conditions of radical finitude.[144]

The destruction of the gift also implies that it must not be recognized and must immediately be *forgotten as gift* both by the donor and the donee. This forgetting of the gift is an *absolute forgetting*, which "exceeds even the psychoanalytic categoriality of forgetting."[145] The annulment or destruction of the gift is not repression in the sense, for instance, that Bourdieu understands when he claims that the agents repress the truth of the gift, which is interest and exchange. Repression does not destroy anything, it keeps by changing place, whereas "the thought of this radical forgetting as thought of the gift should accord with a certain experience of the *trace as cinder or ashes*."[146] It is important to clarify that Derrida speaks here of "a certain experience of the trace"—that is to say, an *experience*. Absolute forgetting (which absolves, unbinds absolutely) has to do with absolute memory, that is, the memory of that which is radically forgotten and yet still experienced, still here: body as absolute past.

As a monotheistic tradition, always rewriting finitude in the infinite, time is given by a transcendent exteriority, God, in Islam. Historically sharing the ancient Greek philosophical tradition, Islam has not only the concept of habitus (*malaka*) but also the concept of absolute past: *azal* (immemorial past), which comes paired with *abad* (eternity). In early Mutazilite scholarship, *azal* is "eternity *a parte ante*" (limitless past) and corresponds to the Greek term ánarchon, while *abad* is "eternity *a parte post*" (limitless future) and corresponds to Greek *atéleuton*. Interestingly *azal* is said to be derived from the Persian word *a-sar*, that is, "without head."[147] Although *azal* and *abad* appear as the two ends of time to the finite human consciousness, both are *present* to Allah and are at the same time under His transcendent gaze. Does the word *azal* keep the memory of a *time without beginning*, a *time before time*, in all its ambivalence, and even though this time without temporalization is constantly translated into the terms of presence and the present time, through transcendent infinity? In the Qur'an, *azal* is often narrated as a time in which things happened and decisions were made; that is to say, it is given an *originary* status. It is impossible not to lose the absoluteness of absolute past. Another closer word is *qidam* (a derivative of the word *qadama*: to precede, implying also level and hierarchy). It refers to the time that precedes, ancient time or immemorial time, or eternity; it is employed widely by Sufism (especially in the sense of "level" or "station"); and it signifies an archive of all that which is actualized. Further, *Al-Qadim* is one of the divine names and attributes of Allah. It is nevertheless important to underline the difference of these concepts, especially *azal*, from a series of other temporal terms all of which can be directly reduced to the present time.[148] It seems as if language bears within itself the *trace* of a time without temporalization, ever past, always-already to-come, through its strata and through the movements of its strata (of its *qadama*), "without head," even though *in exchange* with words, of gifts and counter-gifts.[149] In turn, it is in this sense, that is, in the sense that the past is never reducible to the actual, that religion as the discourse of the absolute might have a power of absolving itself from any given meaning, from any historical and actual given.[150]

His own ethnographer

This absolute memory cannot be appropriated. As I have already argued in the first chapter, all appropriation and reappropriation produces *ex-appropriation* as it is already determined by the logic of trace.[151] Hence the absolute memory already ex-appropriates the one who is in remembrance. We have seen traces of this event of ex-appropriation in "the rhythm of a line of verse whose words have been forgotten," or in the "incommensurable islands of time," in the very operation of Bourdieu's singular and signature contribution, the concept of habitus. Like postmodern ethnography, Bourdieu too believes in a good appropriation that can be achieved by a reflexive approach to practice, but the exchange between past and present is inscribed otherwise in his text, pointing to an ex-appropriation denied by correcting the natives' time and by locking them in the horizon of anticipation.

Bourdieu noted more than once how his own childhood experience in the rural region of Béarn helped him to understand the Kabyle rural community, and indeed he went back to do ethnographic research on his own community after the ethnographic work on the Kabyle community, while making his work in both places an essential aspect of his methodological concept of "participant objectivation."[152] Can the Kabyle and the Béarn communities be compared along the axis of modernization or urbanization, or in terms of what happens to rural communities in a process of rapid social change? This kind of comparison is possible and is perhaps even useful from the point of view of economic sociology; and indeed it may reveal a number of similarities. Yet its effect would be to homogenize very different temporalities and very different trajectories of Algeria and France; and more importantly, it would make disappear the fact that Algeria was a colonized country.

Although Bourdieu himself had drawn our attention to the fact of "imposed change" in the case of Algeria, why did he constantly compare Kabyle and Béarn, as if they belonged to the same condition and experienced the same history? Why this double work? What is under the research here? It seems difficult to follow the track of time and/or the way from sociological knowledge to native knowledge or vice versa. As Bourdieu himself made clear, in his fieldwork in Kabylia he "constantly" used his experience of the Béarn society of his childhood, both to understand the practices that he observed and to defend himself against the interpretations that he spontaneously formed of them or that his informants gave him. Of course, he also conceded that his native knowledge was already "subjected to sociological critique."[153] *Then he returned to Béarn* to do research on changing marriage patterns.[154] As he put it, "having worked in Kabylia, a foreign world, I thought it would be interesting to do a kind of *Tristes Tropiques* (Levi-Strauss 1970) in reverse . . . to observe the effects that objectivation of my native world would produce in me."[155] This second research was not simply about the Béarnais peasants' changing marriage practices, then; it was also about Bourdieu's experience of objectivation—that is to say, Bourdieu was now an ethnographer who conducted two researches at the same time: a research about the "tragic" destiny of his fellow countrymen *and* another one on the effects of objectivation on the ethnographer, who was the native at the same time. Likewise, the "object" of his first research was his fellow countrymen ("older youths, about my age at the time"), while the object of the other, no less significant research was himself as native turned sociologist. Both subject and object, both ethnographer and native at the same time, who objectivates and who is objectified in this research? In Béarn, he should have been able to measure the effect of objectivation of his own world on him, which required that he must have had both sociological truth and the native half-knowledge as well as a means of measuring their distance. Paradoxically, *already before going to Kabylia*, he must have subjected this half-knowledge he had as native to sociological critique and must have transformed it into the truth of full sociological knowledge, by his education in philosophy and social theory. Perhaps we must say that he had done this in Algeria, that is to say, he had transformed his native Béarnais half-knowledge into sociological knowledge by studying the foreign Kabylian knowledge. For after all, they were similar; yet the Kabylia was *different and therefore necessary*. But then did he not himself tell us that, in Kabylia, he *constantly* used his native Béarnais (half-)knowledge in order to understand the Kabylian practices and his own spontaneous interpretation of them? It seems very difficult to maintain any distinction between ethnographic and native knowledge, or the difference between Kabyle and Béarn cultures. I do not aim to demean Pierre Bourdieu's veritable contribution to sociology and anthropology, which speaks volumes. But Bourdieu can produce ethnographic and sociological knowledge insofar as he acts as if these distinctions, differences, cases, and temporalities are solidly established and work unproblematically. Most important of all, do we ever learn the result of the other research, "the effects of objectivation of his native world on him"? This should be the question at the heart of reflexivity: can one make an ethnography of oneself? Can one be one's own ethnographer? No doubt, Bourdieu did not study himself, but others, in Béarn and in Kabylia (though not the same others). But since he himself brought up the question of the effects of objectivation of his native world on him, dividing and uniting himself in the same gesture, the question is legitimate. One's ethnography of oneself is one's appropriation of one's origin, one's ownness and one's proper, hence identity between past and present. And yet what happens to others? For, after all, the others come first, they are where this origin is found, at a distance (which, it seems, took time to give itself, if ever): this is the privilege of Kabylia in the theory of practice—a privilege that the Béarnais do not have, for the Kabylia is their origin too, even though Béarn and Kabylia *are* "incommensurable islands of duration." We need to keep in mind then that the search for origin is made available by colonialism, which destroyed the roofs of the Kabylian houses, displaced their inhabitants, and let the light in for the ethnographic, photographic, and sociological record. As we have learned from Spivak, anthropology is the naming of the other in the Western Man's search for his origins: "the encrypting of the name of the native informant as the name of Man." Or, as I have argued above, Bourdieu's work itself must be working "in analogy with the rhythm of a line of verse whose words are forgotten" by its author.

Part II

Literatures: Crossing Culture

Resonance of Light: Reading T. E. Lawrence

T. E. Lawrence's *Seven Pillars of Wisdom*, a canonical text of modern English literature, has received two very different readings by Edward Said (1978) and Gilles Deleuze (1997). While Said reads *Seven Pillars* in terms of Orientalism and colonialism, as a text that is inseparable from Lawrence's role as a British spy in the Middle East, Deleuze reads it as a politically motivated, vanguard literary work.[1] There can be no possible exchange between these two radically different positions. Although I agree with Said, I would like to read each of these readings a little more carefully, with the hope of producing a different angle on Lawrence's text.

Said: Imperial affect

Before moving on to Said's reading of Lawrence, I want to offer a general view of his *Orientalism*. Said's paradigm-constituting text has rightly been criticized for its methodological shortcomings. Nevertheless, I would like to argue that Said's critics are also misled by the intelligibility of his contradictions, and criticizing Said's totalizing view has become an academic ritual that effectively prohibited reading him in more detailed, different, and positive ways. This might have some relevance in the case of Lawrence.

Since Said confined the citational practice of Orientalism to a question of citing authority and having authorization,[2] he missed what Vicki Kirby nicely called "the empowering mutability" of the Orientalist mark.[3] If he were able to "make an inventory of the traces of orientalism upon him, the Oriental," the hegemonic inscription of Orientalism could not have been as unitary as he claimed.[4] This approach to Orientalism as a material practice in an open force field of citation and repetition can take us beyond a narrow view. Orientalism is no longer a merely methodological problem but a real force that must be taken into account in the analysis of a multiplicity of social, historical, and cultural practices. There can be no clean and once-and-for-all methodological break but a constant engagement with Orientalism, which aims to re-mark its mutability.

Although this criticism is certainly valid for Said's book in general, I am not so sure if it is straightforwardly applicable for his reading of Lawrence. General response to Said's reading of Lawrence has emphasized his neglect of the contradictory and plural nature of *Seven Pillars*. Dennis Porter argued that Said's reductive reading was blind to Lawrence's literary sensibility and romantic attitude, which enabled him to produce a text fissured with doubt and contradiction.[5] In a lengthy psychoanalytic reading, Kaja Silverman criticized Said for discarding Lawrence's homosexuality: it was through his erotic identification that Lawrence was able to discover himself in the Arab Other and sympathize with the Arab cause.[6] Porter's evidence for the heterogeneous nature of *Seven Pillars* is everything "good" Lawrence said about Arabs. His defensive prose depends on a rhetorical employment of the figures of contradiction, plurality, and heterogeneity. In Silverman's psychoanalytic approach, it is Lawrence's homosexuality that makes his case different. While she rightfully brings up the complexity of Lawrence's desire for the Arab, there is a visible tendency in her argument to read this complexity back into a moral distinction under the general claim of the split nature of desire. Silverman reads, for instance, Lawrence's cross-dressing as his effort of disidentifying with his own national group and forming an attachment with the one his nation wants to dominate. This is an unexpectedly categorical judgment coming from a psychoanalytically nuanced and careful reader of Lawrence's homosexuality. These critics present themselves as advocates of the complexity of subjectivity or literature, yet it does not seem possible for them to have sympathy and love for other people, and act, at the same time, in oppressive ways toward them or to get involved in political practices that are harmful to them.

Although Said acknowledges the importance of the libidinal dimension of Orientalism (the fact that it could "elicit complex responses" and "frightening self discovery"), he finds this type of analysis tending to be speculative.[7] Said's fear of losing control of the analysis in the foreign territory of desire should be criticized especially to the extent that this exclusion disables his criticism. Yet insofar as Lawrence's love of the Arab culture is concerned, he engages with what these critics see as lacking in his analysis. The problem identified as Said's reductionist reading was already a particular moment and form of Orientalism for Said, who read Lawrence's love of Asia in a very different way. Lawrence belonged to a special breed in the official genealogy of Orientalism, that is, experts who brought to the coercive framework of Orientalism their "private mythology" by producing a personal vision of the Orient while expressing contempt for official knowledge about it.[8] But this in no way eliminated the traditional Western hostility to and fear of the Orient. It only refined it by giving it a stylistic elaboration.

In fact, this intense subjectivization of involvement with the East turned these people into "White Orientals."[9] When the Orient was made to enter history as a result of World War I, its knowledge had to be translated into action. In such a risky moment, control had to be asserted directly. The Orientalist scholar had to change dress and enter Oriental history to make it. Lawrence was a man of this moment: not a bureaucrat but an expert-adventurer-eccentric. As the moment implied change, for Said, it was also witness to the conflict between vision and narrative. An Orientalist used to offer a vision of the Orient by transforming his encounter with difference into an imperial survey from above and creating a static, unchanging entity; but now the war between European powers caused them to "turn the Orient from unchanging 'Oriental' passivity into militant modern life"[10] and called for narrative history. The conflict was particularly acute, according to Said, in the *Seven Pillars*:

> The great drama of Lawrence's work is that it symbolizes the struggle, first, to stimulate the Orient (lifeless, timeless, forceless) into movement; second, to impose upon that movement an essentially Western shape; third, to contain the new and aroused orient in a personal vision, whose retrospective mode includes a powerful sense of failure and betrayal.[11]

What Porter and Silverman regarded as the personal and dissident aspect of Lawrence's vision of the East, his sympathy for and identification with the Arabs, was, for Said, a historical product of imperialism. Said does not reject that Lawrence had a personal, intense, and sympathetic relationship with the Arabs and Orientals. He rather argues that it was a particular moment of Orientalism that selected and produced him. But he also underlines that Lawrence's singular situation had in no way prevented him from seeing the Arabs as inferior. If we do a favor to Said by distinguishing the content of what he says from his bitter tone, we might trace a nuanced reading of Lawrence's complex constitution. Lawrence sees himself as responsible for "hustling into form . . . the new Asia which time was inexorably bringing upon us."[12] Said carefully emphasizes Lawrence's sense of dominative benevolence, which he describes as a feeling of "triumph": "a mood of enlargement," writes Lawrence himself, "in that we felt we had assumed another's pain or experience, his personality."[13] The sense of triumph had to do with the fact that the Orientalist was no longer the participant observer but now "the representative Oriental."[14] But, Said adds, Lawrence also saw an irresolvable conflict between the West and East. The only thought that did not occur to him was that the Arabs would fight for their independence without him. A friend of Arabs, an advocate of the Arab cause, Lawrence felt a deep and intimate sense of betrayal after the war when his own government did not realize its promise. Equating himself fully with the struggle of the new Asia to be born, his voice becomes history: the effect is that the Orient was brought closer to the West, but only for a brief moment. In the end we are left with a sense of distance, "still separating 'us' from an Orient destined to bear its foreignness as a mark of its permanent estrangement from the West."[15]

In his "Introduction" to *Orientalism*, Said referred to Raymond Williams's well-known phrase: "unlearning of the inherently dominative mode."[16] The mode of thinking this formulation implies must have played a significant role in Said's transformation of the sense of "Orientalism" from an intellectual and human interest in the East into a hegemonic formation. His conceptualization of Orientalism as an "epistemological and ontological distinction between the Orient and the Occident"[17] is a perfect instance of a "deep assumption of inherent inequality."[18] There is, however, a nuance between the words "dominative" and "domination."[19] The dominative is "tending to dominate," that is, a quality and a tendency, implying a force field, while the dominant has the certainty of an actual or complete subject, language, or social form. I would like to argue that the "dominative" is inherent to a cultural or subjective world in a particular way: it comes before material, political, or ideological domination of which it might also be an effect on a subjective level. Although Said does not pay much attention to the possible implications of this nuance, his reading powerfully demonstrates the presence of this singular force or affect in Lawrence. Said certainly does not deny that Lawrence sincerely believed in a new Asia, as he stresses Lawrence's feelings of frustration and shame for betraying Arabs as well as his feeling of triumph. This "oscillation" (Said's word) between the West and East, this mixture of shame and victory, of betrayal and glory, of cunning intelligence and benevolence, is also not far from what Deleuze's favorite philosopher Spinoza would have called *fluctatio animi* (fluctuations of the soul). If the possibility of this reading is not excluded in Said's text, he certainly does not follow the implications of this new aspect of the imperial soul.

Deleuze: Ideas, or passages of life

I have tried to elaborate Said's approach by reinjecting Williams's notion of "dominative" structure of feeling into it, but given that I take this notion of the dominative in terms of affect and force, in terms of a differential force field, Deleuze is already with us.

To begin with, what does Deleuze set out to accomplish in the *Essays Critical and Clinical*? In his previous works on Masoch and Sade, Deleuze argued that, in isolating a group of signs and naming a mode of existence in their literary writing, these writers acted like clinicians or symptomatologists who are themselves already writers, for symptomatology is the literary aspect of medicine.[20] Hence the critical means literary or artistic for Deleuze, whereas the clinical refers to its corresponding phenomena taken as signs (not to mention the rhyme the two words make). What is at stake is the material, bodily, or immanent nature of the literary sign. In the *Essays*, then, Deleuze's effort is to demonstrate the critical, that is to say the literary or literature Lawrence's work produces. The critical power of Deleuze's own work lies in extracting philosophical concepts from literary works and, for Deleuze, the literary or literature has a direct relationship with life: it is "a passage of Life that traverses both the livable and the lived."[21] But what is life here? As the becoming-other or minorization of language, literature decomposes the mother language and invents a foreign one within it (Lawrence's granular English is a phantom German). This is pushing language to its limit, to "an outside or reverse side that consists of Visions and Auditions that no longer belong to any language."[22] These Visions and Auditions that the writer sees and hears in the interstices of language are called "Ideas" by Deleuze. He insists that the Idea is immanent, not transcendent. At the level of experience these Ideas keep happening as oscillations and heterogeneous mixes, that is, the fluctuations of the soul. It is the nature of these Ideas that interests Deleuze.

If the Idea is immanent, the life or "experience" that is at stake in Lawrence's text, especially in his landscapes, is one that is *at the edge*, "a passage of life." This is not culture in the ordinary social scientific sense, but rather nature: light and heat, solar haze, the play of shadows on the rock, changing colors.

In Lawrence's Goethean universe, pure light is invisible: "pure transparency, colourless, unformed untouchable." *On the one hand*, Deleuze argues that this is the Idea, the abstract that has no transcendence, but extended throughout the space, God or revolt as movement.[23] *On the other hand*, it is the Light that opens the space, and what is at stake seems to be the emergence or genesis of the visible. Deleuze never uses the word "genesis" here—even though he used it before in *Difference and Repetition*.[24] He refers to Lawrence's descriptions of "solar haze," "gas," or "vapour" as "the first state of nascent perception,"[25] and white and black as "the conditions of perception, which will be fully actualized when colours appear, that is, when the white darkens into yellow and black lightens into blue."[26] While genesis ordinarily means the origination or coming into being of something, the sentence immediately following Deleuze's use of this term shows that what is at stake in the becoming-visible of the visible is not at all a linear, developmental appearance of a visible form out of the invisible and the unformed. Deleuze's analysis is profoundly Goethean in taking opacity as a condition of seeing, which implies that the passage in question is one that is passed and is not passed at the same time, a passage without resonance between its ends:

> . . . sand and sky, whose intensification produces a blinding crimson in which the world burns, and eyesight is replaced by suffering. Sight and suffering, two entities . . . From gray to red, there is the appearing and disappearing of the world in the desert, all the adventures of the visible and its perception. The idea in space is vision, which passes from a pure invisible transparency to the crimson fire in which all sight burns.[27]

If this is "the first state of nascent perception," then no Gestalt is formed in what might be called the becoming-visible of the visible. Deleuze told in *The Logic of Sense* that becoming moves and pulls in *both directions at once*.[28] Indeed vision is not just a blurred vision, it is one in which all sight burns. Referring to Deleuze's own expression "a silence in the words," Bogue "cautions against a ready equation of auditions and actual sound effects in words."[29] Similarly, visions are not perceptions, but apparitions. Seeing happens for a brief moment, "through a haze" and in a passage that itself is invisible, between the pure light and the crimson fire in which all sight burns.[30] Outside language, these burning sights and deafening sounds touch its edges; they also appear and disappear in and through it. This nonexternal outside is called *literature*, a delirium of language when it is *touched* by these extremes or thresholds of experience. A writer has the power to see and hear, or to "sense" these "subrepresentative" visions and auditions. Lawrence's literary sensibility is a response to the maddening vibrations or resonances of desert light, the gas, or vapor melting his skin when his private desert meets the public/natural one—a body without organs. For Deleuze, the conceptual or virtual Lawrence he extracts from the *Seven Pillars* expresses a kind of "originary" universal experience at the edge of seeing.[31] While, in Lawrence's landscapes, Said would probably read the return of an essentialist static vision of the Orient that interrupts the necessity of making the Oriental Arab enter history and naturalizes the historical, Deleuze sees in them a nearly universal experience of the becoming-visible of the visible, which he reads as an essential aspect of Lawrence's fabulation of Arab freedom.

It is not difficult to see that the vision or audition is also what Deleuze called "sense/event" in *The Logic of Sense*. Especially as landscape, vision has an affinity with the concept of simulacrum in the appendix to the same book—a concept Deleuze finds in Plato and then subjects to a reversal.[32] Landscape here is not something delineated, not an objectified view, but sensory space just before it has become a perceived place. This is why Deleuze describes it as a passage of life: in fog or darkness, or in pure light, I no longer know where I am in the sense that I cannot determine my position geographically: I am in a landscape—becoming-lost or invisible. I wonder if Deleuze's simulacrum is also a return of this condition. If, as a copy of a copy, as an image without resemblance, simulacrum is built upon disparity and difference, this difference is surely not a different identity (in which case it would be the copy of a model) but ". . . simulacrum includes the differential point of view; and the observer becomes part of the simulacrum itself, which is transformed and deformed by his point of view."[33]

This is where Deleuze's philosophical operation can be useful. Lawrence has to locate himself and learn to move around in the desert—a space that is home to the Arabs whom he has to lead and manipulate. The experience of the desert is an experience of difference for the British man, a difference that is both cultural and climatic. Indeed how to distinguish the cultural and the climatic, as the experience of difference is a bodily affair? (And how to distinguish Lawrence's erotic adventure and his experience of the desert?) Speaking of the objectively arisen need for a new kind of Orientalist who is an expert and adventurer "White Oriental," Said quoted the Orientalist travel writer and geographer Charles Doughty: "The sun made me an Arab."[34] Is there an "originary" mimesis that is then controlled? A mimesis that is both cultural and natural, and at the same time, neither natural nor cultural? If, in his landscapes, Lawrence sublimates or sublimes an experience of seeing which is inseparable from losing sight, his cross-dressing can be read as an(other) effort of inscribing and controlling what he desires and mimes, that which has already caught him, that is, the difference registered as the "Orient," the desert, the Arab. How does Deleuze read this cross-dressing?

> In Lawrence, there is a private desert that drives him to the Arabian deserts, among the Arabs, and that coincides on many points with their own perceptions and conceptions, but that retains an unmasterable difference that inserts them into a completely different and secret figure. Lawrence speaks Arabic, he dresses and lives like an Arab, even under torture he cries out in Arabic, but he does not imitate the Arabs, he never renounces his difference, which he already experiences as a betrayal. Beneath his young groom's suit, "suspect immaculate silk," he ceaselessly betrays his Bride. And Lawrence's difference does not simply stem from the fact that he is English, in the service of England; for he betrays England as much as Arabia, in a nightmare dream where everything is betrayed at once. But neither is it his personal difference, since Lawrence's undertaking is a cold and concerted destruction of the ego carried to its limit. Every mine he plants also explodes within himself; he is himself the bomb he detonates. It is an infinitely secret subjective disposition, which must not be confused with a national or personal character, and which leads him far from his own country, under the ruins of his devastated ego.[35]

This is a condensed passage. First of all, Deleuze's focus on Lawrence's private desert is preempted by Said's formulation of a new historical moment as producing a new imperial subjectivity in which private mythologies of eccentric intellectuals play a prominent part. Having solely focused on *symptomatology* (the reading of signs), Deleuze's interpretation has taken *etiology* (the study of causes) for granted: Lawrence is there for a social and historical reason, and he acts in a historical context that selected him. Of course Deleuze is not entirely unaware of this, as he specifies that at no point Lawrence ever thinks of giving up his British identity and the requirements of his national duty. Yet for Deleuze, Lawrence's sole aim is to liberate Arabs, as if he does not choose to return to the British army in the end. Deleuze wants to say that Lawrence's singularity was his impossible position between the British and the Arabs, which created *a nonmimetic, simulacral immanence inscribed as revolutionary fabula* by Lawrence. Yet contrary to his aim of depersonalizing Lawrence's desire in immanence, this approach results in his over-privatizing it. Looking for a singular solution in what he considers to be Lawrence's nonmimetic duplicity, Deleuze overlooks the multifaceted inscription of his desire. Lawrence's desire or fantasy itself is formed by a colonial power spacing and writing that also enables him to be there. This aspect of Lawrence's desire seems to have no relevance for Deleuze except in creating a nonmimetic opportunity. Although his complex notion of immanence as outside is supposed to destroy any "subject vs. object" kind of distance between the private and natural/public deserts at one stroke, Deleuze does not follow all the consequences of this and fails to think (or undo) the "private" desert further. Is Lawrence's private desert not also traversed by the natural/public desert *as imperially fantasized, marked and mapped*? Who is the narrator, who speaks in the *Seven Pillars of Wisdom*? As we learn from Angus Calder, Lawrence was modernist in his literary taste, but also one of the most important stylistic influences on him was Doughty's *Travels in Arabia Deserta*, a founding text of British Orientalism and imperial imagination of the Arabian desert.[36] If Lawrence's desire is in search of a good burn in the desert, "to embody his wound"[37] in a singular, secret manner, he does so as the child of an illicit relation without the aristocratic title he deserved, as an enthusiastic reader of medieval knights while a young boy, as an Oxford graduate archeologist who has completed a thesis study on the crusaders' castles and as having lost two brothers on the Western Front in 1915; that is, as a subject of his *imperial* culture.

Yet it might also be important to keep in mind here that, in his Goethean search of what the blinding power of sun can make Lawrence see (i.e. the "vision" as sense/event, a "simulacral" vision), Deleuze's aim is to fight mimesis understood as a hierarchical model-copy relationship: the task of reversing Platonism. The becoming-visible of the visible implies such a nonhierarchical relationship, as it is inseparable from invisibility and opacity, in the rhythm of appearance and disappearance, sight and blindness.[38] But also the significance or "sense" of the virtual Lawrence extracted from the *Seven Pillars* is the principle of an operation that does not work according to the Platonic mimesis: when Lawrence leaves his British national origin/model in his cross-dressing and speaks Arabic, he does not replace it with another model: "he does not imitate the Arab." Betraying "England as much as Arabia" his difference is not personal either, but "a cold and concerted destruction of the ego carried to its limit" through which is produced "an infinitely secret subjective disposition." In an interesting passage toward the end of the *Seven Pillars*, Lawrence spends his thirtieth birthday alone, contemplating the consequences of his "craving for good repute," his desire:

> This craving made me profoundly suspect of my truthfulness to myself. Only too good an actor could so impress his favorable opinion. Here were the Arabs

believing me, Allenby and Clayton trusting me, my bodyguard dying for me: and I began to wonder if all established reputations were founded, like mine, on fraud.[39]

Too bad to be true? When Lawrence takes up his "mantle of fraud," he betrays both sides, hence his shame. (Nonetheless there is an interesting nuance: the Arabs believe, the bodyguard dies for, but Allenby and Clayton trust him.) From the point of view of Deleuze's antimimetic/anti-Platonic argument, this passage reminds us of the actor in the *Logic of Sense*, who "acts out something perpetually anticipated and delayed."[40] Counteractualizing rather than actualizing, the actor's power is that of the "false."[41] We may describe Lawrence, who is "hardly a man of action . . . interested in Ideas rather than ends and their means" according to Deleuze, as a character close to the "seer" of the "crystalline" regime in his *Cinema 2: Time-Image*, which describes the postwar cinema in terms of the collapse of the sensory motor schema and a crisis of action.[42] Is a similar condition not applicable in the case of Lawrence who is, full with desert-desire, given the mission of leading natives in a foreign land? The European's sensory-motor schema goes through a small sweet collapse in the desert, and his "sensory-motor situation" gives way to "pure optical and sound situations," which turn him into a "seer" who cannot or will not react.[43]

Lawrence's singular literary sensibility shows that the imperial subject he actualizes is not the standard one, hence complicating this historical constitution itself. But what kind of a seer is he? He is there in order to react to a historical situation (war), to start an action, as the organic intellectual of the imperial British state and bourgeoisie, with their organic historical narrative, which he completely internalized. If we follow Deleuze's argument, as Lawrence's aim is to liberate Arabs, he would have to be closer to the Quebecois director Pierre Perrault, a prominent figure of anticolonial cinema in *Cinema 2*.[44] But, unlike Perrault, is Lawrence not colonizer rather than colonized?

Lawrence has an imperial mission to accomplish. Deleuze describes Lawrence's power of the false as a "projection machine." Although the difference is "unmasterable," Lawrence's profound desire is his tendency to project into reality "an image of himself and others so intense that it has a life of its own: an image that is always stitched together, patched up, continually growing along the way, to the point where it becomes fabulous."[45] The image that is projected is that of the movement of revolt. It is, again, nonmimetic by nature: "it has no need to correspond to a preexisting reality."[46] If this projection (political, erotic, and literary) is successful, must it not leave an impression on the reality it is projected onto? Is it not then the repetition of the same mimetic gesture in reverse, projection itself constituting an origin of the projected reality, even though according to Deleuze the images projected on the real live a life of their own? The absence behind the image bears witness to a dissolved ego, but there is also, Deleuze argues, "the mind that regards them with a strange coldness."[47] The mind's abstract ideas are "entities that inspire powerful spatial dynamisms" that are intimately linked up with the projected images in the desert. The entities offer "the weapons of their ruin."[48] At a strategic moment, Lawrence gives a long, "half-delirious" speech to the Arabs, declaring the two of these entities, Omnipotence and the Infinite, major enemies. The audience joins the revolt immediately.[49] Of course we cannot know anything about the factual correctness of whether Lawrence had enlisted new people as a result of his speech or not; but it is certain that Said's "eccentric adventurer" does not operate by linear reasoning or plain moral statements: "what we hear in Lawrence's style is the shock of entities."[50]

Two of these entities are particularly important: shame and glory. The latter is examined by Said in some detail. Deleuze seems to be particularly interested in the former. Shame is a composite feeling, "many shames in one, and also others": shame of betraying both sides, shame of battles, shame of armies, shame of commanding people, of stealing their souls, and, last but not the least, shame of the body.[51] Deleuze presents an analysis of shame as an affect that teaches us that spiritual entities or abstract ideas are affects or passive syntheses.[52] Literature or art is in contact with them in an experience of difference; and out of this contact, which is actualized by extracting intensive qualities or evental powers from things, a new people can be fabulated: a new earth, a desert island, exceeding human vision and audition, which Deleuze also called "a world without others," a radically noncolonial world.[53]

But then why does shame occupy such an important place in Deleuze's reading of Lawrence?

> And it is through this profound shame that the Arabs set about playing the glorious role of an expiation, a voluntary purification; Lawrence himself helps them to transform their paltry undertakings into a war of resistance and liberation, even if the latter must fail through betrayal (the failure in turn doubles the splendor or purity). The English, the Turks, the whole world distrusts them; but it is as if the Arabs, insolent and cheerful, leap beyond shame and capture the reflection of Vision and Beauty. They bring a strange

freedom to the world, where glory and shame enter into an almost spiritual combat.[54]

The world to which the Arabs brought freedom is Lawrence's. The poor, imaginative, mutilated Oxbridge man is expiated by his shame and glory; the Arabs will have to face the consequences of his government's betrayal for a whole century that follows the war. But did not Lawrence invent the guerilla war and transform "their paltry undertakings into a war of resistance"? Interestingly, in the introductory chapter as well as the whole Introduction (chapters 1–7), Lawrence offered a general picture of the political situation and extensive descriptions of the Arabs, especially Bedouins, the desert condition, and the nomadic life. His style is clearly dominative and dominating in the introduction. As "the problem of guerilla warfare merges with that of the desert,"[55] the "invention" might be considered as an effect of his mimesis of the nomadic way of life.

Mimesis and fabula

I do not mean that a more careful, attentive reading of the introductory part would give Deleuze the sense of that other affect that I have called "dominative" above. Deleuze seems to have made a decision: Lawrence's text is the instance of a vision before perception, a kind of simulacral difference. As Aracagök has argued, a major question with Deleuze's philosophy is whether he privileges simulacrum over mimesis.[56] According to Aracagök, "if there is no model . . . the act of copying . . . does not disappear: on the contrary, what we are left with is only the act of copying, yet without a definite model. An indefinite copy with respect to an indefinite model."[57] Imitating or copying was certainly an issue for Lawrence. When he makes distinctions between the two classes of Englishmen and the Frenchman, he gives an interesting description of the "intellectual group":

> Class one, subtle and insinuating, caught the characteristics of the people about him, their speech, their conventions of thought, almost their manner. He directed men secretly, guiding them as he would. In such frictionless habit of influence his own nature lay hid, unnoticed.[58]

The second group showed the complete Englishman abroad; failing to hide himself, he presented "a rounded sample of our traits."[59] Both groups, however, saw the Englishman as inimitable and copying him as impertinent. Although the French started from the same assumption of "the perfection of mankind," they encouraged their subjects to imitate them. While the perfection of mankind was a dogma among the French, it was instinctual with, hence an inimitable character trait of, the Englishmen.[60] The whole passage is about the theater of leadership under the condition of cultural difference. It is not for nothing that the words "copying," "imitating," and "inimitable" keep appearing in this interesting passage. In a disavowal of mimesis, the intellectual Englishman confesses its necessity: in cross-dressing, in taking up his mantle of fraud, in delivering the shock of entities, Lawrence is profoundly Platonic, though in a modern and eccentric way. For Plato mimesis was not simply dangerous; it was dangerous and it needed to be controlled because it was necessary for the education of guardians.[61] If the Englishman were inimitable it was because he naturally possessed and represented this ideal of controlled mimesis—"a frictionless habit of influence."[62] I wonder if the process Deleuze has so brilliantly described in Lawrence, the process of the becoming-visible of the visible, appearance and disappearance, sight and blindness, might be the shadow play of a mimesis or rhythm that is "originary" or "originarily" unstoppable, and further, one that gives him maybe a fear of becoming-Arab, of changing skin under the effect of the sun ("A man who gives himself to be a possession of aliens leads a Yahoo life, having bartered his soul to a brute-master. . . . At the same time I could not sincerely take on the Arab skin"[63]). As Deleuze refers to "the passionate life of entities in the jerking rhythm of a camel's gait," Lawrence himself imagined that the push and pull of this rhythm would be finely inscribed into the Idea of a new Arabia—"hustling it into form," in his words, as "these tides of men" were drawn into his hands. Yet what will be inscribed in the rhythm of his hand moving on the blank (blindingly white?) page of his desert desire, "across the sky in stars"?[64] If the ultimate aim of literature is the setting free of a people, then whose fabula is this?

> Before Lawrence insisted on withdrawing it from sale, for typically complicated reasons, *Revolt in the Desert* sold 30,000 copies in a few weeks in Britain—and 120,000 in the U.S.A. . . . When a popular edition came out very soon after Lawrence's mysterious death in a motor-cycle accident in 1935, that too was an immediate best-seller, and the book has never since been out of print.[65]

Although Deleuze attributes to Lawrence the revolutionary role of producing a fabula for the missing Arab people, what we actually have is English literature. Lawrence's work constructed an incredible fable for the English nation: the spectacular adventures of the young survivor displaced the massacres and losses that characterized the Western front (where Lawrence himself lost his two brothers). The text's power of fabulating a missionary, selfless, benevolent British subject was reinforced by Lawrence's passion for modernist prose. In the end, the dominative and benevolent British subject might be much more vulnerable than he appears in his self-staging as moral victim.

By way of a conclusion, I would like to suggest that the fable, whether British or Arab, cannot employ visions and auditions in order to transform them into something else, but indeed such visions and auditions, inescapable as they are in their dizzying vibration or resonance, are precisely what cause all projection to stray, or to "live" (to speak like Deleuze) as they remain indifferent to that which they nevertheless inscribe. It is in the unlocatability of their "rhythm" that Lawrence's text loses its ends, in resonance with that which no longer resonates it: in the disappearing figure of another story, in the untold story of another figure, of a missing Arab people to come.

Nomadism, or Sovereignty: Location of Culture

The works of Deleuze and Guattari have been subject to close scrutiny in terms of their possible colonial implications. In a lengthy essay, Christopher L. Miller argued that Deleuze and Guattari's references to actual ethnographic works make them complicit with conventional anthropological discourse, which is itself complicit with colonialism. While the concept of the nomad is offered as an alternative to the concepts of identity and representation, what Deleuze and Guattari actually do is to *represent* a concept of nomad that they have unproblematically extracted from ethnographic texts *without questioning* their colonial context.[1] Their concept of nomadism is *authorized* by a colonially contaminated anthropological form of knowledge.

Disturbed by Miller's strongly polemical and unforgiving tone, Eugene Holland responded to this criticism by emphasizing the *philosophical* relevance of Deleuze and Guattari's distinction: their nomad is not the same as the ethnographer's nomad but an abstract conceptual entity, that is, what they have called "conceptual personae" in *What is Philosophy?*.[2] Such abstract entities might be extracted from historical actualities but once abstracted in the way Deleuze and Guattari suggest, they are not reducible to them. Holland's insistence on the nature of Deleuze and Guattari's philosophical intention is a step in the right direction. But is it satisfactory as an answer to Miller's criticism? Holland does not engage the nature of the relationship of *authorization*, which constitutes the core of Miller's accusation (that the concept of nomadism is authorized by ethnographic knowledge that is complicit with colonialism). Further, when he refers to the real or actual postcolonial field, Holland's argument is surprisingly modest and not Deleuzian, as his defense depends on another distinction he makes *within* this reality: critical of Miller's opposition of nationalists versus nomads, he distinguishes between certain "geosocial circumstances where appeal to geographical and traditional rootedness may make sense" and others where "such appeals are not viable"; similarly there are "sociohistorical periods for which thinking in terms of binary oppositions make sense . . . but in most postcolonial circumstances, social relations are likely to be far more complex and require less polarized forms of thought."[3] It appears that there are places and times we should be Deleuzian and other times and places where we should not be, but mostly we should be. This is not helpful in thinking through Deleuze and Guattari's philosophy or concept of nomadism in the field of postcolonialism, nor is it an adequate response to Miller's pointed criticism. Lost in the trap set up by Miller—that is, the unproductive opposition between nationalism and nomadism—Holland's response remains on the defensive, provoking more questions than answers.

Perhaps we need to change the tenor of this debate. In fact, how would it be possible for two prominent French intellectuals' work, as philosophically challenging, radical, and innovative as it might be, productively drawing on multiple disciplinary sources, not to be implicated in colonial references, notions, knowledges, and forms of thought? Deleuze and Guattari do not affirm colonialism or imperialism.[4] Yet, given the incredible complexity of the philosophical and historical narratives in which they are engaged in the volumes they produced together, there is surely no reason to avoid questioning the degree and forms of their unconscious or unintentional complicity with it, or failure to avoid complicity. For reasons that must be thought separately perhaps, Deleuze and Guattari's constantly shifting and dynamic works have often been taken as a "theory" (both by followers and critics) rather than as a certain philosophical or theoretical *practice*, which aims to produce new angles, problems, and ways of thinking. The unfortunate result is that their philosophical or theoretical performance is often treated purely constatively (what is the correct concept of nomadism?). This is a destiny that is hard to escape. It leads to "applying" Deleuzian concepts in reading a novel or in understanding colonial discourse—a conventional disciplinary practice, depending on a non-Deleuzian understanding of philosophy on the basis of a model-copy relationship.[5]

The problem in which Deleuze and Guattari find themselves calls for a theoretical effort of working through the binarisms that are constantly engaged in their texts, an effort that should involve a careful "unworking" of these oppositions in the ways they have initiated or sometimes have failed to initiate.[6] Reducing the question of binarism to one of predicament, and looking for a solution to it, Miller finds the alternative that Deleuze and Guattari's concept of nomad offers to be insufficient, since it is tainted with colonial knowledge. But his own antagonistic investment in Deleuze and Guattari's text disables him to read the extent to which his own criticism suffers from a problem similar to the one he identified in *A Thousand Plateaus*. If, by declaring nomadic thought nonrepresentational, Deleuze and Guattari clean their hands with high philosophy and erase the ethnographic authorization of their reference, Miller himself too has to *erase*, in the same gesture that he is critical of them, the same ethnographic authorization:

> . . . this claim [the claim that nomadology is nonrepresentational] liberates Deleuze and Guattari and their followers from the ethical burden of representing *the real, actual nomads, who might eventually have something to say in response.*[7]

Not only is this position the same as postmodern anthropologists in demanding that the other speaks, but it also evokes a number of serious questions of representation. *Who* are the "real, actual nomads"? *What kind of access* does Miller have to the discourse of "real, actual nomads," if not ethnographic? As Miller points to the possibility of colonial complicity in Deleuze and Guattari's referential world, he would not like to fall back into the assumption of a pure and clean referentiality, which is the colonial assumption as such.[8]

In another essay titled "Deleuze in the Postcolonial: On Nomads and Indigenous Politics," Julie Wuthnow argues that the Deleuzian concept of the nomad proposes a new abstract universalism of the fragmented subject, which must be corrected with a politics of location based on *situated knowledge*.[9] Unfortunately, Wuthnow's criticism is more about a discursive construct which she calls "Deleuzian philosophy" than the actual texts of Deleuze and Guattari.[10] She describes the nomad as a "vague apparition . . . who can loosely be referred as a subject and who exists as force, movement, difference, change . . . [the nomad] is unmarked, unlocatable, and disembodied by virtue of its grounding only in movement."[11] This identification of the Deleuzian nomad with movement, difference, and change is perhaps not untrue in general terms but depends on an impressionistic reading. As Deleuze and Guattari have clearly underlined:

> The nomad distributes himself in smooth space: he occupies, inhabits, holds that space; that is his territorial principle. It is therefore false to define the nomad by movement. Toynbee is profoundly right to suggest that the nomad is on the contrary *he who does not move*. Whereas the migrant leave behind a

milieu that has become amorphous or hostile, the nomad is the one who does not depart, does not want to depart, who clings to the smooth space left by the receding forest, where the steppe or the desert advances, and who invents nomadism as a response to this challenge. Of course the nomad moves, but while seated, and he is only seated while moving (the Bedouin galloping, knees on the saddle, sitting on the soles of his upturned feet, "a feat of balance"). The nomad knows how to wait, he has infinite patience. Immobility and speed, catatonia and rush, a "stationary process," station as process—these traits of Kleist's are eminently those of the nomad.[12]

The concept of the nomad is strangely closer to the concept of the schizo in the previous volume, *Anti-Oedipus*:

the schizo knows how to leave: he has made a departure into something as simple as being born or dying. But at the same time his journey is strangely stationary, in place. He does not speak of another world, he is not from another world: even when he is displacing himself in space, his is a journey in intensity, around the desiring-machine that is erected here and remains here.[13]

Schizo and nomadism are surely different concepts with different genealogies and actual connections. Yet they have common elements: knowing how to leave or how to wait, the schizo's journey in intensity or the nomad's intensive speed rather than movement. In both figures, Deleuze and Guattari seem to be involved in extracting and abstracting certain elements from the actual clinical and ethnographic entities and produce the concept of "something" that is irreducible to them. I would like to describe this as formulating the problem of a collective or singular body's being located, situated, and distributed in space. Without entering into a full account of Deleuze and Guattari's complex treatment of this problem thoughout their works, and leaving aside the potential problems with their unique philosophical operation (which would require that we discuss the status of the concepts of the virtual and actual and their relationship in this philosophy), we might observe that the question of location and position for Deleuze and Guattari is not a simple matter of being situated. What is a solution for Whutnow (a sense of being situated, an appreciation of limits and relativity) is a *problem* for them: how space is occupied, how a "self" is situated, how a collectivity is distributed, etc. We need to understand the notions of concept and problem here in the sense that Deleuze and Guattari mean. For them, a concept is always created as the function of a problem. The concept of nomadism is connected to the problem of inhabitation. In *What is Philosophy?* they write that "concepts are connected to problems without which they would have no meaning and which can themselves only be isolated or understood as their solution emerges."[14] Whutnow suggests that a "politics of location" based on "situated knowledge" is capable of accounting for the crisscrossing plurality of struggles. There is a myriad of stories each of which produces, from its own location, an excess beyond the hegemonic representation. With regard to such a transparent pluralist framework of partial views, the concept of the nomad is in fact an insistence on considering inhabitation as a problem, that is, on the irreducible complexity of the very acts of locating, moving, and situating selves and bodies in space, and on the infinity of the coordinates that produce the locatability of a body.[15]

While the concept of nomadism is produced in a historical context that is inseparable from Western colonialism, there might well be a way of using it in the opposite direction. In a critical reading of Paul Bowles's *Sheltering Sky* and Bertolucci's film adaptation of this novel, Deborah Root argued that "within the colonialist construct that has come to be called Orientalism, the Orient exists as the terrain where a particular kind of experience is available to the Western subject, an experience at once mysterious, dangerous and compelling."[16] In the colonial fantasy of Bowles's bourgeois protagonists, the desert is seen as a cure for the alienation from which they suffer, a place for forgetting all they have left behind in Europe. The originality of Root's analysis lies in the way she reads the structure of the Western subject's desire through Deleuze and Guattari's notions of nomadism, line of flight, and becoming-invisible. At an initial level, the problem of Bowles' characters appears to be the familiar illusion that authentic difference is available over there in the desert:

> *The Sheltering Sky* would seem to fit neatly into Deleuze and Guattari's description of *becoming-invisible* and the dangers involved in moving too quickly across space: the characters seek to become nomad, and embark on a line of flight that skitters across the expanse of the desert into the twin black holes of death and madness.[17]

But, more importantly, Root argues, the end of their adventure in death and madness means that this search for an intense experience itself has assumed an originary, absolute, and radical difference. In the eyes of Bowles and his protagonists, cultural difference is not simply cultural difference but it has an originary status. Accordingly, people of this originary space are seen as mysterious, wild, and dangerous. The European travelers believe that they can have access to what they see as the absolute otherness of the originary by manifesting their unquestionable privilege and authority in experiences of nomadism, sexuality, and hashish, but they become disoriented and ill *when* their authority is shaken in various encounters.[18] As the protagonists exoticize the nomad in familiar Orientalist terms, Root draws our attention to Deleuze and Guattari's concept of nomadism. If, as we learn from them, it is false to define nomadism by movement, and if, instead, nomadism is an art of occupying, inhabiting, holding space, "then the colonialist dream of escaping Western culture through nomadic wanderings and incursions into nomadic territory raises questions about the relation between movement, appropriation and colonial authority."[19] Root concludes that what is problematic is Western thinking and imagining of cultural difference as a radical outside, which is geographically available and appropriable by means of escape. She thus demonstrates how Deleuze and Guattari's concept of nomadism can also be usefully employed in a critical study of Western colonial discourse and subjectivity.

Isabelle Eberhardt's sovereignities

I would like to follow the track of this Western desire in the work and life of a voluntary nomad, Isabelle Eberhardt (1877–1904). A Swiss-born travel writer, anarchist, and Sufi, this amazing woman's writing does not seem to perform the appropriative gesture that is found in Bowles's protagonists. An outsider to common norms and dominant culture, she was also critical of French colonialism. Isabelle Eberhardt was the daughter of an aristocratic Russian couple. Her mother left her husband who was a general and moved to Geneva with the children's tutor, Alexandre Trophimowsky, an ex-priest anarchist who gave Isabelle a nonconformist education. Later Isabelle and her mother moved to Algeria, where both converted to Islam. Following her mother's death, Eberhardt became a journalist and writer in Algeria. What makes her story so unusual is not only her nomadic incursions into the desert and her beautiful travel-writing but also her cross-dressing as an Arab man, her strong sense of freedom and sexual adventures, not to mention her devout Sufism as a member of the Qadiriyya sect, her intellectual ideas, and her addiction to hashish. Leaving behind many unpublished pages, she drowned in a flash flood at the age of 27. Eberhardt is commonly accepted today as one of the most important travel writers of Francophone literature in the twentieth century and is regarded as a feminist heroine by many.

Isabelle Eberhardt was certainly not a mere adventurer; like Lawrence, from the very start her project was becoming a writer. Given her very limited financial means, she used every opportunity and everyone, including the colonial administration, for her single purpose. In terms of given literary classifications, Eberhardt's writing belongs to the genre of romantic Orientalism. Hence her writings fall within the general movement of those texts depicting the search for an originary, authentic experience; but the way this search is conducted seems to be different than Bowles' protagonists or Lawrence. Although Bowles himself was sympathetic to Eberhardt and translated and introduced her work into English, there is a significant difference between the two authors, as I hope to demonstrate below.

Eberhardt's work is not simply travel-writing but also a reflection on space, time, freedom, love, and life. In a short but powerful intellectual statement titled "Pencilled Notes," she expresses her personal perspective as a writer.[20] She begins by defining the essence of freedom as vagrancy, which she sees as a right. Freedom is solitary freedom, or not freedom at all: "no one is free who is not alone."[21] This has nothing to do with a cult of individuality. If vagrancy is deliverance, it is deliverance from sociality, or perhaps deliverance from a form of sociality in which one is "a useful cog in the machine."[22] Deliverance is then a deliverance from the world of *work* in which one is part of a functional whole, and therefore unfree, suffering from "a different form of slavery that comes of contact with others, especially regulated and continued contact."[23] It is not that she is antisocial or even asocial; on the contrary, as we understand from her writing, she has a great skill of easily starting a conversation with foreign people whom she has just met. The issue at stake is *desire*, what she calls her "torturing need" and identifies with a certain transcendence specific to being human:

> Not to feel *the torturing need to know and see for oneself what is there*, beyond the mysterious blue wall of the horizon, not to find the arrangements of life monotonous and depressing, to look at the white road leading off into *the unknown distance* without feeling the imperious necessity of giving in to it and following it obediently across mountains and valleys! The cowardly belief that a man must stay in one place is too reminiscent of *the unquestioning resignation of animals*, beasts of burden stupefied by servitude and yet always willing to accept the slipping on of the harness.[24]

Vagrancy is then identified with human transcendence and knowledge, separated from the animal's slavery, which is also one of work. This is an interesting passage in terms of Eberhardt's own familiarity and closeness with animals, whom she used in her travels; animals working under her yoke, camels and horses who took her from one place to another. As we shall see, her writing is never free of the figure of "Man," the humanist discourse of Enlightenment. Although her sympathy and love for the North African people is beyond doubt, a form of racial prejudice clearly rooted in Enlightenment humanism, and evolutionism is not absent in her texts.

Nevertheless, vagrancy is not only motivated by knowledge. It seems to be *driven by something else*: as soon as she arrives at a town with "many familiar folks . . . many friendly greetings of exchange," she knows she will leave: "and all the time the secret joy of knowing that I will leave at dawn, leave all these things which are still pleasing and dear to me this evening." This is her "double rejoicing" (arriving and leaving), which only a nomad, a vagabond can understand.[25] Although she "knows" her secret joy of continual displacement, this is a figure other than knowledge. Whenever Eberhardt attempts to represent it, she falls back into the figure of an appropriation, which is clearly not appropriation:

> To be alone, to be *poor in needs*, to be ignored, to be an outsider who is at home everywhere, and to walk, great and by oneself, toward the conquest of the world.
>
> The healthy wayfarer sitting beside the road scanning the horizon open before him, is he not the absolute master of the earth, the waters, and even the sky? What housedweller can vie with him in power and wealth? His estate has no limits, his empire no law. No work bends him toward the ground, for the bounty and beauty of the earth are already his.[26]

And,

> There are limits to every domain, and laws to govern every organized power. But the vagrant owns the whole vast earth that ends only at the nonexistent horizon, and his empire is an intangible one, for his domination and enjoyment of it are things of the spirit.[27]

A master who is poor and alone; an outsider who is at home everywhere; a conquest that conquers everywhere hence nowhere; a property owner whose estate has no limits and therefore is not an estate; and a world that ends at no horizon, therefore is not a world—in sum, an appropriation that is not an appropriation. It is a spiritual rather than physical or merely geographical appropriation.

There is a clear affinity between Eberhardt's vagrant and Deleuze and Guattari's nomad. According to Deleuze and Guattari, a distinguishing characteristic of the nomad lies in the relationship between the *points* (of arrival and departure) and the *paths* it constructs: it is the former that determines the latter while it is subordinate to it. Points are relays in a trajectory for Eberhardt too, as she calls this her double rejoicing (arriving and leaving).[28] When we consider the other aspects of Deleuze and Guattari's concept of nomadism, however, we may have a few difficulties. If, for instance, the nomad is "he who does not move," or if he is the one who "occupies, inhabits, holds" the smooth space (as opposed to a space striated by walls, enclosures, and roads), how do we explain Isabelle Eberhardt's first movement from Europe to North Africa?[29] There is also a further problem: what exactly is Eberhardt's relationship with colonialism? She might be critical of French colonialism, but she might also be involved in Orientalist or colonialist discursive problematics. For instance, Laura Rice brought convincing evidence that Eberhardt was persuaded by the French colonel Lyautey's plan for colonizing the Western region.[30] In order to better understand how she located herself in North Africa, how she inhabited the desert and how she positioned herself with regard to French colonialism as well as Western sovereignty, we need to examine the relationship between the two more carefully.

First as a European and then a French citizen after her marriage to an Algerian-French husband, Sliman, Eberhardt's presence in North Africa was determined by the unequal relationship between Europe and North Africa. Colonialism was not comfortable with a transgressive and critical figure such as Eberhardt, but especially in its more cunning and liberal moments it also attempted to employ her in its own schemes. In turn, Eberhardt's response was to use every opportunity, without realizing any promises on her part. In 1897, following her mother's unexpected death, an afflicted Eberhardt bought a horse and flew off toward the Sahara desert. Dressed as an Arab man (the first travel, the travel before the travel is crossing the gender line in order to reverse the relationship of the looking and the looked, which is essential to writing), and fluent in Arabic, she aimlessly wandered from town to town in the desert.[31] After a trip to Geneva upon Trophimowsky's illness and death, she returned to Algeria in 1899, decided to live there and continued her explorations in the desert, smoking hashish, consuming alcohol, and having an uninhibited sexual life—as the legend goes. Meanwhile she met and fell in love with an Arab soldier in the French military, Sliman Ennhi. While cross-dressing frequently, she also took an Arab male name, Si Mahmoud Essadi. She was accepted in to one of the oldest Sufi sects, the Qadiriyya (despite being a woman). Her Qadiri faith and belonging also provided her with free and secure travelling in the whole of North Africa, as it was the duty of every Qadiri to feed her, give her shelter, and protect her when necessary. Naturally the French colonial administration did not like this strange, adventurous young woman who became a Muslim, and found her ubiquitous presence irritating.[32] Nor did colonial society like her liberated character, a woman who seemed to have only contempt for their mannerisms and etiquette (even though she made what are perhaps the most sophisticated analyses of the colonials). In 1901, she was attacked by a member of the rival Tidjanis sect and was wounded seriously. In the days following the trial, however, the colonial government expelled her from Algeria. Her criticisms of the French colonial administration, as well as her habit of sleeping with Arab men, surely played a major role in this grossly unfair decision.[33] She had to go to Marseilles where her brother lived. Desperate to return to Algeria, she eventually had her lover Sliman, who had French citizenship, post himself at Marseilles. They married there and returned to Algeria. French colonial society was doubly frustrated with her reappearance as a French citizen.

This time she was protected by a well-established writer of leftist conviction, Victor Barrucand, who published a newspaper called *Akhbar*. Barrucand would later be the editor of her posthumous publications. Admiring Eberhardt's talent, he wanted her to work for him as a war correspondent. The nomad writer did not miss the opportunity and left for Ain Sefra, where she was going to meet Colonel Lyautey. Soon Lyautey developed a plan of using this intelligent woman—a faithful Muslim with a perfect command of Arabic. It was essential to the French success that they win the marabout of Kenadsa, Sidi Brahim, over to their side. But it was impossible for a Christian even to imagine approaching the Sufi center for learning in Kenadsa where he lived. As a Qadiri, Eberhardt was naturally qualified to enter the center, gain access to Sidi Brahim, and persuade him that the French occupation was preferable to the conflict between the Muslims. Eberhardt accepted the plan without a blink of the eye, since this was another opportunity for her to depart for the nonexistent horizon and to write about the earth and its wandering people. As Laura Rice demonstrates in her careful study, however, Eberhardt was also convinced by Lyautey's plan because she thought that this would bring some order and prosperity to a territory that was torn by the internal conflict between the nomads and the agriculturalists.[34] There is no evidence as to what exactly she had done for this purpose in Kenadsa. She became very ill soon after her arrival, but she continued to work on her manuscript in spite of her diminishing physical capacity. She returned to Ain Sefra and was hospitalized there. Soon after leaving the hospital, she drowned in a flood.

This short biographical sketch shows that Eberhardt was an outsider with a strong sympathy for the natives and a needy writer who used every opportunity to realize her own project of travelling and writing. She had manifest criticisms of the injustice of the colonial system, and she despised the colonial administration and the bourgeois culture of colonial society.[35] But the question remains whether she was critical of specific present colonial policies of expropriation, authoritarianism, and repression, *or* colonialism itself, going as far as supporting anticolonial nationalism. No less importantly, it seems that Eberhardt also shared the hierarchical, cataloguing, and stereotyping tendencies of the evolutionism of Enlightenment and post-Enlightenment discourses. A certain dislike and disturbance with the natives appears as a spontaneous reaction in the following passages, as she does not hide her feelings. For instance, this is how Eberhardt feels in her first days in Kenadsa, close to the Moroccan border:

> To be always surrounded by black faces, to see them everyday anew, to hear only the shrill voices of slaves, with their drawling accents: this is my first impression of daily life in Kenadsa.
>
> Apart from some rare Berber families, all the inhabitants of the *ksar* are black Kharatines. At the *zawiya*, the Sudanese element adds further to my feeling of dislocation.[36]

There are some places, it seems, where the vagrant does not feel at home. Eberhardt finds the Sudanese "robust and often handsome, with a completely Arab type of beauty" whereas "those who are offsprings of marriages with Kharatines are, in contrast, often puny and ugly, with angular faces and skinny, ill-proportioned limbs."[37] In the nineteenth century, this familiar race discourse was often shared in the progressive circles as well. Eberhardt appears to regard black people's "non-humanity" as an objective fact, which naturally and instinctively emerges from their bodies and imposes itself on her helpless white "humanity." In the same passage she calls them "my brothers":

> I find the blacks to be disconcerting and repulsive, mainly because of the extreme mobility of their faces: their ferret's eyes, and features plagued by ticks

and grimaces. They bring out in me a stubborn sense of their non-humanity, a lack of kinship which I succumb to childishly, every time, in the face of these blacks, my brothers.[38]

There is only one among them who she finds likeable. The reason is that, "in his expressions, his gestures and in his regular features, there is nothing of the ape-man, grimacing and crafty; or of the animal cunning which passes for intelligence among blacks."[39] Black women also have their share of non-humanity in this racial parade. The "coloured women" constitute a special category, as their

> . . . morals are extremely loose. For a few sous, for a scarf, and even for pleasure, they give themselves to whomever, Arab or negro. They make open advances to guests, offering themselves with casual forwardness which is often funny to watch.
>
> The male savages manage to contain somewhat the urgings of their blood, but all of black womanhood abandon themselves to instinct, and their quarrells are as frivolous as their loves.[40]

This is a sovereign affect that Eberhardt inherited from her European or Western imperial culture, in which non-Western culture is pushed back in time and cultural difference is read in terms of the origin of the Western Subject/ Man. This sovereignty is not identical to a particular colonial government, and clearly goes beyond the particular troubles that Eberhardt had with French colonialism in North Africa, or her criticisms of it. This general imperial sovereignty is a violent reworlding of the native's world, reducing it by temporalization. But it is also an *opening*, in which difference (of their world) *survives* the epistemic violence of its reduction in the grand narrative. This survival leaves a trace in Eberhardt's text, beyond the question of her being "for" or "against" colonialism. Although, as we have just seen, Eberhardt is unoriginally Western in her trouble with the African presence around her, she gradually has to confront her own feelings. Her initial description of the only black man she likes, Ba Mahmadou, is negative ("nothing of the ape-man"), but we realize that something else in this unusual servant's character and behavior attracts her attention. Her following description, appreciative of the black man's autonomous power of forming himself, carries the trace of a different view of difference:

> he has discovered within himself, or in his slave culture, the secret of deliberate gestures and respectful attitudes, without displaying any of the depressing servility one might expect from a slave. He puts nobility in his

greetings—whereas most other negroes don't even know the formula for a proper greeting.[41]

Ba Mahmadou's secret of producing gestures and attitudes of respect is not learned from the Europeans; it is a secret he discovered *within himself* or *in his slave culture*. Implicit here is a view of culture that attributes to it an immanent productivity and creativity. It is not that he merely pretends to be servile or imitate servility without believing it. He is fully and spontaneously embodied in his act, yet withdraws from it "something" of himself. That is to say, he does not repeat what might be expected of a slave. The others do not know "the formula for a proper greeting," because they have never "formed" it in their minds, as he did. By (re)inventing the formula, what Ba Mahmadou produces is *not simply servitude, but the act of servitude* that gives the effect of a *distance* between his individual person and his act, hence a production of himself as distinct and autonomous, as capable of acting on his own, as having *dignity*—this is what Eberhardt means when she describes his behavior, in surprise, as putting "nobility" into servile greeting: "He puts nobility in his greetings . . . bowing three times in front of them . . . however his respectfulness in no way diminishes him."[42] Puzzled by this unusual black man's silent and invisible withdrawal from the act that is expected of him as he performs it (because he is the one who has devised it), Eberhardt begins to develop other ideas and is reminded of her own prejudices:

> It would be a very interesting study to write about the slaves who live here. For this attempt I should have no prejudices in either direction; it should be a natural history as well as a social history. I should first have to be cured of my prejudices about superior races, and my superstitions about inferior ones.[43]

This is followed by a few observations on the double life of the slaves: free outside, slaves within the *zawiya*, etc. If realized, what would Eberhardt's study look like? We cannot tell. Nevertheless Ba Mahmadou's apparition in the text is marked, and it is this trace of cultural difference freed from its temporalization that makes Eberhardt remember to question her own prejudices and superstitions.[44]

This sovereign affect takes us away from a nomadic relationship with the earth, as it is an imperial one. But perhaps there is another sense or affect of sovereignty that will take us closer to nomadism. Eberhardt's nomadic journeys into the desert are her transgressive search for an authentic, originary experience. Rather than depending on some external ideal, she is after discovery. "I am quite aware," she writes, "this way of life is dangerous, but the moment of danger is also the moment of hope."[45] Although Eberhardt's views of the Africans and Arabs carry these signs of danger, she is much more open to the people of this land and more intimate with them than Bowles' protagonists. And this cultural intimacy is not used directly for the benefit of an imperial politics as it is in the case of Lawrence.

On an initial level, the authentic, originary experience unfolds itself as a spatial experience of immensity: a vast and empty horizon and wide-open sky with accompanying feelings of monotony, loss, tranquility, and solitude.[46] But this experience is not static or external, nor simply an aesthetic matter. It is closer to the immanent concept of landscape that I have discussed in the previous chapter. Eberhardt's spatial experience can be read in terms of Bachelard's concept of "intimate immensity": a feeling of loss of dimensions in radically homogenous environments such as forest, desert, and sea. Eberhardt often conveys a similar feeling: "Under the blazing sun, perspective becomes deformed. Impossible to gauge distances: a kind of dizziness blurs our vision. . . ."[47] Bachelard develops this concept in his *Poetics of Space*. His "phenomenology without phenomena" is critical of the Orientalist Pierre Loti's landscape: "a schoolboy's desert" written "in the shade of a tree."[48] For Bachelard, the immensity of a desert must be lived in the way it is reflected in the wanderer, or as a "concentration of wandering," quite similar to Eberhardt's experience indeed. Referring to Philippe Diolé's interesting work, Bachelard speaks of an "inner space" annexed to spaces such as the desert or the ocean. Under the surface of the water, Diolé discovers absolute depth beyond measuring, which Bachelard describes as a "conquest of the intimacy of the water."[49] We have various descriptions of this kind of intimacy with the earth and the sky in Eberhardt's pages:

> When I sleep under the starry skies of this region, religious in their vastness, I feel penetrated by the earth's energies.[50]
>
> What anguish! I am on the verge of wrestling the warm earth itself. . . .[51]
>
> I am at the heart of the earth; a surge of immortality flows through my veins; my chest expands; I am free, existing above death.[52]

We already feel that the sense of intimacy with nature has a further dimension in Eberhardt's writing, which does not exist in Bachelard's concept of intimate immensity:

> I hear. There are sighs and catchings of breath there in the cinnamon-scented night. . . . The hot night's languor drives flesh to seek flesh, and desire is reborn.

It is terrible to hear teeth grinding in mortal spasms . . . I feel like sinking my
teeth into the warm earth.[53]

The senses of intimacy and continuity with the natural environment has
erotic as well as religious dimensions. It is associated with a socially and
ideologically produced sense of *originary human experience* that she finds
expressed in a number of social and cultural phenomena in the North African
territory: music, chanting and drums, religious rituals, the experience of
smoking hashish, the Sufi version of Islam, and eroticism and love, not
to mention nomadism.[54] This supposition of an originary experience is
impossible without the Orientalist and colonial temporalization, that is,
pushing cultural difference back in time:

> All their ancient negro blood stirs and overflows, triumphing over the the
> artificial habits of reserve imposed by slavery. They become themselves again,
> both innocent and wild, eager for childlike games and barbarous frenzy, *very
> near now to our animal origins.*[55]

Despite this spectacle of savagery, Eberhardt also finds a desirable aspect in
the desert and its people: "what many dreamers have searched for, simple
people have found."[56] This is something she wants to appropriate, all the more
knowing that it remains beyond appropriation. She is "saturated with Islam"
but "still far from the serenity of fakirs," and in fact, it appropriates her: "I
wanted to possess this country, and this country has instead possessed me."[57]
With this statement written in Kenadsa toward the end of her short life, we
are back to the major preoccupation of "the pencilled notes" on vagrancy and
nomadism. This possession by the other is a dispossession of the self. I will
call it Isabelle Eberhardt's other sovereignty. I have no intention of separating
it arbitrarily from the imperial sovereignty. They are inseparable, always
working together, but they nevertheless remain different figures.

   This other sovereignty is one that does not govern itself. It is telling that
Eberhardt sees vagrancy or nomadism as human transcendence and thus
mistakes the second sovereignty for the first. This is the historically determined
production of her desire. The originary experience she is after is perhaps better
understood in terms of Georges Bataille's concepts of intimacy and immanence
than Bachelard's. In his *Theory of Religion*, Bataille suggests that religion is a
return to lost intimacy.[58] Our given condition is *servility*, that is, the world of
work and rationality in which I exist as "a useful cog in the machine," as Eberhardt
puts it. This means for Bataille that I have lost my intimacy and my continuity
with other living beings and with death that I used to have in the immanent

world of nature and animality. Nature is also characterized by excess energy that is destructive and spent extravagantly; life is indistinguishable from death and loss. Human rationality and work introduces discontinuity into it, breaks with the immanent world of animality and nature, and represses excess energy in order to make it useful. But although human beings turn nature into property, they cannot master the destructive forces of death and sexuality, the excess of nature. *Sovereignty* is the return of this immanence, a form of self-consciousness that does not depend on knowledge and discursive articulation, but one that simply "enjoys the present time without having anything else in view but this present time."[59] In sovereign experiences such as eroticism, sacrifice, poetry, or religious ecstasy, I touch this lost intimacy, and I communicate with life from within (rather than externally as it is in the act of knowing that belongs to the world of work and rationality).

Mystical traditions in all religions can be seen from this perspective, including Islamic mysticism. What Sufism calls *wajd*, an ecstatic state of rapture, experienced through poetry or reading the Qur'an, is a perfect instance of sovereignty in Bataille's sense, and one cannot imagine Eberhardt not to know or experience this (though there is no description of any ecstatic ceremony or scene in her writing, which might be because of a refusal to turn the sacred into a spectacle). It is important to emphasize here that implicit in the above view of immanence is the notion of the One. It is common to mystical traditions to see the Divine as manifested in the material world.[60] We are also reminded of Eberhardt's "double re-joicing," according to which the important thing is to be on the path, that is, continual departure rather than arrival, which is similar to the aimlessness as well as the momentary nature of Bataille's sovereignty. Eberhardt's frequent references to spending time as a great enjoyment is yet another instance of sovereignty in Bataille's sense, as well as her descriptions I have cited above, descriptions in which she experiences her body in continuity and intimacy with the earth. Given all this, especially the immanent tendencies implicit in Sufism must have made this religion a metaphor of authentic relationship with the alterity of nature for Eberhardt.

Eberhardt's version of nomadism can be read as a figuration of this return to intimacy and immanence, a primal, original way of inhabiting the earth. We need to keep in mind that this is *inseparable from writing* for Eberhardt. It is therefore also a sovereignty associated with writing as well as the sovereignty of writing, in which there is a movement from the known to the unknown: a continual departure, which sacrifices the language of reason in "seeking oblivion" rather than seeking knowledge.[61] Have we moved away from imperial sovereignty rooted in the evolutionary discourse of Enlightenment Reason? But Eberhardt's first journey, based on her own decision, was the one that took her from Europe to Algeria. (She was already sympathetic to Islam and she convinced her mother to move to North Africa.) Remembering Deborah Root's reading, it is an external movement rather than nomadic inhabitation in the sense of Deleuze and Guattari, as it is also one that aims this nomadism. Hence Eberhardt's version of colonial desire reveals the productive tension implicit in thinkers such as Deleuze and Guattari or Bataille. Although Deborah Root showed us how we can usefully employ Deleuze and Guattari, the demonstration does not cancel the tension between the problem and the concept. Similarly, if Bataille's reading of religion in terms of concepts of immanence, intimacy, and sovereignty communicates with Eberhardt's writing, this is most probably because Bataille's theory, as complicated and critical as it is, is not formed very far from a certain anthropology and sociology whose evolutionism is clear (Durkheim, Mauss, and numerous other similar references in his works). The tension between historical and theoretical aspects has been much debated in Bataille's work.[62]

A no less interesting aspect is the role of women in his theory of religion, which is mostly forgotten in the commentary on Bataille. Bataille accepts Levi-Strauss's analysis of the exchange, that is, control of women, but Isabelle Eberhardt was a woman who refused to enter the circuit and paid a heavy price for it.[63] It is not for nothing that Eberhardt's writing is full of various women figures: Yasmin and Achoura, both of whom are betrayed, Taalith, the "Rebel" (a Muslim woman who hanged herself), Lella Khaddoudja the travelling woman (whom she was never able to meet, because she had already left), Sidi Brahim's mother, a young woman deceived by the magician, Jewesses.[64] Like in Assia Djebar's reading of Delacroix's and Picasso's paintings, we owe their distant figures and voices to Isabelle Eberhardt's other sovereignty, her secret joy of writing, one imagines, between arrival and departure.[65] The legend about her own erotic adventures aside, and certainly more important than that, is her attention to the scenes of eroticism. She hears people making love in the middle of the night; she secretly watches how a nomad seduces a beautiful young woman, and how men and women find each other at the well where they apparently go to water their horses.[66] As she makes them breathe and live in the flow of the everyday, North Africa also appears as a space of transgression, danger, and freedom. This image of North Africa as a space of authentic experience is never far from Eberhardt's writing. The relationship between the two sovereignties are well put by Gayatri Spivak: "It is a truism to say that the law is constituted by its own transgression; that trivial intimacy is the relationship between nineteenth-century feminism and the axiomatics of imperialism."[67]

In the last section of *In the Shadow of Islam* titled "Reflections on Love," Eberhardt reveals the most singular aspect of her nomadic sovereignty as a woman.[68] She is hopelessly sick, suffering from malaria in Kenadsa. In moments of calm, she feels a "vast serenity," having reached "the end of her wandering, tormented existence" and can now see that the distance between her present perspective and that of the newspapers comes from a "geographic illusion," from her "having broken into the past, across countries frozen in time." What is there, in the ancient past? The issue about which Eberhardt seems to reach a final conclusion is *love*. "The Pencilled Notes" declared that slavery is produced by regulated and continued contact with others, which implied being part of a functional whole, a cog in the machine. Now true slavery is announced to be individual love, whether carnal or fraternal: one renounces oneself to become a couple; one sacrifices one's freedom. This is not a denial of sensuality, however, since love and passion are indistinguishable and sensual passion is not all coarseness. But there is a choice to be made:

> The most deceiving and pernicious love of all seems to me the western tendency towards the "sister soul." The beautiful, devouring, Oriental flame has nothing in common with equality and fraternity between the sexes. The Muslim can love a slave and the slave can love her master. This authentication of the natural order completely reverses the social systems.[69]

For Eberhardt, the natural order authenticated by Islam must be one that depends on a mere difference of force, a natural difference (such as we have in the world of immanence understood in Bataille's sense), and love is in this difference. Its nature has nothing to do with the deceptive and destructive formal equality of Western culture. It is a reversal of it (hence her cross-dressing as an Arab man: to reverse the relationship, to be able to look at him who is the looker, to be his comrade, not his plaything). But perhaps Eberhardt is not so sure. Her reflections on love then take on a sudden *spiritual* turn. She introduces a new element by writing that whenever she feels herself in true sympathy, she is in nature or in humanity, "never in the throes of passion" (as if passion is not part of nature!). And she further confesses that she has always guarded herself during sexual abandon, and has possessed "divine wealth," for at such moments she feels that she is "at the heart of the earth," free, existing above death: "Glory to those who go alone into life!"[70] This restraint has nothing to do with asceticism but with a question of protecting oneself from the bondage of love:

> I have found a great talisman of purity, permitting whoever possesses it to pass through any condition of life unsullied by any contact: "Never give your soul to a creature, because it belongs to God alone; see in all creatures a motive for rejoicing, in homage to the Creator; never seek yourself in another, but discover yourself in yourself."[71]

Religion, Islam, is her solution to the question of love: in a relationship that is impossible to reverse, you can be free and sovereign only when you submit your soul to God.[72] The problem itself is more interesting than the solution. For in this last turn of her journey in time and space, the problem of inhabiting the earth has unfolded itself as the problem of love for this remarkable woman writer of the nineteenth century.

Part III

Psychoanalyses: The Voice of the Other

Orphan Religion

Not a day passes without new research being published on Islamic social and political movements in the fields of political science and sociology. Yet there seems to be a problem of naming this new object: Islamism, fundamentalism, Islamic radicalism, religious extremism, political Islam . . . Does this "proliferation of names" indicate a difficulty of coming to terms with an unprecedented political phenomenon? Fethi Benslama sees in it the continuation of "an old repulsive force in the history of Europe," which reinforces "the resistance to the intelligibility of Islam" despite the Muslim scholars' centuries-old efforts. But this is not all, because in his eyes, "this problem of naming is . . . a *symptom* of the internal upheavals within Islam and the chronic crisis of its relationship to what is referred to as 'the West.'"[1] In his psychoanalytic exploration of Islamic language and subjectivity, *Psychoanalysis and the Challenge of Islam*, Benslama's subject of study is this symptom. The problem of European resistance to the intelligibility of Islam is a methodological error that can and must be removed, that is to say such resistance is not considered to be a symptom. It is the intellectual and epistemological question of a restricted empiricism, and not subject to psychoanalysis. Political sociology takes the "political" at face value and fails to see that it is sustained by subjectivity and language, which requires a "psychoanalytic angle," especially in the case of political mobilization of a religious symbolic structure. Identifying Europe with an epistemological problem (resistance to the intelligibility of Islam) and Islam with a historical symptom (the internal upheavals within Islam and the chronic crisis of its relationship with *what is referred to* as the West), Benslama effectively says that *the European problem of naming can be epistemologically solved by the very act of studying the Islamic problem of naming properly*. The European problem is both acknowledged and obliterated as a problem, while the problem of naming is reconstructed as the proper psychoanalytic (instead of merely sociological) knowledge of Islam's own problem of naming (internal upheaval, chronic crisis).

The name is divided into four categories: Muslim religion and doctrine, Muslims in their diversity, fundamentalist Islam, and Islamic political movements that aim to control the state.[2] Islam is "a multiform reality of a billion people on several continents . . . heterogeneous cultural regions . . . Islams behind Islam" and "has attempted to acclimatize itself, allowing itself to be transformed by them, except for an invariable theological and judicial core."[3] Therefore, diversity and heterogeneity are always accompanied by *an invariable core*. Insofar as the recent political wave is concerned, surely not every country has had the same experience, but "the fact that similar protests broke out across the extent of the Muslim world implies that a single shock wave made its way through a *single substructure*."[4] Benslama makes a clear decision by choosing to focus on the invariable core and the single substructure. But what is "invariable"? And what is a "core"? As the diversity and variations are excluded by this decision, the double bind of essentialism follows him throughout his book and the specter of diversity continues to haunt his analysis of the invariable core or single substructure.[5] I will give a few examples of this diversity, especially with regard to the potential threat that it produces for Benslama's argument. But the problem of essentialism itself should not be underestimated: it is not always sufficient, nor liberatory or democratic in itself, simply and directly to oppose the plurality and diversity of an identity or entity to its sameness. This kind of antiessentialism is a rather easily won victory. Indeed, it is often Benslama himself who performs this kind of liberal antiessentialism by *simply stating it as an obvious fact* (as in his statements quoted above), and this is why the specter of diversity haunts his argument. It is only by developing a notion of sameness that is minimal and open that we can come to terms with complexity.

In this chapter, I will be critical of Benslama's psychoanalytic approach. To briefly frame my reading in advance, I do not mean to say that Benslama's psychoanalytic reading is "wrong" in any straightforward sense. On the contrary, I find psychoanalysis indispensable. But, as I cannot possibly imagine a theoretical discourse on Islam that excludes psychoanalysis, I am equally wary of making psychoanalysis justify a reductionist form of essentialism. Benslama's analysis tends to reduce Islam to fundamentalism, despite his explicitly expressed wish to the contrary. I do not think that it is simply a question of giving a quasi-clinical judgment on Islam, reproducing what is received on the screen in the name of and by means of theory. My effort is to understand and use psychoanalysis in terms of ethics, that is to say, as a means and theory of learning how to read and listen to the otherness of desire, in order to not simply reveal its truth in a sovereign manner, but to keep it open where it is blocked.

A story of modernity

Belonging to the young postcolonial generation of Tunisians, Benslama has a bitter story to tell. Just as he thought they had left Islam behind, it came back with a vengeance. Bourguiba's nationalism tried to break with traditional Islam by *translating* Enlightenment values into its language. After independence, Bourguiba created an internal contradiction within Islam by arguing that *jihad* (external anticolonial struggle) must now be replaced by *ijtihad* (internal struggle of interpretation and knowledge). But "the twofold burden of the rapid expansion of technology and the mechanics of expropriation of global capitalism" rendered it insignificant and thus made it impossible to experience modernity through an accessible language.[6] The scientific prosaism of developmentalist expertise claimed to operate directly on the real and to provide immediate access to a bright future. This liquidation of speech and meaning prepared the ground for the new language of Islamism, which addressed the anxiety of existence and promised to restore what is proper. But there is an important difference: while modernity has managed to create "*the desire to be an other*, sustained by the effectiveness of technology and its discourse,"[7] the impulse that drives Islamist extremism is its inverse: "*the despair that wills to be itself*," in an expression borrowed from Kierkegaard.[8] In a dramatic passage, Benslama summarizes the whole story:

> In fact, while an elite thought it had full access to modernity, that it had traced the outlines of free thought, the minarets were rising and their shadows growing. Modernization was no more than imitation (not mimesis) of the modern through which a trompe l'oeil was constructed.[9]

Compared with his very sophisticated psychoanalytic readings of the Qur'an, the hadith, or the *Thousand and One Nights*, why is Fethi Benslama's account of the emergence and rise of contemporary political Islam so brief? His emphasis on the linguistic and cultural alienation is particularly important, since political Islam emerged as a response to this failure of language and translation. Unfortunately, the implications of this point are not followed by Benslama, as he retreats to the familiar formulation and image of political Islam as "the political desire for origin and the terror that accompanies it."[10] Benslama emphasizes the violence associated with political Islam rather than its language (unlike Abedi and Fischer's or Mahmood's attention to the languages of Muslim women, Shariati or Khomeini). Political Islam expressed itself in quite violent and fundamentalist forms in a number of Muslim countries, from Algeria to Afghanistan, but it is methodologically problematic to reduce its analysis simply to fundamentalist violence, as it is a far more complicated phenomenon by any reasonable estimate. The same applies for the concept of return to the origin or foundation, or the "torment of origin" as Benslama calls it. Actually Benslama makes a very useful and meaningful theoretical distinction between two forms of return, that is, the return as the invention of a relation and the delusional return to the origin.[11] But this calls for specific analyses and discussion of the varied field of the discourse of political Islam. Strange as it may be, Benslama has already decided that contemporary Islam's return is delusional *without* making any analysis or discussion of its varied field. For Benslama, any figure of return turns out to be a symptom of the torment of origin. Hence his argument dangerously *mirrors* the fundamentalist form of return.[12] To give one example, the Turkish Muslim intellectual Ali Bulaç brought up an interesting document he had found in the archives of Islam: the "Charter of Madina," which was drafted by the prophet Muhammad during his exile, was a formal agreement between Muslims, Jews, Christians, and pagans living in Madina. Bulaç presented it as a model of civil society, a paradigm of how Muslims can and should live together with Jewish, Christian, and pagan communities.[13] This engaging historical document was widely discussed by Muslim, liberal, and socialist intellectuals in the Turkish public sphere in the early 1990s. The debate had put its stamp on the development of a significant part of Turkish political Islam in a decidedly nonviolent and civil direction.[14]

Such an example cannot have a place in Benslama's analysis, for he insists that contemporary Islam is incapable of distinguishing between the logic of birth and political logic.[15] As Hegel has shown, this is the achievement of the modern state. In the case of pre-modern subjectivity, the paternal imago provides the ego ideal with a capacity for integration and belonging, and this is why pre-modern subjectivity is not a proper ego.[16] Freedom is introduced by the liberation from the figure of the patriarch as father and leader, which is achieved by separating political logic from the logic of birth. Now a multiplicity of the objects of identification is possible, including, Benslama argues, "leaders who want to be fathers, which is not at all the same thing as fathers who are leaders from the start."[17] Can the distinction between the first (modern) case and the second (traditional) case of fathers-leaders be easily made for Islamism? Should the same multiplicity not be open to Muslim subjects in the modern world? Benslama insists that the logic that produces Islamism or political Islam cannot belong to the modern. This isolation of Islam from modern history and this desire to see it as belonging to a previous stage in humanity is rather suspect. Indeed, when he cannot isolate Islam this way, when he has to show that it actually emerges out of an objective history, Benslama tries his best to give the least harm to modernity:

> . . . the modern state *in the hands of the postcolonial elite* (with the relative exception of someone like Bourguiba) has triggered an uncontrollable process of the hidden destruction of the old order of primary identification, replacing it with constructed simulacra, without managing to realize anything other than a series of disconnections. The immediacy of tradition to itself is broken and uncoupled from its awareness. However, there is no new *Kulturarbeit* available to concentrate for the destroyed modes of transmission, bringing about a destructive interference by repressive substitutes than those of the patriarchate. Islamist ideology is the response, in the form of a blend of illusions, to the subjective revocation that this ceasure has brought about en masse.[18]

Is it really an inept postcolonial elite who brought about the hidden destruction of the old order of primary identification? It seems much more reasonable to say that it is *global capitalism* that led to the destruction of primary identification and a series of disconnections, while the postcolonial elite (who were its allies and guardians) actually and paradoxically tried to maintain an authoritarian political order on the basis of *keeping the primary identification intact*, because their structural alliance and global connection could only have been maintained on the basis of an authoritarian hegemony.[19] Lack of *Kulturarbeit* is the insidious hegemonic cultural work of authoritarianism. Contrary to Benslama's attitude of isolating Islam as a singular case from the whole modern history in which it is so deeply embedded, we must insist that contemporary Islamism is a product of postcolonial global and national orders. Although Benslama uses the concept of the postcolonial, his reading of it is indifferent to the structurally unequal nature of this order. But his two major examples of "modern literature" that "consistently bears witness to this multiple ego,"[20] James Joyce and Salman Rushdie, are both authors who emerge from *postcolonial* contexts and their works bear witness to it rather than some abstract notion of modern liberal ego.

The reason why Benslama does *not* offer a reading of contemporary political Islam or "Islamism" as he calls it (except its notion of science) is indeed part of his analysis of it: because it is a return to the origin, Benslama returns to the reading of the originary texts and narratives rather than studying the discourse and form of this return. Despite his reference to the problem of language, Benslama avoids underlining *the crisis and failure of secular nationalism*—as the above innuendo of "the modern state in the hands of the postcolonial elite" makes clear. Bourguiba's strategy of translation seems to be a failed ideal, but we do not know how it actually failed, what the "hands" kept really. Supposing that this was indeed a certain kind of solution, Benslama does not explain how the developmentalist discourse of the positivist experts replaced the strategy of cultural translation that was supposed to help the masses make sense of their experience. Benslama calls developmentalism and capitalism a "burden." Are developmentalism and global capitalism merely pragmatic requirements without social and political consequences? Given the immense socioeconomic division that global capitalism has created, hand in hand with authoritarian nationalist elites in the Muslim periphery, should one not ask whose *perverse* command is embodied by the "rising minarets"?[21] What if "Islamism" is a Western command? (And we do *not need* to mention the support given to Islamic movements by the West during the Cold War) Is turning the West into a natural, untouchable ideal not another way of maintaining primary identification in politics?[22]

If there must be a failure somewhere, something that does not quite work in secularist nationalism, does this not mean that "cultural translation" has its limits too? *And should we not discuss this failure to derive lessons from it?* Benslama's "modernity" does not know finitude; it is transcendent, free, and victorious—even though it seems to have lost ground to political Islam in the Muslim periphery (though it remains debatable if capitalism has lost ground). As we have read above, his framework is based on a distinction between a true modernity (which can be achieved by mimesis) and a false modernization (which is mere imitation and trompe l'oeil). As everyone familiar with this field should know well, "positivism" (developmentalism of the experts) and "imitation" are *the two main charges* that Islamicist criticism has typically directed against elitist-authoritarian nationalism in the Muslim periphery. Benslama repeats almost word for word the same criticism that political Islam has been making for four decades now.

It is not that this criticism is wrong or has no relevance. There might well be a sense of truth in the discourse of political Islam or Islamism (it can perhaps be said that the criticism of imitation or copying is often quickly made and superficial, though it is effective; as for developmentalism and capitalism, this is the test for the emerging political Islam, to put it mildly). It is because Benslama sets up an abstract and categorical opposition between modernity and Islam that he fails to read various aspects of the emergence of the latter as a political movement in the late twentieth century. A good example of this is his previous statement that modernity creates a desire to be an other, while Islamism forwards the inverse affect: the despair that wills to be itself. We have on the one side, desire and change, that is, freedom; and on the other side, anxiety and obsession with self-identity under the appearance of rebellion. It is difficult to understand, especially when it is stated by a *psychoanalyst*, how the "desire to be an other" is a modern invention, as if, for instance, Islam (or any pre-modern ideology, religion, culture . . .) has been one huge monolithic doctrine without divisions, differences, interpretations, and internal conflicts from the seventh to the twenty-first century. Is desire ' not always and *universally* a desire to be an other, and are difference and otherness not the very dynamic of desire, according to psychoanalysis? What distinguishes modernity is something else: it is what Deleuze and Guattari have described as a generalized decoding and deterritorialization of desire. They emphasize that deterritorialization is often immediately reterritorialization.[23] Islam itself is part of this global logic and movement of capitalist modernity: decoded and deterritorialized by the abstract general movement of capital, it is reterritorialized under the new miraculation of its identity, due to its global position in the world order of things. As a social and political movement, it has to do with the failure of decolonization and the double crises of nationalism and socialism. This is why one has to distinguish the traditional from the new Islam, not in order to save the former but to recognize the *newness* of the latter. The formulation Benslama borrows from Kierkegaard, "the despair that wills to be itself," appears to be fitting the identity politics of Islam, especially in its fundamentalist version, but in insisting that it is pure despair and opposed to modernity understood as change, we may be distorting a significant part of the reality of contemporary Islam.[24] For instance, the new political Islam has articulated science as an essential part of its discourse; indeed it would not be wrong to say that it repeats the nationalist formula in a different way as the synthesis of universal science with the religion and culture of Islam.[25] This was possible because neither science nor rationalism have ever been entirely alien to Islam in its doctrine or in its history. This is why the argument for science might actually be affirmative, going beyond a mere episode of justification of religious faith. Benslama's oppositional approach would have to focus on the concepts of cleanliness and prohibitions. A major example he gives is a text by a Muslim woman in which she constructs the common body as infected, sick, having lost its immunity and its dignity. The manifestation of this, a tumor in the subject's own body, is removed by God. She did not cover her head with a veil, now is it covered with a bandage. With the guilt and sacrificial debt involved, we have the reign of the anguished "obscure God," whose order is revenge.[26] This is indeed a common metaphor in many religious communities, and under the new modern conditions, it should be seen as the fascistic tendency in an emerging field of Islamic biopolitics. The other example Benslama gives is a young Muslim man who justifies the Islamic prohibition on eating pork in reference to the medical discovery of parasites in the pig's muscle tissue: "hygiene is used to justify the rites of ablution."[27] But why is ablution only a rite, a prohibiton merely a prohibition? If we approach ablution or diet (fasting too) in terms of Michel Foucault's concept of "self-care," following his suggestion that such a practice is not specific to the Ancient Greek culture,[28] then an entirely new area of struggle, transformation, and research is opened up. Indeed, we can and must speak of a varied field of *Islamic biopolitics*, from the Lebanese Hezbollah to the Turkish moderate Islamic government. Articulating biopower with everyday practices: this is an emerging new and complex political field.[29] We should be wary of a kind of analysis that forecloses the multiplicity of paths of development open to contemporary political Islam or Islamism—whether such developments are positive or negative, whether they concern hegemony or resistance, they are precisely what is new in it, what is already under transformation. Since Benslama tends to reduce the whole field to a fascistic and totalitarian tendency, he cannot really elaborate his claim that the Islamist "use" of science is an example of "autoimmunization" in Derrida's sense[30] and admits this in a footnote.[31] Since he has decided that contemporary political Islam or Islamism can and should be taken in isolation, as a symptom of Islam itself, there is no possibility for him to see this contemporary phenomenon itself as the Western Subject's autoimmunization—and why not?[32] But more importantly, the logic of autoimmunization is not only suicidal. If one were to understand this concept deconstructively, one should see that it also has a positive aspect in keeping the community *open* to otherness.[33]

Literature as the truth of religion: *The Satanic Verses*

Cultural translation is a strategy of negotiating discrepant cultural practices and discourses. Is there another implicit ideal of modernity in Benslama's text, apart from the strategy of cultural translation? As the above passage implies, this other strategy must be a form of mimesis that is *not* imitation and trompe l'oeil.[34] Rather than an external effort of staging modernity, this form of discourse must have an internal relationship with the religious; its articulation and repetition of the religious must be potentially disruptive and capable of transforming it from within. For Benslama, this discourse turns out to be literature. Like Abedi and Fischer, Benslama too reads Salman Rushdie's *The Satanic Verses* as a paradigm of literary rewriting of a religious narrative. Benslama finds in the Qur'an a conflict between the truthful discourse of God and a poetic or false discourse, fiction, or fable. For him, the extreme manifestation of this conflict is the well-known case of the Satanic verses. A small verse in which Satan assumes the identity of the Archangel Gabriel and praises the pre-Islamic female goddesses was temporarily included in the Qur'an and was later removed by the prophet. Satan used a particular moment whereby the prophet of Islam was in search of a political negotiation with some of his polytheistic adversaries. He realized Satan's game upon Gabriel's reprimand and removed the verses.[35]

In order to go on with Benslama's reading of *The Satanic Verses*, I need to briefly mention his concept of the torment of origin in Islam. Reading a dream of Muhammad, Benslama argues that, although Islam depends upon an originary openness, "an initial withdrawal, which established a void in the heart of the child Muhammad,"[36] and therefore although "openness" is the originary signifier of Islam and its spirituality, the "institutionalized theology and, even more so, extremism are based on forgetting the truth of this experience and on the reversal of its meaning as victory" (the word *fath* is both openness and conquest).[37] Hence the first word the prophet heard from Gabriel, *iqra*, that is, "read" or "recite," means to read from the hyper-originary text of the Other, the mother of the book in the seventh heaven. This means that, instead of offering redemption from an original sin, Islam's first act is to open an internal difference through a separation in the flesh. Since the intruder is thus language, there is nothing like a proper "subject" form in Islam: "man is never entirely man" but "intimately foreign to his species."[38] (In the next chapter, I will present Abdelkebir Khatibi's different approach.) However, Benslama also draws our attention to a *beginning* in the Biblical story of Hagar, the maid in exile: his son, Ishmael is the *father* of the Arab nation. Benslama derives from this the conclusion that "the concept of origin in Islam is split between a cut and a beginning" and argues that "the cut precedes the beginning; it is always an opening and a trace in the memory of the Other and can therefore wait a considerable time for reading to begin."[39] The cut is both before and beyond the beginning; no beginning can heal it and therefore can never begin properly.[40]

Hence the strategic position of the question of origin in Islam according to Benslama. Since this question of origin also involves the opposition between the truthful discourse of origin and the fictive discourse of literature, Rushdie's return to the origin destroyed its theological truth by playfully demonstrating that the truth might have been only a lie in disguise and everything a fiction. When Benslama refers to Rushdie's self-defense in terms of a *right to literature*, it is impossible, indeed criminal, to disagree with him. Rushdie's novel is a reappropriation of the origin, a "snatching" of it from the guardians of tradition. Rushdie's self-reflexive Oedipalism (Benslama calls him "Oedipus the writer," "Oedipus the autobiographer") determines the subject as the origin of the truth of origin.[41] Right to literature thus becomes, for Benslama, the truth of the (modern) subject. Literature, and the subject in his right to literature, reveal the truth of the origin as fiction. In this way, Muslim man overcomes his pre-subject status (his intimate foreignness and his consequential failure of humanism) and becomes *a full or proper man*. Similarly, Rushdie's principal character, Saladin Chamcha, finds himself in reconciliation with his *father* at the end of the novel.[42] Saladin finds his *name* pleasing for the first time at the deathbed of his father whom he begins to like now as the old man is dying. "The voice is revealed" Benslama stresses, "so that the subject welcomes *the return of the letter in his name*."[43] This also provides a symbolic connection between his dead father and the founding father of Islam ("An orphaned life like Muhammad's, like everyone's," says Chamcha). As a result of this "fictionalization of religious truth," the son finds his place in the symbolic: "by passing through the letter and the body of the father, it exposes the subject's consciousness to the name of the father as a determiner of his existence."[44]

Is the cut healed by this reconciliation, and the beginning successfully established? The reconstruction of the truth of religion as fiction would at the same time mean for Benslama *a reconciliation with the father of religion*, with finding or refinding him as father. His rhetorical question confirms this: "isn't it strange that a novel that was denounced as blasphemous and considered to have harmed the figure of the prophet should end up identifying with the founder of religion and the assumption of his name?"[45] Literature is the only discourse that is capable of restoring religion to its true essence, to *the truth of its origin as fiction*. It is, for the subject, the only possible way of enacting what he *owes* to the symbolic: "what we consider literature makes use of diversion to enact, outside religious truth, what the existence of the subject owes to *the naming that established him in language*."[46] The original sin or error of Islam is redeemed or corrected by the modern (literary) son and is hence brought back into its proper place in the symbolic.

The fictionalization of religious truth determines the truth of religion as fiction and thus restores it to its proper place in the symbolic. It determines the subject of this fictionalization as the origin of the truth of origin as fiction (or rather fiction is this subject's self-determination, and his determination as self-fiction, Oedipus the auto-bio-grapher, self-life-writer); and finally, the subject and his act of fictionalization, or the subject through his act of fictionalization, recognizes himself in the name-of-the-father, which means not only that the proper genealogy is established but also that the religion in question is properly established in the symbolic as its permitted perversion (the son sanctioned by the father, who thus becomes, in sanctioning the son, a proper father). Further, Benslama wants us to realize that "it is through the literary subject and not the subject of science that this subversion is bursting into public view."[47] While "we had in mind the model of Enlightenment and the great historical demystifications . . . the shock, in the case of Islam, came from where it was least expected: literary fiction that presented the truth of fiction as an artifice."[48] And while the institution of Islam attempted to seal the crack, Rushdie's novel is the return of the repressed. We need to understand that "the action of the literature he is a part of surpasses his individual case. It is part of the *historical process of modernity.* . . ."[49]

Benslama suggests that we think this modernity in the sense of Lacoue-Labarthe's reading of the subject of philosophy through Nietzsche.[50] I would like to argue that Lacoue-Labarthe's reading of Nietzsche is different than Benslama's use of Lacoue-Labarthe. In *The Subject of Philosophy*, Philippe Lacoue-Labarthe's project is "an inquiry into the 'form' of philosophy, to cast upon it a suspicion: what if, after all, philosophy is nothing but literature?"[51] To this purpose, he goes back to Nietzsche's well-known comment on Parmenides' statement that "one cannot think of what is not." For Nietzsche, we are at the other end: "what can be thought of must certainly be a fiction."[52] Quoting Lacoue-Labarthe, Benslama considers this reference to fiction to be our "modern condition": the belief that being can be thought only because it is a fiction and literature is the experiment responsible for this claim.[53] Hence the Rushdie affair refers to a *historical mutation* for Benslama. But, he immediately reminds us, it is not sufficient to say that religion is fiction; because, as Lacoue-Labarthe shows, fiction cannot be taken apart from its reference to the truth: speaking of religious texts, Benslama asks "if Salman Rushdie did not believe in their truth, why did he want to eliminate that truth, turn it into its opposite, and propose its distribution? Aren't the reversal of a truth and the subjective sharing of its text still this truth, if not its fulfillment?"[54]

It is impossible to disagree with this point, on the condition that its opposite (Rushdie's disbelief in the truth of religious text) should also be true. The reason is both Rushdie and Benslama actually follow a figure of reversal, which inevitably remains limited. If, as Benslama argues, Rushdie had to believe in the truth of the religious text *in order to eliminate it,* to show that it is fiction, this means that he *also* had to believe in the *factual* truth outside of and contrary to the *religious* textual truth (namely, it was not the word of God, but of the prophet). In order to show that religion depends on fiction, *not fact,* Rushdie's fictional writing must have involved a comparison of the textual (religious) with the factual truth and a moment of belief in the factual truth (hence the unintended ambiguity of Benslama's expression "the truth of religion"). When we say "fact" and "fiction" here, we are entirely within the terms set (or accepted) by the author himself. We may consider, for instance, the passage in which Gibreel explains how the words are forcibly taken from him by Mahound: "then he did his old trick, forcing my mouth open and making the voice, the Voice, pour out of me once again, made it pour all over him, like sick."[55] That is to say, the prophet did not recite the original word of God, but he was the origin himself. No doubt, this is fiction, and indeed Gibreel's dream in the fiction. But Rushdie also felt the necessity of warning his reader about the nature of his text already in the text itself, in the following conversation (about the theological movie that uses Gibreel Farishta's dreams):

> "It is a film," the producer, Sisodia, informed *Ciné Blitz* "about how newness enters the world."—But would it not be seen as blasphemous, a crime against . . . "Certainly not," Billy Battuta insisted. "Fiction is fiction; facts are facts. . . ."[56]

Rushdie's purpose was to subject all faith to doubt. It was surely not to overthrow the religious point of view but to show that it is of the same nature as fiction, and therefore it should be subject to the same freedom of reading and interpretation. As the above passage shows, he already predicted the possibility of the accusation of blasphemy. But this is also to admit the possibility of the subtle working of the oldest metaphysical belief, which comes before the difference between fact and fiction: *the world is what is said about it.* No sacred text can work without this belief, which comes before its explicitly stated belief. Fact and fiction meet at the spontaneous operation of metaphysics in (and as) language. The moment I have said "fiction," I have also said "fact," especially in the case of fictionalizing a religious text. No doubt this does not invalidate the demand for toleration, and for a certain minimal acceptance of the fictionality of the fiction. But every such demand also maintains the duality of fact and fiction. Benslama treats Rushdie's text *as if* it does not involve this moment of comparison of the religious with the factual and the belief in the latter; but he must have already acknowledged this moment of comparison, which is akin to an effect of *demystification* in Rushdie's text. Benslama's reading has to assume this factual moment while it cannot openly admit it. This double bind is originated in a *simple reversal* of the hierarchical relationship between truth and fiction by substituting truth with fiction and registering this reversal-substitution as the definition of modernity as a privileged historical period.

There is, indeed, a striking difference between Lacoue-Labarthe's careful reading of Nietzsche and Benslama's *use* of this reading. While Benslama insists on the historical mutation and the specific nature of modernity, Lacoue-Labarthe's reading of Nietzsche unfalteringly moves away from history. For Lacoue-Labarthe, if we read Nietzsche simply historically (though there is enough in his texts that will push us in this direction), we cannot see that he wants to speak a language that is *not* dialectical. When Benslama says that the truth of religion is fiction, but this means that we also believe in the truth of religion, he is still within a dialectical language because fiction remains a *concept* of truth. Indeed, Benslama's quote is highly selective and makes Lacoue-Labarthe an accomplice of his historicist universalism. For Lacoue-Labarthe, it is necessary "that the 'concept' of *fiction* escape conceptuality itself, that is, not be included in the discourse of truth."[57] Unless we make a move to break with the opposition between truth and fiction, or appearance and reality, we remain limited to a *reversal* of Platonism, hence within metaphysics. "To think fiction," writes Lacoue-Labarthe, "is precisely to think without recourse to this opposition, outside this opposition; to think the world as a fable."[58] Benslama has not destroyed the apparent world with the true world; *he made this opposition survive under the concept of fiction.*

Making a rigorous reading of Nietzsche's well-known statement "with the true world, we have also abolished the apparent world,"[59] Lacoue-Labarthe opens his argument by *asking* if it is possible to think outside the opposition.[60] It is such thinking that cannot be historical in any simple sense, as if one simply can step into it in modernity. While Nietzsche's decisive move is "to abolish appearance, that is to let appearance abolish itself, and to risk this vertigo, to thus renounce presence and refuse to repatriate it as an appearance promoted to the level of appearing or epiphany,"[61] Benslama precisely *repatriates* presence as an appearance promoted to the level of appearing: he first determines truth (of religion) *as* (literary) fiction and then makes (literary) fiction dependent on the truth (of religion). Benslama thus safely steps into the secular space by substituting the truth of religion with fiction (a secularism by substitution). But in abolishing the true world with the apparent one, Nietzsche's move is a strange "leap," which "is as though one were 'penetrating' into an unlimited space that is the same as the space one has (not) just left, but in which the ground gives way. . . ."[62] Lacoue-Labarthe insists that the leap is *not spectacular at all*, but, on the contrary, "the ground is ultimately (more or less) the same. There is only a brief and, so to speak, *unapparent difference*."[63] What is the unapparent difference of Nietzsche's leap? To follow Lacoue-Labarthe's argument, while Benslama argues that the world is what is said about it (appearance or fiction), he has forgotten that this is what metaphysics has already said. Hence he has forgotten *"to undo the tailoring of the saying to the truth."* Once this is undone, however, there is nothing left but pure saying, and nothing can ever begin.[64] This is an experience of "dispossession."[65] In *substituting* the truth with fiction, Benslama produces a fictional access to the truth of religion, and leaves the hierarchical difference of truth and fiction untouched. Forgetting that Lacoue-Labarthe poses a problem rather than offering an answer, he makes a fast move from the restricted to the generalized sense of writing: otherness (desire to be other) is *given* in the modern act of fiction.[66]

Nevertheless, this substitution teaches us something valuable: does the episode of *The Satanic Verses* not too easily lend itself to the metaphysical economy of appearance versus reality, falsity versus factual truth? Surely we must also ask: is there any occasion that would not lend itself to the metaphysical economy? Without forgetting this question, I have to remind once more that, when Benslama writes that the shock came from literature rather than demystification in the Enlightenment style, he had already approached the literary fiction in terms of a presentation of the *truth* of religion.

One may nevertheless object to my criticism by reminding me how Lacoue-Labarthe ends his essay:

> We could, in the end, reformulate the question in this way: Are we capable of no longer believing what is *in* books or of not being "disappointed" by their "lie"? Or, as Nietzsche would have said, can we cease to be "pious"? Are we capable of atheism?[67]

Is this not what Benslama meant indeed (even though he reconstituted, at the same time, the truth of religion as the son's fiction sanctioned by the name-of-the-father)? We must note however that, first of all, Lacoue-Labarthe does not mean the religious but the philosophical text here, even though he uses religious terms such as piety or atheism. Secondly, the "books" in the above quote would involve *The Satanic Verses* as well, to the extent that it articulates the *truth* of religion in and as fiction. Thirdly, and most importantly, Lacoue-Labarthe does not answer his questions; he is only posing them, inviting us to see a *problem* where Benslama sees the *truth* of metaphysics as literature. This questioning mode is the very mode of the leap (not of "the fall," which is Benslama's preferred quasi-Heidegerrian mode[68]), or an experience of "dispossession,"[69] and *not* having the proper name sanctioned by the symbolic.[70] As I will try to show in the next chapter, contrary to the anxiety of occupying the (correct) place in the symbolic, the experience of dispossession marks a different opening of the religious text to the generalized writing.

So far I have focused on Benslama's reading of *The Satanic Verses*, and not the novel itself. Indeed, Rushdie's novel cannot be reduced to a moment of demystification, a reversal of truth with fiction, or of fiction with truth. Since Benslama opens his argument in terms of the problematic relationship between Islam and modernity, it should be emphasized that *The Satanic Verses* is too specific to be *the* model of the literary act of fictionalizing the religious truth. Benslama does not seem to pay attention to the fact that Salman Rushdie's novel belongs to a highly specific instance of the postcolonial context. Although Rushdie himself is keen on narrating and representing Indian society and history, *The Satanic Verses* is about the metropolitan British context in its setting and characters. Fethi Benslama's reading is indifferent to the intricate production of the metropolitan *postcolonial* subject in Rushdie's novel. In contrast to this, and only briefly mentioning Saladin's reconciliation with his father, Gayatri Spivak reads *The Satanic Verses* as "a portrait of the author as schizo under the desiring/social production of migrancy and postcoloniality, a displacement of the Oedipal project of imperialism as bringing into Law of the 'favorite son.'"[71]

Spivak's emphasis on "the peculiar authority of the many times repeated 'Gibreel dreamed' . . . and then a noun of event and space . . . the relationship between this and the chain of 'and then . . .' 'and then' that Deleuze and Guattari assure us is the mode of narrativization of the schizo"[72] as well as "the confident breaching of the boundaries between dream and waking in the *text*"[73] is respectful to the text(ure) of the novel, and to the singular historical subjectivity it superbly gives voice to. This is a reading that saves *The Satanic Verses* as a singular literary and historical object from being an occasion for fundamentalist mobilization or liberal commonplace.[74]

The gift of the other: Abraham, Sarah, Hagar

I have criticized Benslama's failure to engage a critical analysis of nationalist secularism, his highly problematic concepts of modernity and fiction, and last but not least, the strong essentialist tendency of his overall framework, which reduces contemporary political Islam into a merely subjective obsession with the origin that he finds in its originary or founding text, in complete isolation from its recent historical context. None of these criticisms should be an excuse for failing to attend to his unique and stimulating reading of the narrative of Abraham, Sarah, and Hagar. The critical response given so far to his book emphasized one of these aspects to the exclusion of the other. The book is either heavily (and quite rightly) criticized for its essentialist tendency, or praised for his original psychoanalytic readings of Genesis, Islam, and monotheism. It seems as if it is hard for readers to reconcile these two aspects of the book. However, this is not a contradiction at all. Benslama's intriguing psychoanalytic reading cannot be overlooked, especially his singular way of putting together the concepts of the gift, the father, and sexual difference, the way in which Hagar appears as the other woman necessary to the patriarchal economy of monotheism. But then one wonders if this reading, despite its revelatory (and to a limited extent "deconstructive," from a feminist point of view) value, or precisely through it, does not reproduce the metaphysical economy of phallogocentrism. Everything seems to depend on how we read *a certain withdrawal* in Benslama's analysis: his reading of withdrawal as well as the withdrawal or forgetting of a certain concept, that is, the withdrawal or forgetting of the concept of *forgetting* itself.

Benslama's psychoanalytic reading is not limited to Islam. As Islam returns to the Abrahamic narrative, he has to cover the whole field of monotheism.

He begins by reminding us of Freud's judgment in *Moses and Monotheism* that Islam is an "abbreviated repetition" of Judaism, which lacked the depth that came with the murder of the founder in Judaism. Benslama is interested in Freud's emphasis on *the recapture of the primal father by Islam*. He sees in this not a mere imitation but a reappropriation of origin, namely Abrahamic faith in the origin, which was deformed by Judaism and Christianity according to Islam. Benslama argues that "originary reappropriation is a very old story in monotheism."[75] This is the patriarchal drama between Abraham, Sarah, and Hagar in Genesis, which he analyzes separately.

If the primal father is the mythic figure of unlimited *jouissance* (excessive enjoyment), as we know from psychoanalysis, it should be difficult to reconcile this figure with the God of monotheism. This is also revealed as the tension between the primal father and Abraham as the Father-of-Genesis, who should actually detach himself from the primal father but who is haunted by its specter. What makes things even more complicated for Islam is that "contrary to Judaism and Christianity, Islam, from its origin, excluded God from the logic of paternity."[76] Hence the problem: how can we conceptualize the question of the father in a religion in which God is not the father? From the very start, the problem is defined as a problem of paternity for Benslama. Or the problem of origin is defined as a problem of paternity, that is, the problem of its mastery and ordering. Benslama's argument will oscillate between the problem of origin or its foreignness *and* its mastery.

Abraham's son Ishmael is also designated as the father of the Arab nation. This is the way Islam can be genealogically tied to the Abrahamic religion. We are reminded of the well-known story in Genesis. Since his wife Sarah could not give a child to Abraham, she offers her servant Hagar to him. Hagar gives birth to Ishmael, and later Sarah also gives birth to a child, Isaac. Since she wants the family heritage to go to her son, Sarah instigates that Abraham send Hagar and Ishmael into exile in the desert. As Hagar is desperately looking for water for her son, God reveals a spring that saves them both and gives the promise to make Ishmael's children a great nation. The abandoned son is turned into the Father of a future nation. Reading the meaning of Ishmael's name (Isma'El: "God hears/understands"), Benslama argues that "the revelatory hearing of the voice . . . existed at the origin of Islam, an origin emerging from the origin of the other or its writing" and that "the status of alterity in Islam is marked by the voice, by a 'letter-voice.'"[77] This relationship, Benslama insists, is not imitation (as Freud says) but translation. Muhammad's declaration that "Ishmael is Arab" is a speech act, an appropriating translation, that turns him into an Arab.

According to Benslama, the prophet was aware of this power, but the institution of monotheism erases the translation, the foreignness in the origin, by making the Father-of-Genesis (Abraham), the son-father (Ishmael) and the translator-reader-father (Muhammad) reciprocally inclusive, and by thus establishing the monolingual reign of a pure filiation. It is Hagar, "the other woman," whose presence disturbs this story of origin.

Benslama's reading of the narrative of Abraham, Sarah, and Hagar is a veritable application of Lacanian psychoanalysis. This reading depends on the concept of the object of desire, and the generation and circulation of this object. Benslama makes a little change in the writing of this object of desire by reinscribing it as "gift" throughout his text. We realize the significance of this when, in the middle of his text, he makes a connection with what Derrida calls "gift" in his well-known work, *Given Time*. But I should first of all briefly reconstruct Benslama's analysis. The story I have summarized above told us that the future of the origin is accomplished in the borrowed womb of the bondswoman Hagar: she provides "the gift that will restore the patriarch, without which there would be no father, no origin, no memory."[78] When Hagar gives birth to Ishmael, Sarah despises her, realizing that she has elevated a servant to the position of the Other woman who gives the gift of origin to the father. (The initial lack of origin is thus transformed into the question of female *jouissance* in its relation to the establishment of the father.) When Hagar wants to leave following Sarah's harsh treatment, she is warned by the angels to return to her mistress, but she is also given the promise that she will be the origin of numberless descendants. This is how Isma'El gets his name ("God hears" [your suffering]) as the God's seal of his promise. In turn, Benslama carefully emphasizes, Hagar gives a counter-gift by performing a singular act that distinguishes her from all the other women in the Bible: she gives a name to God, "god of vision."[79] Benslama describes this act as "the possibility of writing the origin from below."[80] It is only after Hagar's giving birth to Ishmael that Sarah gives birth to Isaac. As soon as they have their child, their names change: Sarai (*my* princess) becomes Sarah (princess), and Abram becomes Abraham. Benslama reads this loss of the possessive in Sarah's name as an operation of symbolic castration. But the dispossession is also the gift of "procreative universalization" providing her with "the fertility that will engender kings."[81] Hagar has no access to this kind of symbolic universalization and the resulting "phallic *jouissance*"—a kind of *jouissance* that depends on the operation of the signifier's replacing an absence. Hagar remains outside the covenant; her name is not sanctioned by renaming in the symbolic (hence the significance of Shariati's renaming of Hateem as the wall of Hagar, as we have seen in the second chapter). To put it in Benslama's Hegelian manner, Sarah is the spiritual principle or modality of the maternal, whereas Hagar is the flesh or body.

In giving a child to a very old man and woman, God made the impossible possible. Benslama emphasizes the implication of God himself in the conception of Isaac. It is this passage "from an other to the Other" which produces a serious problem for Islam. In Judaism and Christianity, God is the real father, assuming the creative omnipotence of the primal father, and Abraham is a father by proxy, a symbolic father. In other words, in these two religions, "the son's conception is divine, or at least mixed, involving God in paternity, which assumes for Sarah, as much as it does for Mary, a *jouissance* of the son that restricts them to the phallic absolute."[82] As for Islam, his filiation through Hagar is *merely real*, hence "if we stick to the Biblical text, the symbolic father for Judaism and Christianity is the real father for Islam."[83] Benslama insists that Islam never speaks of God-the-father: "the god who hears Ishmael has nothing to do with the human sexuality of his parents, does not intervene in the signifying mechanism of phallic *jouissance*. The God of Islam is not an originary father, he is the impossible: transpaternal."[84]

Benslama's thesis of discontinuity between God and the universe he creates must surely be taken seriously, as it is really a unique aspect of Islam. In reference to the well known Sura 112,[85] Benslama writes that Islam's God is "in the background of relation and non-relation; he is the incommensurable withdrawal of the non-place, through which the place of the father finds its opening. In other words, God is the originary withdrawal of the father."[86] A question is inevitable here: how is Islam's God *both* "transpaternal," "not an originary father" and "the originary withdrawal of the father" at the same time? For the withdrawal requires the presence of the father in the first place. The originary withdrawal cannot be simply originary and cannot be simply withdrawal; it must be the withdrawal of *something* already there *before* the originary, a "father" in our case, so that "the originary withdrawal of the father" (the lack of son) actually means "*there is father*"—"forthcoming," Benslama says, that is, its place is there in the symbolic. Indeed the "there is father" (or "there shall be father") seems to be the organizing statement of Benslama's analysis. But is the originary withdrawal of the father (or the lack of son) not the originary situation of monotheism, what Benslama formulates philosophically as "there is a there-is-not"?[87] If the originary withdrawal of the father is a necessary moment of the unfolding of monotheism, then it is shared by Islam as well. Otherwise, how would it be possible, as Benslama himself says above, "for the place of the father" to find "its opening" "through the incommensurable withdrawal of the non-place" in Islam?

When Benslama writes that Islam's God is the impossible, what does he mean? And what does he mean by the concept of the impossible in general? He writes for instance that "to the impossibility of the gift between Abraham and Sarah, the originary god of monotheism responds with an impossible gift."[88] He then makes an enigmatic reference to Derrida's deconstruction of the gift: "The gift is the impossible."[89] According to Benslama, Derrida's statement is "written in the direction of the fundamental utterance" of the extreme biblical solution, which makes the impossible possible.[90] "This approach exposes the originary challenge of the father," he writes, "as the writing of the impossibility of the possible."[91] But Derrida's approach is quite different than Benslama's. While Benslama talks of a structure and an economy, Derrida is interested in the experience or event of the gift. When Benslama conceptualizes the economy of giving and receiving in the biblical narrative, he uses the notion of the gift as that which is *in* circulation, that is, the absent object of desire as the signifier, or the impossible Real. God is part of this economy as the "Donor" (as he calls him), the Other who makes the impossible possible (but the *place* of the possible is already given in the structure). According to Derrida, however, as we have already seen in the discussion of Bourdieu, the gift is impossible in the sense that the moment it is given it is no longer gift and becomes exchange:

> If there is gift, the *given* of the gift (*that which* one gives, *that which* is given, the gift as given thing or as act of donation) must not come back to the giving . . . It must not circulate, it must not be exchanged . . . If the figure of the circle is essential to economics, the gift must remain *aneconomic*.[92]

This is *not* what happens with "the originary withdrawal of the father," for, as I have shown above, if there is *withdrawal*, then the object is *there* and has a *place* in the circulation, which means that there is already an economy. This economy is governed by the father, by the circulation of his signifier. Islam's God is "the impossible" for Benslama, because this God refuses to create the miracle (i.e. to participate in the circulation and/or the circle by getting involved in procreation). Surely Islam's abstract God has created the universe like a God should, but in this process of creation Islam takes sexual difference for granted; it unsays the enigma of sexual difference rather than the father. More crucially, we could consider Benslama's approach as a certain criticism of Derrida, one that Derrida expects and responds to in his *Given*

Time: there is the excess or dissymmetry of the absolute gift, but (as Benslama also demonstrates) the circle of debt, of exchange, or of symbolic equilibrium reconstitutes itself according to the laws of the unconscious.[93] As we have already discussed in the third chapter, Derrida's response to such criticism is that the paradox of the gift also involves "the keeping in the unconscious" and "the putting into reserve as an effect of repression," so that, for there to be gift, the forgetting "must be so radical that *it exceeds even the psychoanalytic categoriality of forgetting.*"[94] Derrida's concept of absolute forgetting does not link forgetting to the logic of the signifier or to the symbolic order of exchange, debt, and obligation. Nevertheless, Derrida insists, what is at stake is *a certain experience of the trace*, and not nothing.[95] In an intense argument, he shows that the gift and forgetting are actually conditions of each other.[96] As Derrida's analysis takes us, once more, to what comes *before* the subject or his/her determinations, I would like to argue that, from this point of view, absolute forgetting is related to the absolute past, which I have already emphasized. Remembering the connections I made between absolute past, absolute memory, language, and body in Chapter 3, as well as the association established between body and woman in the binary law of given culture, we may try a different reading of Hagar than the one offered by Benslama.

When Benslama refers to the difficulty of taking Hagar's point of view, this is not a theoretical difficulty for him, for his analysis has also repeated all the moves implicit in the unfolding of this patriarchal structure. Hagar is the body, Sarah is the mind, Abraham has a son . . . It is true that he referred to Hagar's point of view "from below," a point of view that is "repressed" in the narrative. But this point of view is from below in a particular sense: the repressed position it articulates presupposes a binary concept of woman according to which the female subject is divided between body and mind. As Benslama's demonstration has implied (though in Hegelian and Lacanian terms), the binarism of mind and body (which is always associated with the binarism of man and woman) is reproduced within the feminine as Sarah and Hagar. Sarah represents the woman of the Other, with her access to the phallic *jouissance* and her place in the Symbolic, while Hagar represents the radical alterity of the flesh, the ineffable female *jouissance* beyond phallus (which Lacan articulated in his *Encore*). The opposition might have significance in referring to the threat femininity poses for the patriarchal order. But it is also one that is already marked and inscribed by this order, even though such inscription refers to something ineffable. Its text must be read carefully, in order to make Hagar begin to speak, and to hear her. It is not for nothing that Benslama's reference to the possibility of a writing from below appears at the moment when he reads Hagar's unique speech act: in the biblical text, Benslama tells us, she is the only woman who "gives a name to god—Lord (El)."[97] This should mean that the possibility of her power of symbolization is already inscribed in the text. Benslama interprets this as "Hagar's countergift to the gift of the name Ishmael,"[98] a name for a name, that is, as part of the circle, of the economy. But if this naming is a singular act that distinguishes her from all of the other women, it would not simply be just another exchange in the biblical economy. It is the moment of the opening of the textual economy to its outside; it is a threshold of the biblical text, where a woman is involved in the act of giving a name. In a Lacanian problematic, this can be read only as a moment in the circle of exchange of the absent object of desire. For, by splitting the woman into two while keeping it as one (by expelling or repressing one of the two), the biblical text assured that (sexual) (binary) *opposition* begins from itself, that is (sexual) *difference* is necessarily hierarchical and the *lack* is localized and constitutive. Benslama's analysis is closer to a reversal here, a legitimation in reverse. If we approach the body as absolute past, however, difference is never reducible to opposition, even though it is never without it either, at least in a certain sense. We should go even further by borrowing the following formulation from Derrida's deconstruction of Heidegger's neutralization of sexual difference:

> one must think of a pre-differential, or rather pre-dual, sexuality—which doesn't necessarily mean unitary, homogenous or undifferentiated . . . Then, from that sexuality, *more originary than the dyad*, one may try to think to the bottom a "positivity" and a "power" . . . Here indeed it is a matter of the positive and powerful source of every possible sexuality.[99]

Given Hagar's exclusion (she is no more than a moment—material, bodily—that is sublated), her act of giving a name is *not simply a countergift*. How can one produce a writing from below if one sees her act simply as countergift, as another moment in the circle? Hagar would not have been able to *give a name to Him*, if the father were capable of governing the whole structure—if, in other words, the sexual difference were entirely governed by *his signifier*, which depends on the *localization* of lack. In such a case, she would have only been thankful to Him, who gives the promise of justice and seals it in the name of her son, that is, she would have only reproduced the circle by this countergift of gratitude. Interestingly, Hagar's speech act is a response to a promise of *justice*, not in the form of *recognition* of the already existing law of the father, but in the form of *giving it a name*, marking its singularity: a justice not guaranteed in the law, but a justice to come. This power or ability of giving a name is *the emergence of her difference*, irreducible to opposition or lack, *in the symbolic*.

The biblical text cannot but mark this moment. Islam simply does not. While in Judaism and Christianity Hagar is only disapproved of but present as a figure, the Qur'an never mentions her. Although both Ishmael and Abraham are cited numerous times in the Qur'an, "Hagar was kept out of the text, unreferenced."[100] Benslama first draws our attention to the level of historical and sociological reasoning:

> To rally the Arab aristocracy, or even simply the proud people of the desert,
> by giving them for an ancestor a female slave expelled by the man one wishes
> to make the father of the new religion, was no doubt a difficult maneuver to
> enact—even more so given that the Jews and Christians of the region apparently
> did not fail to remind the Arabs of Ishmael's "impure" heritage.[101]

But the internal or structural reason is more important. In Benslama's argument, the removal of Hagar from the Qur'an is immediately related with her status as the Other woman, that is, a figure associated with the radical alterity of female *jouissance* as opposed to the woman of the Other, Sarah, who is easily appropriated by the Qur'an. Islamic institution is bent upon containing and controlling the radical excess of the "Other woman," and it is this containment that is at stake, according to Benslama, in the contemporary debate about the veil or *hijab*. Before discussing Benslama's reading of the French debate, I would like to emphasize that, if it is important to underline the eradication of Hagar's name in the Qur'an, it is an overstatement to say that she is totally banned from Islamic textuality and culture. Although Hagar certainly does not have the credibility of Khadija or Aisha, she is a well-known figure in Muslim cultures as the mother of Ishmael. Contrary to what Benslama says, her name is very commonly found indeed.

Whose name is she? Right(ing) woman

Benslama begins his discussion of the veil with the example of a young woman who defends it on the ground of "modesty before god."[102] From this he immediately moves into a psychoanalytic reading: "The young woman believes in the de-monstration of woman, which indicates that in her system's unconscious she is represented by the monster of erectile visual power and enigmatic knowledge. This is what we encounter in the imaginary of ancient civilizations. . . ."[103] Although this might be a relevant reading, the political field also reveals a variety of struggles and discourses in different contexts. For instance, how to account for various instances in which Muslim women perform a singular agency, totally independent of men, around the issue of *hijab*? It is often said that, although they act independently, insofar as they defend a practice that is objectively oppressive of women in general, this should not be considered as an instance of agency. But this argument cannot be made as easily as it is assumed, in the face of various different forms of politicization that can be found among Muslim women of different social, cultural, and geographical backgrounds, from those who call themselves Muslim feminists and make explicit feminist criticisms of Islamic patriarchy to those who are involved in a rights struggle in alliance with various other minorities. How shall we read the unconscious of a Muslim feminist who criticizes contemporary Islamic patriarchy? Is she in contradiction with her system's unconscious by her creation of a fiction of pure originary Islam when women were not oppressed? But it is also clear that this originary purity is not the same for her as it would be for the Muslim man of whom she is critical. The origin is already divided, already contested. It is not helpful to reduce this complexity to an invariant core of "seclusion." Benslama's French example does not exhaust the whole field, nor the unconscious. And perhaps we need to ask *the degree to which* this kind of analysis creates a fiction of homogeneous origin, suffering from a similar torment.

More importantly, however, singling out an issue of the veil is an oppositional politics of a highly susceptible kind, which often ends up in giving further strength and legitimacy to what is opposed. Benslama's insistence that the veil is not a sign but a filter that protects against the female body's disturbing effects is a criticism of the practice of veiling as patriarchal and sexist.[104] Benslama is critical of the French government's "prohibition of the prohibition of the other."[105] But this prohibition also leads to the increasing and conscious use of *the veil as a sign*, to the extent that the Muslim community interpretes this as an attack against their overall identity (as we know they often do). Therefore, not Benslama's analysis in itself, but the categorically oppositional attitude in which he frames it takes the risk of contributing to the production of the veil as sign.

Benslama suggests that we consider the "textuality" of human rights: in this discourse, the woman is Man as anthropos, that is to say "not only is sexual difference not an essential characteristic of this textuality, but it is precisely one of the forms of discrimination the textuality wants to suppress."[106] The veiled woman's emergence as a sign of conflict is inevitable; these two truths are at war. Consequently, the question of "the prohibition of the prohibition of the other" is "unanswerable."[107] But why is it unanswerable, especially when Benslama has clearly answered it while appearing to be merely providing the terms of the debate between discrimination and anti-discrimination? Because he does not want to give support to "the prohibition of the prohibition of the other," which is, unfortunately, a prohibition! As a prohibition, it is a violation of a basic human right. In other words, there is another possible example here, another Muslim woman, who utters a completely different statement: "Everybody is entitled to their beliefs, and I only follow my own belief as a human individual. As a human subject, I have the freedom to dress the way I like." This other Muslim woman defines herself on the ground of the discourse of human rights and freedom rather than directly on the ground of her specific belief. Benslama *cannot recognize* this possibility; his young Muslim woman can only be a Muslim, never a subject of rights, and never both at the same time. She has never heard the discourse of human rights, she does not know it, she cannot speak it, insofar as she is veiled. But this is what we have heard in the recent social upheavals in the Middle East and North Africa: in Egypt, Turkey, and Tunisia, political Islam emerged as part of a discourse of human rights, freedom, and the rule-of-law state against the arbitrary rule of nationalist authoritarianism. Although what emerged out of the dust seems to be an authoritarian form of democracy, it is not a fundamentalist regime. This is a development that analyses such as Benslama's could not predict. It surely does not mean that Islam is democratizing itself without any problems. But it means that the situation is far more complex than a simple return to the purity of origin, an obsessional traditionalism, etc.

More importantly, *how is it possible* for the Muslim woman to articulate her practice of veiling in terms of a right to veil? When Benslama writes that the subject of human rights is neutral with regard to sexual difference, his reference is Man as species. But what is "Man" supposed to mean here? Benslama reads the *practical* discourse of human rights in terms of the *philosophical* category of Man. He speaks of the "textuality" of human rights, but he does *not read* the text of human rights. Under the stylish password of "textuality," his approach is a defense of the ideology of human rights. As for the *text* of the Universal Declaration of Human Rights, it refers to the *dignity* of the human person in Article One: "All humans are born free and equal in dignity and rights. They are endowed with reason and conscience and should act towards one another in the spirit of brotherhood." In his work on human rights, Pheng Cheah provides an excellent materialist reading of this passage:

> The minimal philosophical justification of the human entitlement to rights in these sections of the Universal Declaration seems to be as follows: humans are born with an inherent dignity. This is, however, not a natural justification of human rights. Since rights only come into existence via political instruments which specify and protect them, dignity by itself is not the source for rights. Dignity is rather some contentless human attribute that is the basis of freedom in the world. The second sentence of Article One introduces "reason" and also "conscience" for the first time. The three terms, "dignity," "freedom" and "reason" are related as follows: because dignity is contentless, it involves a practical orientation. Reason is the operator of normative human action (because humans "are endowed with reason and conscience," they "should act") that protects and fleshes out dignity by specifying determinate rights via political instruments. Now, precisely because dignity is contentless, the work of reason is open-ended and interminable and this links reason to freedom. . . . Apparently, this open-endedness is also reflected in the subsequent increase in human rights instruments and in ongoing debates about different views of human rights.[108]

Surely this does not mean that anything goes in the field of rights, but it gives us a much better means of thinking this complex force field. *First of all*, to go back to Benslama's reading of the discourse of human rights, it is true that the sexual difference is not its "essential characteristic," but it is always already there *qua* difference, that is, the contentless human attribute. Otherwise, there would be no possibility of fighting discrimination. There would be no human rights without difference indeed. *Secondly*, an argument that opposes the universalism of human rights to the traditionalism of a specific culture or belief system overlooks the fact that culture is also a defining characteristic of being human, a difference constitutive of human dignity, and an instance of the contentless human attribute. Consequently, as unpleasant as it may look to many, the practice of veiling can well be defended as a right (especially when it is ridiculously prohibited). There is therefore no absolute or final ground on which the rights can be fixed. The rights always appear in finite contexts and are always contaminated. In relation to them, we always go through the ordeal of undecidability, calculate in the face of the impossible, make decisions, choose something, and sacrifice something else. Are they therefore merely relative and contextual? The practical discourse of human rights has no permanent ground, but it is associated with a universal normative force, a force that makes us act morally and politically.[109]

The prohibition of the prohibition of the other, which apparently concerns Benslama, depends on the assumption of a fixed and permanent ground of human rights provided by the Western liberal and secular rule-of-law state. Just as we think that this is the ground of "Man" that Benslama cannot do other than to salute, in a striking turn he interprets the Western desire of producing the prohibition of prohibitions as one of "becoming the difference of differences, thereby connecting with an absolute femininity of the species."[110] Unfortunate as it might be, this is related to Levi-Strauss' rather infamous lament that, if it were not for Islam, the militarizing masculine intruder, the Christian West would have encountered the Buddhist East and would have remained female! It is Islam, in other words, that is responsible for the grand narrative of prohibition.

Benslama's work is really a missed opportunity. Its project of offering a psychoanalytical insight into a significant political-religious movement of our times is sacrificed at the altar of an originary fear of the origin. One of the unfortunate consequences of framing psychoanalysis in such an abstract, categorical, and essentialist way is the reproduction of the sociological empiricism that is criticized in the initial opening of the argument. When conducted in this manner, Benslama's critical analysis of Islamic patriarchy and sexism is too general, and indeed may not be so new for sociologists and political scientists who are familiar with the varied field of political Islam or Islamism. Benslama's own torment is easily readable (originated in an assumption he shares with empiricial social science): it is very difficult to develop a comprehensive understanding and analysis of contemporary political Islam or Islamism *without taking into account its complex and unequal relationship with the West*, which means taking into account not only colonialism, postcolonialism, and neocolonialism, but also the crisis and failure of nationalist modernizing elites. Benslama justifies his desire to isolate the religion and cultures of Islam from its recent history in reference to Islamism's return to the origin, that is to say, by taking Islamism's word for granted.

Determined by this oppositional logic, Benslama's approach involves and produces several figures of reversal (essence vs plurality, unconscious vs history, fiction vs fact, West vs Islam, modern vs traditional). More importantly, his justification by Islamism's discourse of origin hides his violent refusal to see the alien (Western) involvement in the historical production of contemporary political Islam or Islamism. Measured against his own stated wish to place foreignness in the origin, this is a serious, though hidden failure, one that points to his own belief in the transcendent, unquestionable, and absolute paradigmatic value of Western liberal polity and culture, which must be saved from contamination by Islam.

Reciting: The Voice of the Other

The last two decades witnessed a rapidly growing literature on religion and the religious in the humanities. With only a few exceptions, the usual reference for religion is either Christianity or, more infrequently, Judaism. There is a consistent pattern that makes the Judeo-Christian tradition the instance or the site of an analysis of the religious, or sometimes the political. Such a pattern demonstrates that we are living in an intellectual and political culture that could be described as Eurocentric. This is further reinforced by the marginalization of other religions, including Islam, in the departments of so-called area studies—a specialization that requires the learning of languages.

Islam's increasing politicization went hand-in-hand with its expulsion from the philosophical, theoretical, or theological debates. The Abrahamic, monotheist tradition is conventionally named as Judeo-Christian, and never as Judeo-Christian-Islamic. When Islam is other-ed in ways that resemble the anti-Semitic aggression of the 1930s, it is rather sad to see that political intelligence as well as scholarly learning is still fascinated with the so-called universal form of the subject that is found in Christianity, as in the influential works of Slavoj Žižek.[1] In an important recent book titled *The Rebirth of History*, the philosopher Alain Badiou offers a comprehensive study of the current popular uprisings throughout the globe from France and United Kingdom to Tunisia and Egypt (2012). Badiou's study is particularly instructive in its focus on the stages and forms of these uprisings, how they develop, unfold, and organize themselves, especially what kind of possible or potential future is implied in these forms and organizations. A significant number of these recent popular uprisings and revolts have occurred in the so-called Islamic geography, with a serious involvement of political Islam and often resulting in a transfer of power to this movement. Throughout his analysis Badiou rightly draws our attention to the spontaneous pluralism of these uprisings, how they have involved oppressed people from all views, religions, groups, and social strata—often under a single banner such as "justice" or "freedom." Especially depending on the example of the great rallies in Egypt, Badiou writes toward the end of his book: "by 'justice' today is also, or even primarily to be understood *the eradication of separating words. We must affirm the generic, universal and never identitarian character of any political truth.*"[2] I have nothing against a criticism of identity politics. But, supposing that the universality of political truth can be maintained unproblematically, how could it have any hold on the actuality of politics without a serious analysis of the historical and social conditions that often put identity politics at the forefront of social movements and struggles? The free and equal collectivity at Tahrir Square was gradually appropriated and replaced by a classically organized political Islamic leadership. No doubt this expected victory of the "state form" did not stop the organized mass resistance against the new government. But the point is that Badiou has *no analysis of political Islam*, which has been such a significant part of this whole process. In Badiou's understanding, there is no structural difference between places such as the United Kingdom or France and Egypt or Tunisia. They are all the same capitalism, the same political structure, the same culture, the same history.

Badiou's complicated theory of political truth also involves an aspect that can perhaps explain this. In another well-known work titled *St. Paul: The Foundation of Universalism*, in which he develops an original interpretation of the Christian ideas of St Paul as an instance of revolutionary universal truth, Badiou argues, following St Paul, that universality should not present itself under the aspect of a particularity. If differences must definitely be transcended, then this must be by a "benevolence" that presents itself "as *an indifference that tolerates differences.*"[3] But then in his "Conclusion," in reference to the universalism conceived of as the production of the Same, Badiou speaks of "indifference to secular nominations . . . to particular subsets," for according to St Paul, Christ is "the name which is above every name" and "it is always to such names, rather than to the closed names proper to particular languages and sealed entities, that the subject of a truth lays claim. All true names are 'above every name.'"[4] This is not a contradiction for Badiou or St Paul, because those differences that Pauline benevolence tolerated were customs and opinions, that is, not truth but something inferior indeed.[5] The question remains: what makes Christ the true (universal) name when there are other (particular) names and when Christ is just one of the names? If this is a truth procedure, the question then becomes: can we write Muhammad in the place of Christ, as a true name above every name? For reasons internal to Islam, we cannot because Muhammad is not regarded as the son of God, nor is resurrection expected in the way that St Paul articulates. Does this put Islam outside universal truth? Is it therefore incapable of producing universal truth? Or, does it have other mechanisms, procedures, and modalities of universal truth? (But then there is no universal truth.) If we can write Muhammad in the place of Christ, is universal truth merely a form? What makes it universal then? Badiou's model for universal truth is derived from St Paul's text. It is according to this model that he studies uprisings in the Middle East and North Africa where the majority of the population are Muslim and where there is a strong Islamic movement. I am not at all arguing that this is by definition an illegitimate methodology. I am only asking for some awareness so that difference is not simply an object of benevolence.

With the new images of Tahrir Square, and by extension with the "Arab Spring," are we now beyond the images of bearded and armed men in strange garb, women under seclusion, visions of the desert and dust, bombs and ruins? In the face of these familiarly strange images, which must be called "strategic" in Michel de Certeau's sense,[6] one is tempted to render the voice of Islam audible. Although this voice is brought nearer to us in the prime time news as the event that interrupts our normality, it is also distant for the same reason, as a sign of disturbing otherness. We have seen, however, that the desire to render the Muslim voice audible is already everywhere, from the media and publishing industry to the academy. It is time to remind ourselves of Edward Said's fine warning that Orientalism will not blow away once the truth about it is understood.[7] Speaking of audibility, that which is audible is so because it has a proper form, free of noise. But what if we find in the very heart of the so-called true and proper Islam, of that which is proper to Islam, a constant preoccupation with and an inescapable failure of audibility itself?

The primal word

In the previous chapter, Benslama has drawn our attention to Muhammad's biography: orphaned by both parents at four, a void is opened at the heart of the child Muhammad. Benslama followed the track of this cut or opening in

Muhammad's dreams, in Arabic language and in the revelation. The last one is of great significance. According to Benslama, Gabriel's command *iqra*! (read!) means "read the Mother of the Book," that is, the guarded tablet in the seventh heaven. Revelation is basically a reception of the hyperoriginary text of the Other. Benslama draws a number of conclusions from this:

> Origin would then be merely an operation of deciphering an ancient text that the prophet embraced in the cut in the Self, from which a future text would come into being. To read is to bring the text of the Other to gestation. It is the first operation of the Law. The Law in Islam does not offer redemption from any original sin, and yields to universal reason and law only as a secondary matter; its initial action is to open an internal difference and the field of the possible through a separation in the flesh. The intruder in the heart of man is language. It follows that man is never entirely man. He is intimately foreign to his species.[8]

Hence to read is to repeat a text that is already written, already embraced in the cut. The intruder is language. It seems that there is a short cut in Benslama's argument from the cut and the openness (*fath*), which embraces the letter (*harf*: also "edge"), to the victory (*fath*) of institutionalized theology and extremism.[9] "Read!" or "Recite!": how to read or recite this command? Obviously the only reference could not be the Mother of the Book (though this allegory is not insignificant in establishing a foundation), especially when Abrahamic biblical narrative was available to Muhammad. Hence Benslama draws our attention also to a beginning (as different from a cut): Muhammad's declaration of Ishmael as the father of the Arabs is placing a foreignness in the origin (his "translation" of the Abrahamic narrative). According to Benslama, since "the cut precedes the beginning, it is always an opening and a trace in the memory of the Other . . . there is never any beginning."[10] Of course. But this is because, before the beginning, before this authorization and origination, the cut opened by the command is also a question: how to read? how to recite? And, what am I to read? Did Muhammad not run back home to Khadija, in *fear and trembling*?

Islam begins, then, by Muhammad's hearing of the voice of the other, the angel Gabriel who gave a command: "Read, in the name of your Lord!"[11] The first meaning of the Arabic word *iqra* is "read." It also means "recite" and it is often translated as to "read," to "recite," or sometimes to "proclaim." I suggest that we hear the word as to "read/recite" in order to be able to link this primal scene of Islam with the Islamic practice of learning the Qur'an by reciting and chanting it. The proper word for the latter practice is *tajweed* (recitation). Reciting or reading the Qur'an is an essential aspect of the pedagogy of the Qur'an course, which produces the Muslim subject.

With the command, a text is in the making. Given the availability of biblical narrative, we must also emphasize Islam's acceptance of previous religious monotheisms and of the Abrahamic tradition in general, the voice of the Other as One and the Same.[12] In the linguistic register, this is an example of performative contradiction. The command implies a text that is both there and is yet going to be produced; it refers to a "before" that is going to be performed in the future. In the historical register, the text signified by the command is not just in the past, but it will have to be invented. Having many references to the previous texts of the Old and New Testament, the Qur'an places itself firmly in the biblical grand narrative. Interestingly, in spite of its unconditional acceptance of Abrahamic narrative, something like the kind of conflictual exchange between Judaism's "Law" and Christianity's "Grace," that is, something like Islam's differential place vis-à-vis the other revealed religions, has never been granted to the last religion in the historical narrative of ethical monotheism. It is as if its word had no value in the history and economy of revelation, as if it did not read or did not even know how to read the narrative of revealed voice.

In the beginning, then, a reading as reciting, a re-citing, a repetition, or doubling, not one but two words or voices: the one who commands and another who reads. Attending to the imperative of this command, I suggest that we read/recite it as referring to an uncanny "before" that is demanded to be performed and given shape in the future as a reading or book. It is a pure command, which recites itself as one recites it.

Levinas: Event and transcendence

How are we going to read or hear this command, the voice of the Other? Emmanuel Levinas' philosophy has become a model in the interpretation of the revelation of the Other. Rather than offering a detailed presentation of Levinas' readings of Descartes' Third Meditation[13] or his analyses of the revelation or placing of the Other in the Same,[14] I would like to offer a brief critical account of his approach through Lyotard's attentive reading in his *Differend*.[15] Lyotard's reading emphasizes that what is at stake in Levinas' argument is an announcement or address that is violent, traumatic, and expropriating in character. (Is this not what Benslama meant by the cut?) Its precise nature is that it expels the self from the instance of addressor to that of addressee. The dispossessed self will then try to take hold of itself by forming another sentence that enables it to frame and overcome the dispossession. It will re-gain the position of the sender so that it will be able to legitimize (or refuse) the disrupting command of the other. But the second sentence cannot put an end to the prior event of dispossession that has a force to prescribe prescriptions; it is only an attempt to master it, and in mastering it, it forgets what Levinas calls the transcendence of the Other. It is cognitive and descriptive, articulating a truth, prescription described, whereas the first one has a pure proscriptive force, taking hold of the self prior to the possibility of description. The first sentence, which Levinas calls ethical, immediately creates an obligation. It is this strange, prior ethical obligation that is forgotten in the second cognitive and descriptive sentence. The voice of the other is heard before it is listened to (or it cuts before it is read). It is something that happens to the self or the subject. But if the subject transforms itself from being an addressee to an addressor in the face of a violent expropriation, what makes us assume that there is a voice addressing or interpellating me in a sentence? Is it not the self's attempt to produce a cognitive mastery, which has to take the form of a sentence, and clear the prior noise by giving the violent force of event a description, attributing it to a subject as Other and turning it into a command or law?

In the trajectory of Levinas' thought, it is possible to follow a movement from the alterity of what he called the "there is" in his early work to the human face and the voice of the Other in his later works. This is important because, in early Levinas, the "there is" (the pure event of existing that is left after everything is reverted into nothing) makes itself felt through a feeling of the "world in pieces" or "a world turned upside down"[16] that is clearly an overturning event. Further, what makes itself felt in this way is audible for Levinas. But this is a strange audibility, quite out of the ordinary indeed. The "there is" is not only "the impersonal field of forces of existing,"[17] which "no longer composed a world"[18] but also it is "a rumbling silence," "something resembling what one hears when one puts an empty shell close to the ear, as if the emptiness were full, as if the silence were noise," [. . .] "a noise returning after every negation of this noise," and an unstoppable music.[19]

In Levinas' later work, however, this overturning event, the dispossessing force of the event of existing, is given meaning and intelligibility by a concept of the transcendence of the Other.[20] This is Levinas' criticism of ontology in favor of ethics as primary philosophy. In *Totality and Infinity*, Levinas follows

Descartes' demonstration of the transcendence of the infinite with respect to the "I," while this is at the same time related to the notion of the face of the Other in conversation. The face "bring[s] us to a notion of meaning prior to my *Sinngebung* (sense giving)."[21] In his later series of lectures, *God, Death and Time*, Levinas' search for a God outside of what Heidegger calls onto-theology is indeed a search for "a new model of intelligibility."[22] The placing of the idea of the infinite in us is called "heteronomy," "inspiration," or "prophecy which is not some kind of genius but the very spirituality of the spirit."[23] He emphasizes that the meaning and intelligibility of the transcendence of the Other is of a unique kind. It is before cognition or knowledge;[24] and it is not that of a content, or of the "Said" of discourse, but of "Saying": escaping both objectification and dialogue, God is "a third person or Illeity" whose "command, to which, as a subject, I am subjected" and which "comes from the understanding that I hear in my Saying alone."[25] Levinas further argues that the word "God" is an excessive utterance that prohibits itself and does not allow its meaning to be conceived in terms of presence or being. This is why its thematization in a cognitive and descriptive sentence cannot erase its proscriptive force, as Lyotard underscores. Yet such a prohitibion, that is, this sense of a God prohibiting its own being, is still tied to meaning and intelligibility by Levinas. If the Other is incommensurable in Levinas' philosophy, Lacoue-Labarthe is quite right in describing this as the idea of a "vertical incommensurability."[26] Insofar as the voice of God is understood in its transcendence, it must have intelligible form. With this passage from the "there is" to the Other as God, what is at stake now is no longer simply an overturning and expropriating event that decomposes the world; on the contrary, it is the promise or word of order, even if delayed or prohibited.

Are we then supposed to say that, contrary to such an approach, the originary expropriating event is not linguistic, that it should have nothing to do with language? Rather than taking a quick decision, I am reminded of Althusser's reading of Spinoza's theory of prophecy: ". . . these incredible prophets," Althusser writes, are "men who climb the mountain at the summons of the Lord but who only understand in the thunder crash and lightning flash some partially incomprehensible words."[27] For Althusser, it is the community who tells them what they have heard, and all understand except "the imbecile Daniel" (who represents resistance to ideology as internal to it). As a volunteering imbecile, I cannot except hear that the event of "interpellation," the so-called voice of the other, is never without a good deal of noise that the hearers or readers are bound to clear up. Can we think of the citationary structure of monotheism as noise, between thunder crash and incomprehensible words, supposedly in the uncanny and undecidable passage between nature and language? Citation, recitation, quote or mention are perhaps indissociable from noise. And the question has always been: how to avoid it? It is in this sense that the self tries to master the violent event of the hearing of the other in a cognitive and descriptive sentence.

This mastery has to do with the composition of a form that is supposed to clear up the reciting throat. Its articulation can be found in the following account by everyone's sophisticated Orientalist Louis Massignon, who is, unlike Althusser, faithfully committed to the originary purity of the voice and vision:

> The experience of inspiration begins in Islam with the "internal upheavals" felt by Muhammad at the beginning of his prophetic mission. According to Aisha, the prophet of Islam first had a vision of isolated, luminous letters (several examples are cited at the head of certain chapters in the Qur'an) and simultaneously an audition of isolated sounds; the letters corresponded to the sounds, as with the child learning to spell. Then the prophet, having learned to spell, was enabled to recite inspired sentences. They were "breathed" into him by the Spirit, *Ruh*, a vague word which can designate the angel as well as God or the Prophet himself.[28]

"Internal upheavals," that is, the opening of an unknown, noisy and destabilizing "before" in the event of hearing is immediately lost in such confident belief in the perfect correspondence between letter and sound, in the clarity of meaning as vision and the child as the metaphor of an innocent beginning. Recitation is conceived within a restricted economy of mimesis, that is to say, as recitation of a pure and clear originary form, of an audible or readable sentence, that has to forget the violence of hearing, its strangely obligatory and interpellative force.

Haunting: The lost book

As an alternative to Massignon, I follow Gayatri Spivak's advice and offer the Morrocan psychoanalyst and writer Abdelkebir Khatibi's fascinating reading of Muhammad's biography in his essay "Frontiers" (2009). Khatibi's problem is Freud's dismissal of Islam as an "abbreviated repetition" of Judaism, an imitation, which lacks a "murder" in *Moses the Man and the Monotheistic Religion*. According to Khatibi, Freud, who was a professional outsider, showed that there is a borrowing of names in the origin: the founder of Judaism and of the monotheistic law, Moses, was an outsider, an Egyptian.[29] However, in discarding Islam as a mere repetition of Judaism, Freud turned it into a frontier of his theorization. Rather than applying psychoanalysis on Islam, Khatibi's aim is to use the singular adventure of Islam as a "frontier position" by turning a psychoanalytic account of the Islamic imaginary into a problem for psychoanalytic narrative.

Like Benslama, Khatibi's psychoanalytic reading also draws on the prophet's biography. But Khatibi follows a completely different route than Benslama by directly challenging Freud's claim that Islam lacks depth because there is no murder or sacrifice within it. On the contrary, there is sacrifice in Islam, but in a very different form. Khatibi asks how Muhammad the orphan, the one without proper family romance, was to maintain the proper name. As the revelation in the form of the letter was illegible to Muhammad (though legible to his wife Khadija), he had to *sacrifice* his signature, "gave it as offering to Allah."[30] Khatibi interprets Gabriel's order as "recite!"—that is to read it without understanding it. He shows that there are two voices who are unified, according to a symmetrical and circular logic, to transmit the same message. Allah the addressor is the other voice of Muhammad, whereas the addressee is Muhammad the prophet as recognized by witnesses. Muhammad occupies sometimes one place, sometimes the other. This creates a singular problem: identifying himself with the message of the Book written by no one, Muhammad is inhabited by it and becomes the Book, which he can neither read nor write. Khatibi emphasizes that, since there is the illegible as soon as there is writing, Muhammad sacrifices his signature by attributing the Book to the Other—an unusual murder. Khatibi calls the sacrificed book "the lost book." In Muhammad's unconditional subjection to the letter, to its unity and transcendence, another letter is hidden. Following Nicolas Abraham and Maria Torok's concept of cryptonymy,[31] Spivak interprets Khatibi's analysis as "transform(ing) the historical pathology of Islam into a negative cryptonymy—the encrypting of the sacrificed signature as something that cannot be avowed."[32] The result of the sacrifice would be, as Spivak emphasizes, "the consolidation of the difference at the origin of monotheisms."[33] In Khatibi's words, "the unicity of Allah and of the Arabic language marks this frontier, in the Islamic imaginary, as the founding signature, the emblem."[34]

Depending on our prior discussion, we might say that Muhammad's mastery takes the form of a circular address, which is structurally under threat of separation. The power of Khatibi's reading is in its opening of the illegible pages of the lost book. Recitation here is not learning to spell, as in Massignon, but rather *the unification of two voices that remain separate* in imitative repetition, even though it seems to obey the circular logic of communication or address. What Khatibi calls the lost book, or Spivak the encrypted signature, is like Levinas' "noise returning after every negation of this noise," an uncanny "before" or past haunting and discontinuing language.

We should remember here our criticism of Abedi and Fischer's reading of the Qur'an in Chapter 2. Recitation is circular, hermeneutic, and dialogical on the institutional and pedagogical level where it works as a power relationship between the imam and the student in the Qur'an course. The technique of learning is the same as that of the Ancient Greeks: the breaking up of utterances into memorizable, imitable, and manageable units that give form to the voice as the "Gestalt" of the audible. As recitation is also chanting, an Islamic typography as phonography stamps, marks, and seals the voice in the letter: "Move not thy tongue concerning the Qur'an to make haste therewith. It is for Us to collect it and to promulgate it: But when We have promulgated it, follow thou its recital (as promulgated)."[35] It is the recitation manual that controls and tames the tongue. But, as an instance of mimesis, recitation cannot be reduced to a mere effect of such techniques of governing, shaping, and disciplining the voice, since, as we learn from Derrida, "imitation does not correspond to its essence, is not what it is—imitation—unless it is in some way at fault or rather in default."[36] The noise of the event, of the lost writing, continues to haunt and encrypt the sacred word of the self. What makes a language what it is and is not, this flow of voices and silences, always in plural, is also irreducibly singular, as it includes all kinds of "intonation, elocution, tone, inflections, melisma, rhythm, even timbre (or what Barthes calls 'grain')."[37] In this second sense, recitation is indeed what Derrida would call an "infrastructure," that is, a structure of generalized writing: "the irreducible complexity within which one can only shape or shift the play of presence or absence: that within which metaphysics can be produced but which metaphysics cannot think."[38] There is no hermeneutic/dialogical circle without this "infrastructural" process; for instance, the play of interpretation is usually based on the "proper" recitation of a certain word.

This generalized recitation cannot be artificially separated from recitation in the narrow, pedagogical sense. Their positive conflation is a permanent enabling of the social text. Speaking of the voice in the context of mimesis, Lacoue-Labarthe reminds that "the voice, the lexis concern not only psyche, desire . . . but equally an investment that is social, historical, cultural, aesthetic— in short ethical, in the strict sense of the word ethos."[39] It is the social condition, the suffering of the world as it is known and lived, which throws the poor, the oppressed, and the alienated into the beyond, into "the soul of a soulless world" in Marx's well-known phrase. There a language is finally found, it seems: the word is fixed, the tongue is bound, in a beyond that is sanctified by the letter of the sacred text. The genealogical transformation of alterity into identity cannot dissolve the singular passing of the voices of the submitted, each of whom should be hiding or crypting the wound of a broken letter/voice in submission to the letter. What is commanded in and by this transformation or translation should survive the command and should maintain a silent echo, vibration, or resonance that somehow departs from it: sounds of an unspoken, unknown language. I imagine that, in every Qur'an course, there must be children of the kind Deleuze and Guattari mention in a different context, those who are "skilled in the exercise of repeating a word, the sense of which is only vaguely felt, in order to make it vibrate around itself,"[40] in a playful "recitation which strips them of their identity."[41]

Reciting: Specters

That which survives in resonance is ghostly, spectral. Is recitation not also spectralization or ghost-calling? Following Derrida's insight,[42] I would like to argue that maintaining a certain noise, a haunted voice, is an ethical thinking of the eventfulness of the event. In her essay on Derrida's concept of the specter, Spivak discusses Assia Djebar's novel, *Far From Madina*, and describes it as an instance of ghost calling or spectralization.[43] Djebar reads Muslim chroniclers of the first three centuries of Islam who write about the prophet's lifetime (Ibn Hisham, Ibn Sa'd, Tabari) and finds the names of 33 women on the margins of these texts. To apply Benjamin's well-known expression, "reading what was never written,"[44] she creates a world for each of these women by questioning what happened and providing alternative interpretations and possible, though unactualized, paths of development of events. I should like to expand the sense of reciting here to one of its oldest meanings as narrating. Since Djebar herself took the Qur'an course as a child (as we already learned from *L'amour la fantasia*), her reciting of the Islamic narrative in *Far from Madina* can also be described as an echo or resonance: by vibrating women's words and names around themselves, she touches a future in the past. As Spivak explains in another essay on Ovid's story of Narcissus and Echo, like Echo who repeats but with a difference (to Narcissus' question "why do you fly from me?" Echo replies "fly from me"), Djebar turns her weakness into the deconstructive power of differing from the utterance she is subjected to recite.[45] In Spivak's words, her re-citing "opens up a liminary time into a counterfactual possible world."[46]

Especially with the prophet's youngest daughter Fatima, we read Djebar's "counterfactual narrative" at its strongest. Literally interpreting the prophet's saying ("From us, the prophets, no one shall inherit! What has been given to us, is given as a gift!"[47]), the new Islamic rule refuses Fatima's share of inheritance. Djebar turns her into an "Islamic Antigone" who challenges the Muslim *polis*. Spivak emphasizes Djebar's struggle "to reconfigure the past, to imagine the ancestors as ghosts."[48] Djebar imagines that Fatima might have unconsciously wished to be a boy: "To be both her father's Daughter (for the affection) and his Son (for the continuity)."[49] This is why, she muses, Fatima must have married Ali, her father's adopted son, which was almost marrying her own self and thus drawing closer to the impossible right of inheritance. But then she stops and asks if this is "to form too free an idea of Fatima."[50] Spivak emphasizes Djebar's cautious use of imagination: "the ghost named Fatima has no more than an anticipatable reality."[51] Djebar carefully conducts the "gender-deconstructive force" of her imagination to open "a fissure in what is merely history, and the ghost can dance in the fault."[52] If Djebar does not merely let her imagination go without setting it limits while continuing to exercise it, what is the result of which she might be wary? I would like to further explore the status of what Spivak calls "the radical counterfactual future past."

This is a concept with a long history in the analytic philosophical tradition.[53] The first counterfactual definition was actually given by Hume, even though it was due to a confusion. He failed to distinguish a regular definition of cause ("an object followed by another") from a counterfactual one ("if the first object had not been, the second never had existed"). If analytic empiricist philosophy had to spend a serious effort in order to manage the ineluctable reference to unactualized possibilities, this was mainly in the context of the question of causation.[54] A significant part of this effort has the aim of controlling a form of thinking that is not based on a simple, stable, and homogenous reference. Imagination gets dangerously close to rational thought by multiplying the reference in terms of other worlds and unactualized possibilities. Insofar as this multiplicity of universes is countable, the relationship between them would have to be one of continuity (e.g. we have counted 33 women). But it is also one of discontinuity at another level, for "the world in which Fatima raises an objection to the Islamic rule following her father's death" is counterfactualizing a narrative that is already regarded as stable and homogenous (i.e. "the world in which Fatima does not raise an objection to the Islamic rule following her father's death"). Following our concept of recitation as differing echo, we can read Djebar's strategy as subjecting the narrative form to the uncanny force of discontinuity. This is not merely discontinuing the narrative in the sense of simply giving it up or denying it and telling another narrative, but it is a recitation that, to make a neologism, *de-cites* what it recites. Gaps in what happened, in the facts of history, open up a future.

In the "Preface," Djebar writes that she used her power of interpretation (*ijtihad*) in the Islamic tradition, and that she is not necessarily unfaithful to the way narratives are generally told or recited. For instance, *Far from Madina* opens with the death of Muhammad: a problem, or a disruption in the normal course of life as the narrative rule of beginning. The first sentence reads: "He is dead. He is not dead."[55] Thus, even there, in the beginning, which announces the disrupting event, there is suspense, an oscillation that gives us a discontinuous sense of time. But the narrative does not follow a regular pattern of the unfolding of a conflict and its resolution. If it did so, it would have to be the story of finding an appropriate successor to the prophet, and it would have to find a political model in the stories of these ghost women. As Spivak warns, Djebar's "rereading of a past for a future—a future anterior . . . is not a formula for a future present. The ghost dance cannot succeed as a blueprint."[56] If Fatima is a "model," then the model is spectralized and the stories are multiplied. Various beginnings are woven into the apparently single grand story of Islam, as if its disappearing ends are disseminated all over the desert. It is as if the past moved by leaving gaps, discontinuously, going backward and forward and then backward . . . The novel ends by going back to the very beginning of the monotheistic narrative, to the other woman in the beginning, Hagar. Women's stories are regularly interrupted by "a voice" (and nothing guarantees that it is the same voice). Others, the *rawiya* (woman reciters or storytellers) intervene; there is a "pause" before the last part. Most important of all is the spectral status of all the characters and voices in the novel. It is the discontinuous nature of Djebar's narrative that produces an overall effect of a multiplication of ghosts, of voices.

The representational economy of recitative mimesis keeps producing the form of a sentence, vision, or narrative. I would like to call it an "onto-typology" that finds its ultimate paradigm in the contemporary fundamentalist urge to preserve the letter in its unity and clarity, in the imprint of its stamping force on the surface of the body, of the throat. By reopening the gate of *ijtihad*, Djebar opens our ears to the vibrating and differing echo of the receptive surface. Her re-citing and re-counting (by *de-citing*) asks if it can make the "aphonie" of these stifled voices reverberate in our ears, and if the tympan of our ears can accommodate such bare audibility of a rumbling silence, of a noise returning, resonating after every negation of this noise. Rather than referring to a mere deviation from a given route, she takes us back to a future implied in the ghostly subjunctive, the contingent verb in the origin ("if she were . . ."), in the womb of a narrative where every newborn child is born into a spectral crowd of voices. What we need to attend to here is that Djebar's narrative strategy does not assume a mere lack of origin but brings up the spectral and cryptic status of the originary event and of the very event of origination of stories. It is the haunting noise of this spectrality that is to be controlled and given form in the continuity and consistency of the sentence and vision as understood by Massignon. Such is the complicity of Orientalism and fundamentalism. Djebar's novel does not offer an alternative history, another factualization, or an actualization, but, while keeping the narrative form on the one hand, most delicately undoes it on the other. Otherwise, as Spivak warns, the work of imagination would turn into its opposite: the reinstallation of a pure origin. Djebar does not finally read the lost book of monotheism; she only moves in its gaps for a future to come rather than the future present.

I am reminded here of Khatibi's insistence on the prophet's first wife Khadija's importance as the *first scribe* of the Qur'an.[57] Before this displacement of the scene of revelation, one cannot but ask: in between voice and transcription, what was the message Muhammad lost in order to state another, to the wife who read the sign of election on *his and her* bodies? If this is unsayable, it is perhaps not merely repressed. It is the ever-written secret with which the Muslim Man/Subject can only negotiate by attending to the echo of his recitation.

Khatibi also writes that the three social figures Muhammad had to fight were the seer (the soothsayer), the possessed, and the poet—the first at least a female figure.[58] Most importantly, I am reminded of what Lacoue-Labarthe writes, speaking of the dangers of mimetic narrative according to Plato:

> . . . mythical or mythopoetic contents, or, quite outright, '*old wives' tales*' . . . are all the more formidable and powerful (which must be translated as: their mimetic power is all the stronger) for the fact that they are without author, anonymous, and spoken, that is to say, *recited*, in nobody's name.[59]

Are women merely the medium, the reciter, or the scribe?

Dual words

If it is not a question of merely affirming plurality, but of discontinuing the continuous, then how should this very discontinuity be maintained or reproduced anew? The problem returns. If Fatima is the voice of contention, of interruption, then Aisha, the prophet's young wife, is the voice of recollection, of the taking-care, the survival of memory. They are like the "dual words" in Arabic language, or the dual voice, the two sides of recitation: maintaining and interrupting, same and other. Djebar calls these women "the daughters of Hagar."[60] Djebar's narrative ends by returning to this exiled woman in the beginning of the grand monotheistic narrative. In her version, Hagar is driven out and driven mad in her search for water for her son Ishmael, dancing, wandering back and forth between the two hills where the Ka'ba, the center of Islam, would be built later. Djebar's passage depends on a beautiful play on the words *Hegira* (emigration), *hajra* (sunstroke), and *Hajjar* (Hagar's archaic pronounciation)—a reciting, a return of what crypt, what noise? In the ending scene of the novel, a voice calls all believers:

> All believers, men and women alike, once a year,
>
> or at least once in a lifetime,
>
> daughters of Hagar and sons of Ishmael, join together,
>
> to re-enact the scene of Hagar's madness.[61]

Hagar's madness is the noise, which keeps passing through the voice of the Abrahamic grand narrative, the revealed religions of ethical monotheism. Islam's so-called historical pathology is also of this lineage. It can be read otherwise, in terms of a singular loss of singularity, a loss that remains open to a re-marking of the otherness in, as well as of, its inheritance.

Conclusion

From nineteenth-century travel literature to contemporary ethnography and psychoanalysis, Islam is approached in terms of culture, religion, and identity. While writers such as Lawrence and Eberhardt searched for authentic, originary experience in the cultures and lands of Islam, ethnographers such as Clifford, Abedi, and Fischer presented a program of research that depended on hearing the voice of the Muslim other. Benslama's psychoanalysis offered a powerful reading, but at the cost of essentializing Islam, closing rather than opening its text. Khatibi's psychoanalytic reading moved in another direction and opened the pages of another book within Islam, while fiction writers such as Djebar re-cited the pages of this other book, which was never written. All these writers, scholars, and thinkers approached Islam in terms of culture and religion. But, intentionally or not, implicitly or explicitly, they also had to point to an otherness within culture and/or religion. Their writings are also influenced by a political agenda that is different than religion in its mundane, ordinary operation. In the case of Lawrence and Eberhardt, anticolonial resistance and struggle for independence in which Islam is involved, and in the case of others, a powerful political and social movement that shook the world in the last four decades—political Islam or Islamism. What is the unique political status of Islam today? And what is the role of the humanities in its perception and understanding? I should like to offer a few dispersed concluding observations.[1]

In "Faith and Knowledge," Jacques Derrida has referred to the "war of religion" in our age of "globalatinization."[2] This war is between the Enlightenment force of techno-scientific rationality and capitalism (which appears as globalization or globalatinization), that is, "knowledge" and the force of religious "faith," which has its own place of truth. It appears that, with respect to the forces of abstraction, that is to say, deracination, deterritorialization, delocalization, disincarnation, and formalization, religion is involved in reacting antagonistically and outbidding itself. On the one hand, this globalatinization (religion that does not speak in its name) is a declaration of war as peace, a pacification without limits: "all the religions, their centers of authority, their religious cultures, states, nations or ethnic groups that they represent have unequal access, to be sure, but often one that is immediate and potentially without limit, to the same world market."[3] Thus religion necessarily participates in and is part of this whole process. On the other hand, religion declares "war against that which gives it this new power only at the cost of dislodging it from all its proper places, in truth from place itself, from the taking place of its truth."[4] And yet this antagonism is not the absence of a bond, not external at all. "In this very place," writes Derrida in the beginning of his essay, "knowledge and faith . . . will always have made common cause, bound to one another by the band of their opposition."[5] As much as religion wants to maintain its purity or truth, the necessity of its communication renders its discourse profane. Religion cannot but maintain itself in and through a rational discourse, by means of tele-technologies. Science and religion are linked by the "autoimmunity of the unscathed."[6]

Derrida underlines the singular place of Islam in this configuration by referring to the absence of Muslims at the conference where he delivered this speech, wherein he offers these thoughts on the status of religion: "No Muslim among us, alas, even for this preliminary discussion, just at the moment when it is towards Islam, perhaps, that we ought to begin our discussion."[7] He also warns: "Islam is not Islamism, never forget this, but the latter operates in the name of the former, and this is the grave question of the name."[8] If it is toward Islam that we ought to begin our discussion, this is because "the grave question of naming" has already begun with the name "religion," since Islam is also a name for religion, or perhaps even the name for religion today, when, for instance, Derrida talks about the war of religion. If, today, "Islam" is inscribed as the religion that cannot go beyond religion, as the one that fails to privatize and secularize itself (and instead produces a movement such as Islamism), then this is already part of a politics of naming religion, which is at the same time, as both Carl Schmitt's and Derrida's works bear witness, a politics of naming politics, of naming sovereignty.[9] Who is inscribed as sovereign in this politics of naming? Derrida's concept of "globalatinization" already tells us that Judaism and Islam do not occupy the same position as Christianity for him. Religion is never one for Derrida. Does this not imply that "the grave question of naming" not only concerns Islam, but the very naming of religion as well as of politics?

The question of the name is also the global (or globalizing?) name of Islam; or Islam as a global name that goes beyond nationalistic particularities. Western ideologues treat religion and culture as if they are the same thing, by relentlessly and dangerously writing one in place of the other—a violent politics of naming. For these ideologues, the difference between religion and culture is only a question of political calculation when necessary. As a religious-political coding, political Islam or Islamism inherits Islam's necessarily global vision as a religion. Islamism or political Islam has been the religious-political coding of a cultural rift between national culture and Western culture (which in the long run might also be seen as a religious rift, a rift or bifurcation within the Abrahamic tradition). This is the way I understand "Islamism acting in the name of Islam." I would like to emphasize that the rift is cultural rather than religious per se, even though religion appears to be the most significant and most powerful coding and production of this rift because of its historic place, and even though the "cultural" here is no more than a shifting and ambivalent signifier of *difference*, with regard to the West. But there is always already difference within culture itself. The cultural rift cannot be separated from a dynamic field of class forces and divisions, which it enables and disables at the same time. Like every political movement, Islamism is an expression of certain social and economic interests. As I have already highlighted in the Introduction, it can be described as a strange alliance of two major social classes in a hegemonic historical bloc: the disenfranchised, subaltern, and poor working people (both rural and urban) and the emergent provincial bourgeoisie (e.g. the so-called Anatolian tigers in Turkey).[10] It came to power in struggle with the old nationalist authoritarian elite, the westernized urban middle-class, and the big industrial and commercial capital located in metropolitan centers in the Muslim periphery. To say this is not to reduce it to these class and economic terms, but it is important to know and understand this aspect so that we will not see it simply as a matter of some fight over cultural identity, or simply as a matter of secularism versus religion.[11]

Political Islam or Islamism appeared as a "fundamentalist" religious movement by advocating a programmatic return to the original word of Islam and by separating itself from all Western culture in a strongly oppositional identitarian manner. But its unfolding cannot be reduced to this single appearance, as its recent turn has been in a parliamentary-democratic rather than theocratic direction.[12] The overthrow of authoritarian elitist dictatorships by massive popular resistance and uprisings in the Arab Spring brought Islamism to power, because it has been the major contestant and the most powerfully organized movement in this process. The resistance movement developed in a highly unique context in which it became clear that political Islam could not immediately establish a paradigmatic Islamic rule and instead the new regime had to move in a parliamentary democratic direction.[13] The mass resistance in Tahrir Square in Egypt offered an unprecedented example of what Antonio Negri has recently called the common.[14] The variety of desires and demands that make it are mixed, shifting, and ambivalent. A passage from dictatorship to democracy in the context of a peripheral capitalist structure is quite different than the Greek or Spanish workers and impoverished middle-classes resisting the monstrous economic measures of finance capital, and from the migrant worker under classist and racist oppression in the metropolitan capitalist centers of Europe and North America.[15] This is also why these uprisings and the democratic transition they mark should not be approached in isolation from the financialization of the globe, the liberalization of economies, and the ongoing privatization of the public sector especially in the North African and Middle Eastern countries in question. With Islamism in parliamentary power now, it seems that there is and will be some democratic improvement in these countries, but a democratic improvement that never completely eliminates the general authoritarian framework. Secondly, the predominant tendency in Islamism has nothing against the global-capitalist imperative. If, for instance, the pace of privatization is slower than expected in Tunisia or Egypt, the only reason is fear of losing legitimacy—and the working-class resistance has occasionally been successful.[16] While the abstract logic of capital is capable of permeating the farthest regions of the earth as well as the body, Islam(ism) is in the position of *moralizing* the markets opened by the global capitalist order, *whether in opposition or protection*, as these emerging markets consumerize its body from Ramadan to the fashion industry and contain it in its global circuit. The search for piety under such a condition takes the risk of justifying what it is against (for instance, consumerist excess) precisely by producing mechanisms of protection and insulation. There is more than the use of tele-technologies or techno-science to Islam's autoimmunization today.

It seems as if no one can avoid naming or writing Islam today, at least on this global measure of things. I would like to argue that de-transcendentalizing Islam and being able to respond to the oppressed within it are separate but inseparable tasks. Some time ago Gayatri Spivak has suggested that

> in order to be able to get to the subject of ethics it may be necessary to look
> at the ways in which an individual in that culture is instructed to care for the

self rather than the imperialism-specific secularist notion that the ethical subject is given as human. In a secularism, which is structurally identical with Christianity laundered in the bleach of moral philosophy, the subject of ethics is faceless. Breaking out, Foucault was investigating other ways of making sense of how the subject becomes ethical.[17]

From fasting and ablution to the more intricate concept of *nikah* (which regulates sexual relationships), a number of Islamic religious rituals and concepts are instances of the technologies of self-care. This is the domain of the relationship of self to self in Foucault's understanding: "I am referring to the development of what might be called a 'cultivation of the self,' wherein the relations of oneself to oneself were intensified and valorized."[18] Spivak interprets Foucault's notion of the intensified relationship of self to self as the "inaccessible" domain of the "absolutely intimate."[19] She also poses the question of the place of these ethical practices with regard to the grand binarism of capital versus social:

> Today Marx's ghost needs stronger offerings than Human Rights with economics worked in, or the open-ended messianicity of the future anterior, or even "responsibility" (choice or being-called) in the Western tradition. The need is to turn toward ethical practices—care of others as care of the self—that were "*defective* for capitalism." Marx must be turned around to those who lost in the capitalist competition again and again; in order to turn this ferociously powerful form of capital around to the social.[20]

Spivak does not seem to be arguing that these ethical systems can provide the answer; I understand her as arguing for a problematization in an unusually Foucaldian sense, in a sense that wants to "turn the ferociously powerful form of capital around to the social."[21] Such a project requires intimacy with the language as well as a meticulous effort of translation. For instance, what Foucault calls "ethical substance" can be considered as *nafs* in Islam. It is a difficult and rich concept, which means variously "self," "psyche," "ego," "soul," or "breath" but also "flesh" and "desire" or "appetite." It means both the self as well as the lowest part of the self that concerns the egoistic, worldly desire and appetite, which must be strictly controlled and regulated. Another such example is the concept of *taqwa*, which means "piety" but implies "self-restraint" or "self-protection" at the same time, and communicates with Foucault's notion of self-care.[22] And yet another example would be the concept of *Haqq*, which means "truth" as well as "right," and which is one of the names of God. The frequent translation of the concept of *mahrem* as "forbidden" overlooks that it also means privacy and intimacy.[23] In highlighting a series of randomly chosen concepts, my point is not to explain a given ethical system or vocabulary but to emphasize the openness of the means of problematization within it. It is perhaps in this sense that Foucault distinguishes between morality as a set of rules and prohibitions and ethics as moral problematization.[24] We increasingly have a moral recoding (not always and not necessarily problematization, or a restricted problematization) of Islamic subjectivity under the exigency of new capitalist markets. Today traditional Islamic practices of self-care and self-making (the constitutive aspects of an Islamic habitus or ethos) are increasingly subject to these new market forces. We should also refer to an emerging and complex field of Islamic biopower and biopolitics: from the health services provided by Hamas in the occupied territories to the privatization of health services and organicist concerns over the health of the social body or population policies in Turkey.[25]

The rise of Turkish moderate Islamism is usually explained by its successful instrumentalization of nongovernmental organizations and its forming of an institutional base in civil society, that is, in processes and practices that remained outside the conventional field of party politics. Despite that this account emphasizes an apparently unusual form of political practice outside party politics, it actually maintains a conventional concept of politics in terms of an instrumental rationality of means and ends. Instrumentalization is certainly an irreducible aspect of politics. It remains debatable, however, if all political language and subjectivity works according to this model. In this conventional problematic, political language or discourse is seen as a *means* of communication with people. This instrumental and rationalizing approach to language overlooks the role played by its *idiomatic* dimension. I have argued that language touches the subject at another level. The Islamic idiom has been able to interpellate the masses alongside the cultural rift I have mentioned above, insofar as it has been able to touch at something like a memory before memory, a preinscribed affect or trace that comes with(in) it. I have also argued that, although coded by religious-political language, this trace or affect survives its command or law as a silent echo (as we have read in Assia Djebar's counterfactualizing literary act). Its departure or differing has always already begun, and I would like to think this departure as *messianicity without messiah*, or *desire for justice* as different than law and as having the structure of *promise* in the senses given to these terms by Jacques Derrida.[26] This messianicity is inseparable from religion, but it is in no way reducible to it. Indeed all religions are permanently marked by this promise, and this is why they must be repeatable. Belonging to the absolute past (a past that has never been present), the promise of justice to come is the opening of an unanticipable future. I would like to think that this movement of time communicates with the subaltern classes, genders, and ethnicities.

The iterability required by the survival of religious text and subjectivity pushes it into an aporetic embrace with the global capitalist techno-rational order. We have been witnessing for some time now how the iterability and survival of religion gradually enters into the order of capitalist management and governmentality, of political calculation and decisionism. Turkish moderate Islamism's ordeal with the Kurdish question is a telling example of the paradoxes and aporias that appear in this process. It gives us a different picture beyond the humanist ("let the Muslim speak") and Islamophobic ("keep the Muslim away," or "destroy the Muslim") views. In the Turkish public sphere, the so-called Kurdish question has been defined as one of terror and violence, which is caused by the terrorist, a transcendent figure of radical evil, who betrays the country that is home to him/her and who expresses his/her illogical demand for territory from the nation in his/her monstrous acts of violence. Racism has never appeared as an alternative concept, except in tiny sections of the most marginalized left. The new program of peace and democratic reform, initiated by the moderate Islamist AKP (Justice and Development Party) in government and accepted by the Kurdish leadership, is defined in conventional liberal terms as one of replacing "violence" with "politics": it depends on a mutual decision of putting an end to armed conflict, accompanied by a process of bargaining. Although this is a courageous attempt under the given circumstances, the government has to continually repeat its commitment to the sovereign principle of an undivided nation (especially under the nationalist attack): it is in order to keep the integrity and oneness of the nation that peace is needed. If this opens up the burning question of the post-reform national identity, it also keeps the terms of the debate under the strict control of the old paradigm of sovereignty, when what is needed is a creative democratic act. There is urgent need for a kind of discursive context that would problematize a century-old Turkish sense of privilege and would unfold the concept of *racism* in a social, historical, and political context that is neither used to it nor receptive of it. Interestingly one does not hear for instance the Qur'an's well-known Surah 30 Ayat 22, which presents "the variations in colors and languages" as the *evidence* of God. Reference to language here is important, as education in Kurdish proves a major demand that is fiercely rejected by Turkish nationalists and the far right. For their own good reasons, however, the Islamists are more interested in the evidence produced by opinion polls: how many people support the peace and reform intiative, and how many are worried about the loss of national integrity. If Surah 30 Ayat 22 were ever to be mentioned, this would be in order to justify an unquestioned moral ideal of plurality.[27] It is not that Islamism ceased to be religious. The religious text is reserved as the site of a self-contained, transcendent goodness, while political decision is made on the basis of cognitive mapping, informatics, and control.[28] As Spivak puts it, "when we confine our idea of the political to cognitive control alone, this does not just avoid the risk of response, it closes off response altogether."[29]

Is it possible to read the religious text in a way that transforms textual evidence into the *ethical problem of listening and responding to the others*, that is, an ethical experience of difference, which is inseparable from a questioning of one's own privileges? I am reminded of Foucault's distinction between moral rules and moral problematization. Political decision based on cognitive mapping reproduces the rule or law without problematization since its aim is to produce knowledge of the other in order give a judgment about him or her. But can one morally problematize without falling back into a mere reproduction of moral truth? Spivak warns that "the ethical cannot be immediately institutionalized."[30] If we were simply to present the textual evidence as if it were a matter of informing the public about the good content of religion, we would only reproduce ideology or morality. The double task of de-transcendentalizing alterity while getting into touch with the other is a question of doing rather than saying or stating.

In a later work written in response to 9/11, Spivak's approach shifted toward a careful reading of Kant's distinction between *mere* reason and *pure* reason in *Religion within the Boundaries of Mere Reason*.[31] The question here is defined as *de-transcendentalizing* the religious text by putting it into contact with the aesthetic. What is at stake is not simply the moral truth of religion, but a "figuration," which evokes the ethical, or the ethico-political. According to Kant, Spivak argues, since *mere reason* "push(es) legally good actions with no attention to the mind's corrupt attitudes," it cannot produce ethical action.[32] Therefore *pure reason* needs religion in order to produce moral capacity. But the help comes from what Kant calls the "effects of grace" rather than transcendental intuitions. The effects of grace are the secondary elements ("parerga") according to Kant. They are not religious knowledge and are not available to cognition. Spivak suggests that we take the word "effect" out of the realm of the theological and into the aesthetic in order to de-transcendentalize the "grace." What Kant calls the effect of the transcendental upon the moral will can only be understood in the realm of the aesthetic. When the "effect" becomes aesthetic, the goal-oriented, epistemologically bound thrust of political decisionism is interrupted. "Grace" moves into the aesthetic, becoming an "unverifiable effect of an effect." Spivak suggests that grace now works through a hidden chain of cause and effect, like the rhetorical figure of metalepsis.[33]

Employing Spivak's approach in a study of the American far right, Erin Runions poses the question of how we shift from political decisionism to ethical action especially when reason cannot apprehend the effects of grace cognitively.[34] This gives her the possibility of unfolding Spivak's notion of *the ethical need to listen to the other*, which remained unexplained in her reading of Kant. The answer to the question is in Spivak's preface to her translation of Mahashveta Devi's work, where she defines love as the impossible experience of ethical singularity. Runions particularly emphasizes ethical singularity as the impossible communication between two people: as responsibility flows from both sides, the communication is open but something (which Spivaks calls "secret") never gets through. This is why ethics cannot constitute a program; it is an impossible single encounter. But it is also an interruption of the epistemological. I have also noted this ethical interruption of the epistemological in the second chapter, following Spivak and Davis.[35] When, for instance, Assia Djebar tells the stories of 33 woman she found on the pages of chroniclers of early Islam, she treats each and every story *singly*. As she presents these women as *counterfactualized figures* (an unactualized wish, a possibility departing from the historical, an outside within it), she disrupts the informative narrative of history.

This disruption of the epistemological by the ethical (through the aesthetic) is also thought by Spivak in terms of Paul de Man's concept of permanent parabasis, which is "a disruptive speaking- and reading-otherwise."[36] Permanent parabasis is the interruption of a figure in the performance of a role by speaking or reading otherwise—for instance, the interruption by the chorus in the Greek tragedy by stepping aside, or the intervention of the author. What is disrupted in this way is the continuity between the cognitive and the performative. In the case of the native informant, which I have discussed in the first chapter, Spivak suggests, according to Sanders, that

> to speak or read otherwise in the name of that to which the philosophical example refers (which is not necessarily the empirical, since the figure is,

strictly speaking, "unverifiable"), projected as the (im)possible perspective of the Native Informant, is to perform the parabasis necessary to disrupt the inscription, in Kant onwards, of the Native Informant.[37]

When the Muslim native informant (not necessarily empirical but an unverifiable figure) is called for performance before the global audience, how is one to speak or read otherwise, or to interrupt the Subject's encrypting of the native informant as his origin?

In the essay on 9/11, in which Spivak discusses Kant's notion of "the effects of grace," she frequently employs a certain notion of *figure*, or *figuration*, which she defines as "representation without concept" in Kant's sense in the Third Critique.[38] In this context, she also makes a reference to Hannah Arendt's well-known reading of Kant's Third Critique in terms of political philosophy: "Hannah Arendt commented on the political potential of Kant's thinking of the aesthetic. What I am proposing links up with that thought."[39] Spivak then reminds us that, in the Third Critique (on which Arendt's account depends), the check on imagination is the understanding; but in *Religion within the Boundaries of Mere Reason*,

> Kant implicitly, and to a large extent without acknowledgement, shifts the task of representation-without-concept—figuration—to the figuring of Grace as near metalepsis—unverifiable effect of an effect—to a parergon or outside-work of pure reason. It is not understanding that is now a check on the Imagination, as it was in the Third Critique. It is figuration that supplements mere reason's calculative moral laziness.[40]

Despite the obvious connection, Spivak's notions of "figuration" and/or "figure" points to a different approach than Arendt's reading of Kant's aesthetic judgment for a political theory. The obvious similarity lies in Arendt's concept of the link between culture and politics: it is judgment rather than knowledge that provides this link for her.[41] Although Spivak agrees with Arendt that the reason is the ground of ethical commonality, she immediately underlines the fracture of this unity in Kant's essay on religion—the difference between mere and pure reason. In Arendt, however, reason remains the common ground without any further specification.

Arendt's approach depends on grounding political judgment on "reflective judgment" (Spivak's "representation without concept") that proceeds from the appreciation of the particular for which no universal rule or law exists, but for which some judgment can be reached universally from the perspective of what is shared in common. Arendt emphasizes "thinking from the standpoint of others" ("listening to the other as if one were listening to the self" in Spivak) and calls it the "enlarged mentality," made possible by the faculty of imagination. Like reflective judgment, political judgment does not determine its particular object under a pre-given universal law, but begins from the particular and arrives at the universal exemplified by it. In this, however, Arendt is committed to an ideal of political community, whereas it seems to me that Spivak presupposes such a community of democracy or reason as a minimal requirement but does not dwell on it as that which is theorized.[42] Because the fractured unity of reason already points to the limits of reason in terms of its ethical capacity, there can be no question of theorizing it.

This is why I wonder if a perspective such as Arendt's would have to accept as given the "immediacy" of Islam's image, which Said mentioned in *Covering Islam* and which I have discussed in the Introduction. The immediacy of Islam's image is what Derrida has called the "artifactual"—a portmanteau word, which refers to an "actuality" (also "news" in French) that is made or produced technologically.[43] The homogenizing aspect of the ideal of political community requires antagonistic images, which become explanatory by virtue of being broadcast. Although it can be argued that the immediacy of this image is a product of technological mediation, and hence of conceptual determination (rather than the immediacy of feeling in the sense of Kantian communicability before communication), it is also the image of a threatening other. The ideal political community is predisposed to such images as its constitutive other.

Contrary to the homogenizing and idealizing aspect of Arendt's reading of Kant, I see Spivak's version of Kantian representation-without-concept, that is, "figure" or "figuration," as radically heterogeneous. It not only disrupts cognitive control, artifactuality, or even consciousness-raising and resonates with a response, but it also has "immense range in space and time."[44] This immense range might be considered as historical, social, and cultural. The figure is also an act of imagination of the heterogeneity of the classed, gendered, and racialized other(s), and figuration is the risk of a response: being able to imagine the other as imaginative, as responsive. But it also implies that, being without concept, the "figure" is a figure without figure, already discontinuous with itself, always remaining singular. Response and responsibility is permanently and positively energized by the impossibility of communicating with it.

Although this is perhaps a somewhat different route, diverging from Spivak, I should also like to think the figure in terms of the concepts of messianicity and event. If religion is marked by the promise of justice-to-come, its repeatability is always already a figuration of the classed, gendered, and racialized others that traverse its movement in time and space. Responding responsibly to the actuality of Islam, to its time and timing, is giving an ear to the untimely and the disadjusted rather than seeing in this actuality nothing but the present image. That which comes to pass through the actuality of religion is the *promise* of justice-to-come in the opening of the inappropriable and the unanticipable. "The event," Derrida writes,

> is another name for that which, in the thing that happens, we can neither reduce nor deny (or simply deny). It is another name for experience itself, which is always experience of the other. The event cannot be subsumed under any other concept, not even that of being. The "there is" ("*il y a*") or the "that there is something rather than nothing" belongs perhaps to the experience of the event rather than to a thinking of being.[45]

I have already argued, in the seventh chapter, how in Levinas' philosophy there is a passage from a thinking of the "there is" as an overturning event to the concept of a vertical Other. De-transcendentalizing the political-religious text passes through the return of this event or experience of difference, which involves figures and figurations of class, gender, and race. This is *also* the moment of calling the Muslim native informant for a performance before the global audience in the emerging conjuncture of democracy. It is the inscriptive moment of voicing difference, of miraculating identity, which can be interrupted by allegorizing class, gender, and race, from within the alterity of the figure. Such an interruption maintains the eventfulness of the event, the to-come, writing for a future unbound.

Notes

Introduction

1 Edward W. Said, *Orientalism* (Harmondsworth: Penguin, 1978).

2 Mahmood Mamdani discussed this as the background of terrorism. See his *Good Muslim, Bad Muslim: America, the Cold War, and the Roots of Terror* (New York: Pantheon Books, 2004).

3 Gayatri Chakravorty Spivak, "Terror: A Speech After 9/11," *boundary 2*, 31.2 (2004): 102.

4 Edward W. Said, *Covering Islam: How the Media and the Experts Determine How We See the Rest of the World* (New York: Pantheon Books, 1981), 37–8, 39.

5 Tiziana Terranova, "Futurepublic: On Information Warfare, Bio-racism and Hegemony as Noopolitics," *Theory, Culture and Society*, 24.3 (2007): 129.

6 Terranova is more careful than Said in avoiding a framework that opposes bodily and unconscious dimensions to discursive articulation: "a hegemony that does not primarily operate at the level of statements, that is not primarily logico-discursive, although it can take that form, but one that considers those statements as part of a primary assemblage that links together statements, images and passions in the duration of a body, whereby affect functions as a mechanism of passage between affective and empirical facts" (Terranova, "Futurepublic," 133–4).

7 The impossibility of this is evident in Said's own analysis of the historical inseparability of Islam and the West in the first part of *Covering Islam* (3–32). But Said never tackled the problem on a methodological level.

8 Said, *Orientalism*, 6.

9 Clifford, James, "Introduction: Partial Truths," in *Writing Culture: The Poetics and Politics of Ethnography*, edited by James Clifford and George E. Marcus (Berkeley, Los Angeles, and London: University of California Press, 1986), 1–27, and "On Ethnographic Allegory," in *Writing Culture: The Poetics and Politics of Ethnography*, edited by James Clifford and George E. Marcus (Berkeley, CA, Los Angeles, CA, and London: University of California Press, 1986), 98–121.

10 Mehdi Abedi and Michael M. J. Fischer, *Debating Muslims: Cultural Dialogues in Postmodernity and Tradition* (Madison, WI: University of Wisconsin Press, 1990).

11 Pierre Bourdieu, *The Algerians*, translated by Alan C. M. Ross (Boston, MA: Beacon Press, 1962); *Outline of a Theory of Practice*, translated by Richard Nice

(Cambridge: Cambridge University Press, 1977); and *Algeria 1960*, translated by Richard Nice (Cambridge, London, and New York: Cambridge University Press, 1979).

12 Abdellah Hammoudi, "Phenomenology and Ethnography: On Kabyle Habitus in the Work of Pierre Bourdieu," in *Bourdieu in Algeria: Colonial Politics, Ethnographic Practices, Theoretical Developments*, edited by Jane E. Goodman and Paul A. Silverstein (Lincoln, NE and London: University of Nebraska Press, 2009), 199–254; Saba Mahmood, "Rehearsed Spontaneity and the Conventionality of Ritual: Reflections on the Egyptian Islamic Revival," *Cultural Anthropology*, 16.2 (2001a): 202–36; and Gregory Starrett, "The Hexis of Interpretation: Islam and the Body in the Egyptian Popular School," *American Ethnologist*, 22.4 (1995): 953–69.

13 T. E. Lawrence, *Seven Pillars of Wisdom* (London: Wordsworth Classics, 1997). Isabelle Eberhardt, *The Oblivion Seekers*, translated by Paul Bowles (San Francisco, CA: City Lights, 1975); and *In the Shadow of Islam*, translated by Sharon Bangert (London: Peter Owen, 1993).

14 Gilles Deleuze, "The Shame and the Glory: T.E. Lawrence," in *Essays Critical and Clinical*, translated by Daniel W. Smith and Michael A. Greco (Minneapolis, MN: University of Minnesota Press, 1997), 115–25.

15 Laura Rice, "'Nomad Thought': Isabelle Eberhardt and the Colonial Project," *Cultural Critique*, 17 (1990–1): 151–76. Deborah Root, "Misadventures in the Desert: *The Sheltering Sky* as Colonialist Nightmare," *Inscriptions*, 6 (1992): 81–96.

16 Fethi Benslama, *Psychoanalysis and the Challenge of Islam*, translated by Robert Bononno (Minneapolis, MN and London: University of Minnesota Press, 2009). Abdelkebir Khatibi, "Frontiers: Between Psychoanalysis and Islam," translated by Burcu Yalım, *Third Text*, 23.6 (2009): 689–96. Assia Djebar, *Far From Madina*, translated by Dorothy S. Blair (London: Quartet Books, 1995).

17 Gayatri Chakravorty Spivak, "Psychoanalysis in Left Field and Fieldworking: Examples to Fit the Title," in *Speculations after Freud: Psychoanalysis, Philosophy and Culture*, edited by Sonu Shamdasani and Michael Munchow (London and New York: Routledge, 1994), 41–76; and "Ghostwriting," *Diacritics*, 25.2 (1995): 65–84.

Chapter 1

1 Jean-François Lyotard, *The Postmodern Condition: A Report on Knowledge*, translated by Geoff Bennington and Brian Massumi (Minneapolis, MN: University of Minnesota Press, 1984).

2   Fredric Jameson, *Postmodernism, or the Cultural Logic of Late Capitalism*
    (Durham, NC: Duke University Press, 1991). Although the former view is not
    specific to Jean-François Lyotard and is shared by many in US academia, one must
    nonetheless underline that it is generally used in the wake of his influential work,
    The Postmodern Condition. Fredric Jameson's work on postmodernism can be
    regarded as an example of the latter view in the same general terms.

3   A similar discussion is found in Vicki Kirby, "Viral Identities: Feminisms and
    Postmodernisms," in *Australian Women: New Feminist Perspectives*, edited by Ailsa
    Burns and Norma Grieve (Oxford: Oxford University Press, 1993), 120–32.

4   James Clifford and George E. Marcus, eds, *Writing Culture: The Poetics and Politics
    of Ethnography* (Berkeley, CA, Los Angeles, CA, and London: University of
    California Press, 1986).

5   George E. Marcus and Michael M. J. Fischer, *Anthropology as Cultural Critique*
    (Chicago, IL: University of Chicago Press, 1986).

6   Johannes Fabian, *Time and the Other: How Anthropology Makes Its Object*
    (New York: Columbia University Press, 1983).

7   Stephen Tyler, "The Vision Quest in the West or What the Mind's Eye Sees," *Journal
    of Anthropological Research*, 40.1 (1984): 23–40.

8   See: James Clifford, *The Predicament of Culture: Twentieth Century Ethnography,
    Literature and Art* (Cambridge, MA and London: Harvard University Press,
    1988) and, James Clifford, *Routes: Travel and Translation in the Late Twentieth
    Century* (Cambridge, MA: Harvard University Press, 1997).

9   Johannes Fabian, *Time and the Work of Anthropology: Critical Essays 1971–1991*
    (Chur, Switzerland and Philadelphia, PA: Harwood Academic, 1991).

10 Stephen Tyler, *The Unspeakable: Discourse, Dialogue and Rhetoric in the Postmodern
    World* (Madison, WI: University of Wisconsin Press, 1988).

11 Michael M. J. Fischer and Mehdi Abedi, *Debating Muslims: Cultural Dialogues in
    Postmodernity and Tradition* (Madison, WI: University of Wisconsin Press, 1990).

12 Clifford Geertz, *Local Knowledge: Further Essays in Interpretive Anthropology*
    (New York: Basic Books, 1983).

13 To the above references, I must add the following: Renato Rosaldo: *Culture and
    Truth: The Remaking of Social Analysis*. (Boston, MA: Beacon Press, 1993). Lila
    Abu-Lughod: *Veiled Sentiments: Honor and Poetry in a Bedouin Society* (Berkeley,
    CA, Los Angeles, CA, and London: University of California Press, 1986) and
    Writing Women's Worlds: Bedouin Stories (Berkeley, CA, Los Angeles, CA, and
    London: University of California Press, 1993). Especially Abu-Lughod's works
    can also be regarded as part of the same general movement to the extent that they
    engage a similar notion of narrative. Abu-Lughod's project, however, is "writing
    against culture" as she is critical of the fetishistic abstraction that characterizes the
    conventional concept of culture. The culture concept makes cultural difference

seem evident and is a tool for making people other (Abu-Lughod, *Writing Women's Worlds*, 6–13). Her sensitivity to especially women's individual narratives opens up new avenues for ethnographic research. But since the anthropological relationship is not ethical singularity, the anthropologist has to acknowledge the impossibility of her task and should interrupt her text rather than making this acknowledgment a part of it.

14 I should also note the fact that ethnography itself is one of the methods employed in the early founding work of cultural studies at the Birmingham Centre for Contemporary Cultural Studies (the working class and/or audience ethnographies of Paul Willis and Dave Morley). Understandably this has led to growing interaction and mutual penetration between anthropology and cultural studies in the later development of these fields, especially in the United States. James Clifford has been one of the pioneers of a productive exchange between the two fields. George Marcus' more recent work (1998) is an example of this tendency of an ethnographic cultural studies.

15 James Clifford, *On the Edges of Anthropology: Interviews* (Chicago, IL: Prickly Paradigm Press, 2003), 11–13.

16 In retrospect, Clifford makes a nice discussion of his emphasis on "the tropological pre-encoding on the 'real'" in his recent book of interviews (Clifford, *On the Edges of Anthropology*, 13–14).

17 Among the other significant theoretical contributions, one must cite Johannes Fabian's *Time and the Other* as well as Marcus and Fischer's *Anthropology as Cultural Critique* and Rosaldo's *Culture and Truth*. Marcus and Fischer's work is closer to the tradition of non-positivist, interpretive anthropology. Although it carries Geertz's argument further by describing the ethnographic aspiration as "eliciting the native's point of view" and the "current problem" as requiring "new narrative motifs" (Marcus and Fischer, *Anthropology as Cultural Critique*, 26, 27), it does not go as far as Clifford in emphasizing the poetic aspect or the native's voice as a singular voice in ethnographic narrative. Fabian's work is original in its inventive and rich formulas such as "pushing the other back in time" or "denial of coevalness" (see especially the first three chapters), but its specific argument requires a separate reading for this reason. All of these works, however, share the general theoretical tendency that I have outlined in this article: a dialogical concern with difference and otherness in terms of speech rather than a merely scientific description of culture. There is a branch of feminist ethnography which is in critical dialogue with and can be regarded as part of postmodern ethnography. As it would require a more particular argument, it remains outside my concern in this chapter. I should nevertheless underline that, to the extent that it repeats the same conceptual gesture as Clifford's, the foregoing criticism should be applicable for it as well. Ruth Behar and Deborah A. Gordon's

important collection *Women Writing Culture* (Berkeley, CA and Los Angeles: University of California Press, 1996) brings valuable criticisms, especially in autonomizing women's voice and writing, but it does not go beyond what Clifford expects from the new ethnographer and remains within the postmodern ethnographic inclusion. A singularly important contribution is Kamela Visweswaran's *Fictions of Feminist Ethnography* (Minneapolis, MN: University of Minnesota Press, 1994). Her particular problematization of the boundaries of fiction and science, or literature and ethnography, as well as her employment of a deconstructive strategy of deferral as ethnographic instrument would require a particular reading. For Lila Abu-Lughod's feminist ethnographies of Bedouin women, see note 13.

18 Clifford has described himself in similar terms in the same interview: "I'm more marginal to the field. I frequent the borders. And that's my basic methodological principle, if one could call it that: never accept, never take as a beginning or ending point, what the discipline says it is. Ask instead: What do anthropologists, for all their disagreements, say they are not? Then focus on the historical relationship that is being policed, or negotiated—the process of disciplining that goes on at the edge" (*On the Edges of Anthropology*, 8). I certainly follow him in asking what scholars and researchers say they are not, and in focusing on the historical relationship (which I describe as his renegotiating the ethnographic contract). But instead of "disciplining that goes on at the edge," I would refer to the problem that keeps returning at the edge.

19 James Clifford, "Introduction: Partial Truths," in Clifford and Marcus, *Writing Culture*, 2.

20 Ibid., 5.

21 James Clifford, "On Ethnographic Allegory," in Clifford and Marcus, *Writing Culture*, 98–121.

22 Clifford, "Introduction: Partial Truths," 7.

23 Ibid.

24 I cannot help underlining a similarity here between the earliest avant-garde movement of modernity, that is, German romanticism, and one of the latest, postmodern ethnography: both depend heavily on a notion of incompleteness in different ways. In their fascinating work on German Romanticism, Phillippe Lacoue-Labarthe and Jean-Luc Nancy have observed a similar deconstruction of romantic incompletion in Blanchot's reading of the romantic journal *Atheneum*:

> Within romantic work, there is interruption and dissemination of the romantic work, and this in fact is not readable in the work itself, even and especially not, when the fragment, *Witz*, and chaos are privileged. Rather, according to another term of Blanchot, it is readable in the unworking [*desoeuvrement*], never named, and still less thought, that insinuates itself

through the interstices of the romantic work. Unworking is not incompletion, for as we have seen incompletion completes itself and is the fragment as such; unworking is nothing, only the interruption of the fragment. (Phillipe Lacoue-Labarthe and Jean-Luc Nancy, *The Literary Absolute: The Theory of Literature in German Romanticism*, translated by Philip Barnard and Cheryl Lester (Albany, NY: SUNY Press, 1988), 57; my emphasis)

See also Maurice Blanchot's essay on "The Atheneum," in *The Infinite Conversation*, translated by Susan Hanson (Minneapolis, MN and London: University of Minnesota Press, 1993), 351–9. The question of continuities and discontinuities between romanticism and postmodern ethnography might be a subject for further research, and it is surely part of the general question of romanticism's huge, complex, and ambivalent legacy today.

25 See: Michel Foucault, *Discipline and Punish: The Birth of the Prison*, translated by Alan Sheridan (Harmondsworth: Penguin, 1978); Michel Foucault, *Power/ Knowledge: Selected Interviews and Other Writings: 1972–1977*, edited by Colin Gordon (New York: Pantheon Books, 1980); Michel Foucault, *History of Sexuality*, Vol. 1, translated by Robert Hurley (New York: Vintage, 1980); and Gayatri Chakravorty Spivak, *Outside in the Teaching Machine* (New York and London: Routledge, 1993), 25–51.

26 Clifford, "On Ethnographic Allegory," 100.

27 Ibid., 99.

28 Ibid.

29 Paul de Man, *Blindness and Insight: Essays in the Rhetoric of Contemporary Criticism* (Minneapolis, MN: University of Minnesota Press, 1983), 207.

30 Clifford, "On Ethnographic Allegory," 99.

31 Marjorie Shostak, *Nisa: The Life and Words of a !Kung Woman* (New York: Vintage Books, 1983), 194.

32 De Man, *Blindness and Insight*, 207. "It is not her child yet, her girl, another self, but 'a big thing', non-self. This immediate aftermath of the birth is a singular moment, which is before a mother is able to say 'My child . . . today my child is no longer nursing'" (Shostak, *Nisa*, 198). "I must also add that a similar expression appears at another dramatic moment. When her husband realizes that Nisa is pregnant (from another man probably), she describes his look in the same manner: 'He looked at me, looked and looked and looked'" (ibid., 191). The expression is employed at dramatic moments when a certain crisis or limit appears. In marking this, the ethnographer is not eliciting or bringing out a native voice present to itself but marking the non-self-presence of the voice.

33 Clifford, "On Ethnographic Allegory," 101.

34 Ibid.

35 Clifford, "Introduction: Partial Truths," 12.

36 Although poetic and scientific dimensions can also be considered in terms of "style" rather than "voice," given the ethical value of the native voice in the new ethnographic text, I would like to suggest that part of the problem is precisely the consideration of the question of style in terms of voice. In other words, the concept of voice is essential to the postmodern ethnographic enterprise precisely because it requires the concept of self-presence that the concept of style cannot communicate directly because of its dependence on "writerly" concerns. In its opposition to the positivistic recording of observation that depends on a simple opposition between the literal and the allegorical, the new ethnographer has too quickly conquered the field of writing (forgetting that it is a force field). Since its ethical critique of representation does not involve the deconstruction of the subject form itself, the question of style can hardly be articulated within its limits.

37 Clifford, "Introduction: Partial Truths," 12.

38 Tyler, "The Vision Quest in the West," 25. For a critique of Tyler's work, especially his claim of following a Derridean approach, see Vicki Kirby, "Re-writing: Postmodernism and Ethnography," *Mankind*, 19 (1989): 36–45.

39 Clifford, "Ethnographic Allegory," 115–16.

40 Ibid., 117.

41 Leroi-Gourhan writes: "in its origins figurative art was directly linked with language and was much closer to writing (in the broadest sense) than to what we understand by a work of art" (*Gesture and Speech*. Translated by Ann Bostock Berger (Cambridge, MA and London: MIT Press, 1993), 190). Leroi-Gourhan's broad concept of writing was carefully read by Derrida himself in his *Of Grammatology* (*Of Grammatology*, translated by Gayatri Chakravorty Spivak (Baltimore, MD and London: Johns Hopkins University Press, 1976), 81–7).

42 Clifford, "On Ethnographic Allegory," 118.

43 Ibid.

44 I thank Trevor Hope for his help with this formulation.

45 Clifford, *Routes*, 167. The comparison of voice with photography in this passage is important. The living and natural character of voice is preferred over photography's attachment to an irreducible past. Does photography not become a metaphor for an absolute past that cannot be brought back in living speech?

46 Clifford, "Introduction: Partial Truths," 7, 15.

47 I am reminded of Gayatri Spivak's careful criticism of "uncritical inclusiveness": if the native voice is strategically excluded by conventional anthropology according to postmodernist ethnographers, it might have been more advisable to keep in mind that "any critique of strategic exclusions should bring analytical presuppositions into crisis" (*In Other Worlds*, 249) rather than trying to correct the anthropological record.

48 Jacques Derrida, *Speech and Phenomena and Other Essays on Husserl's Theory of Signs*, translated by David Allison (Evanston, IL: Northwestern University Press, 1973); and Jacques Derrida, *Of Grammatology*.

49 I thank Johannes Fabian for drawing my attention to this point.

50 For the notion of ex-appropriation, see: Jacques Derrida and Jean-Luc Nancy, "'Eating Well' or the Calculation of the Subject: An interview with Jacques Derrida," in *Who Comes After the Subject?*, edited by Eduardo Cadava, Peter Connor, and Jean-Luc Nancy (New York and London: Routledge, 1991), 105–7.

51 For a brilliant exposition of Derrida's concept of experience, see Zeynep Direk, "On the Sources and Structure of Derrida's Radical Notion of Experience," *Tympanum: A Journal of Comparative Literary Studies* 4 (2000). URL (accessed May 2, 2006): www.usc.edu/dept/comp-lit/tympanum/4/direk.html

52 Clifford, "Introduction: Partial Truths," 8.

53 Blanchot quoted in Mark Taylor, ed., *Deconstruction in Context: Literature and Philosophy* (Chicago, IL: University of Chicago Press, 1986), 1. The anthropologist would like to argue that he or she does not employ an interrogative abstract syntax in his or her interaction with the native. My point is precisely that this moment is bound to arise in the anthropological encounter. If ethnography is research, then it might be more advisable to describe its method as controlled intimacy than participant observation.

54 I thank Vicki Kirby for drawing my attention to Blanchot's uncanny formulation as well as the following quotation from Pierre Bourdieu. I am in debt to her reading of Blanchot in her *Telling Flesh* (New York and London: Routledge, 1997), 87–8, 156–7, and my following approach to "absolute past" is inspired by her argument to some extent. See especially Kirby, "Re-writing," 40.

55 Pierre Bourdieu, *Outline of a Theory of Practice*, translated by Richard Nice (Cambridge: Cambridge University Press, 1977), 81.

56 Ibid., 79.

57 In his work on Bergson, Gilles Deleuze has demonstrated the relevance of the concept of "absolute past" for memory and recollection: "There is therefore a 'past in general' that is not the particular past of a particular present but that is like an ontological element, a past that is eternal and for all time, the condition of passage of every particular present. It is the past in general that makes possible all pasts" (Gilles Deleuze, *Bergsonism*, translated by Hugh Tomlinson and Barbara Habberjam (New York: Zone Books, 1991), 56–7). The notion of an ontological element or condition here is not unproblematic. How could absolute past be absolute, if it did not mean, paradoxically, a radical de-ontologization of past? Deleuze here can only be followed in a sense closer to Derrida's notion of *différance* as "a past that has never been present, and which never will be, whose future

to come will never be a production or reproduction in the form of a presence" (Jacques Derrida, *Margins of Philosophy*, translated by Alan Bass (Chicago, Illinois: University of Chicago Press, 1982), 21–2).

58 In this context, see especially Jacques Derrida's early work on Husserlian phenomenology (*Speech and Phenomena*, 32–70). Bourdieu makes a radical use of the Husserlian difference between the temporality of retention and protension and the temporality of project. Hence his emphasis on a certain notion of "forthcoming reality" or "imminent" or "upcoming future" for creating a dynamic, fluctuating sense of social strategy employed by agents. Although Bourdieu's phenomenological attention to everyday temporality gives his framework a sense of flexibility and dynamism, metaphysics of presence survives the concept of habitus in his sociological adoption of metaphysical certainties. Indeed the Durkheimian reference should put a significant part of his theoretical claim in crisis, especially his ideas on the generative, inventive power of habitus. Bourdieu's materialism, his insistence on the role of bodily mimesis and his great thesis that social practice is not simply the following of an abstract rule or model, but always inscribed and embodied, aims to fight metaphysics in the concept of habitus. But in opposing the abstract to the habitus (as if the former is never part of the latter), and in simply reverting the problematic of mimesis, this sociological materialism reduces the philosophical problematic into a mere question of correct methodology and results in a dismissal of what might be called the transcendental or the virtual. For instance, Gilles Deleuze's work has shown that the virtual is never fully actualized in history, but is always part of it. In terms of Deleuze's work, Bourdieu's framework remains limited with the first passive synthesis of time—retention and protension (Gilles Deleuze and Felix Guattari, *What is Philosophy?* translated by Hugh Tomlinson and Graham Burchell (New York: Columbia University Press, 1994), 70–85).

59 Derrida, *Margins of Philosophy*, 6.

60 I should remind the reader here that in this supplementary economy of repetition (reconstruction, remaking), re-appropriation (information retrieval) is determined as ex-appropriation by absolute past or *différance*.

61 Clifford, *The Predicament of Culture*, 268.

62 Gayatri Spivak's work has persistently drawn our attention to what might be described as the inscription of sympathy in her deconstruction of humanist benevolence. In *The Postcolonial Critic*, she emphasizes that the benevolent subject's desire to do good and to promote the happiness of others involves "welcoming those others into his own understanding of the world, so that they too can be liberated and begin to inhabit a world that is the best of all possible worlds" (Gayatri Spivak, *The Postcolonial Critic*, edited by Sarah Harasym (New York and London: Routledge, 1990), 19). In the performance of such

good intention, the norm remains the benevolent humanist. Being benevolent or sympathetic toward "others" is thus a reduction of their difference and an inscription of sameness.

63 Jacques Derrida, *Aporias*, translated by T. Dutoit (Stanford, CA: Stanford University Press, 1993), 11–12 (my emphasis).

64 Gayatri Spivak, *A Critique of Postcolonial Reason* (Cambridge, MA: Harvard University Press, 1999), 5.

65 Ibid., 6.

66 Clifford, *Routes*. For an astute critical reading of Clifford's (and Homi Bhabha's) problematic of displacement, see Pheng Cheah, "Given Culture: Rethinking Cosmopolitical Freedom in Transnationalism," in *Cosmopolitics: Thinking and Feeling Beyond the Nation*, edited by Pheng Cheah and Bruce Robbins (Minneapolis, MN: University of Minnesota Press, 1998), 290–327. Clifford responds to this criticism in the same collection.

67 Clifford, *Routes*, 11.

68 Ibid., 35.

69 Ibid., 11.

70 Ibid., 182–3.

71 Ibid., 272.

72 Ibid., 10.

73 Ibid., 182.

74 Walter Benjamin, *Illuminations: Essays and Reflections*, edited by Hannah Arendt and translated by Harry Zohn (New York: Schocken Books, 1968), 69–82.

75 Ibid., 70.

76 Maurice Blanchot, *Friendship*, translated by Elizabeth Rottenberg (Stanford, CA: University of California Press, 1997), 59.

77 Benjamin, *Illuminations*, 75.

78 Nicolas Abraham and Maria Torok, *The Wolf Man's Magic Word: A Cryptonymy* (Minneapolis, MN: University of Minnesota Press, 1986); and Nicolas Abraham and Maria Torok, *The Shell and the Kernel: Renewals of Psychoanalysis* (Chicago, IL and London: University of Chicago Press, 1994).

79 Jacques Derrida, *The Ear of the Other: Otobiography, Transference, Translation*, translated by Peggy Kamuf and Avital Ronell (Lincoln, NE and London: University of Nebraska Press, 1988), 104.

80 Ibid., 122.

81 Clifford, "On Ethnographic Allegory," 111–19.

82 Ibid., 113.

83 Ibid., 115.

84 This is an important point that has implications for the so-called process of globalization. In a recent interview, Clifford reiterates the same point in a

criticism of a certain kind of criticism of globalization, of the idea that the spread of American hegemonic culture results in a wholesale destruction of local cultures and a worldwide homogenization of culture (Clifford, *On the Edges of Anthropology*, 33).

85 Tyler, "The Vision Quest in the West," 25.

86 Jacques Derrida, *Dissemination*, translated by Barbara Johnson (Chicago, IL: University of Chicago Press, 1981), 139.

87 For the notion of remark that I employ here, see Derrida's *Dissemination*, 258.

88 In *The Wolf Man's Magic Word*, Nicolas Abraham and Maria Torok argue that it is the incorporation that leads to the formation of a crypt inside the subject. This incorporation is, in their framework, a swallowing of words as opposed to their introjection, that is, the subject's articulation of his or her desire in words. It is in a rethinking of this analysis that Gayatri Spivak has produced the formulation, mentioned earlier, of "the encrypting of the name of the native informant as the name of Man" (Spivak, *A Critique of Postcolonial Reason*, 5).

89 Jacques Derrida, *Positions*, translated by Alan Bass (Chicago, IL: University of Chicago Press, 1981), 81.

90 Smadar Lavie, *The Poetics of Military Occupation: Mzeina Allegories of Bedouin Identity Under Israeli and Egyptian Rule* (Berkeley, CA, Los Angeles, CA, and London: University of California Press, 1990), 304.

91 Ibid., 304–8.

92 In a more comprehensive historical account, this should be taken back to the early ethnographic work at the Centre for Contemporary Cultural Studies in Birmingham, especially the working-class ethnographies of Paul Willis and Dave Morley. It is important to emphasize, however, that these works are stamped by a distinctively Marxist concern, like the whole work at the Birmingham Centre. This point must surely complicate my argument given earlier.

93 Indeed the same argument is also applicable for Lyotard's *Postmodern Condition*, in which the native is taken as the originating model of storyteller, that is, as an allegory of "language-game," which is the strategic concept in articulating the change in the status of knowledge in Western society.

94 Jameson, *Postmodernism*, 1–54.

Chapter 2

1 Sande Cohen, *Academia and the Luster of Capital* (Minneapolis, MN and London: University of Minnesota Press, 1993), 4.

2 Ibid., 3.

3 Abedi and Fischer, *Debating Muslims*, xix.

4   See: Gayatri Chakravorty Spivak, "Ghostwriting," *Diacritics*, 25.2 (1995): 65–84; and Dawn Rae Davis, "(Love is) the Ability of Not Knowing: Feminist Experience of the Impossible in Ethical Singularity," *Hypatia*, 17.2 (2002): 145–161.

5   Davis, "(Love is) the Ability of Not Knowing," 147.

6   Abedi and Fischer, *Debating Muslims*, 97.

7   Bourdieu, *Outline of a Theory of Practice*, 81.

8   Abedi and Fischer, *Debating Muslims*, 130.

9   Ibid., xxiii, xxxi, 148, 341.

10 Although it could be said that Abedi and Fischer's concept of dialogue finds its source in Gadamer, they somewhat differ from him by giving a much stronger emphasis to the "face-to-face" nature of the dialogue in a manner reminiscent of American interactionism (rather than Levinas). In any case, one expects more theoretical elaboration from the authors. To give only one example: in the context of a single passage, Fischer and Abedi put together several theorists and writers around a single idea, which they call a "cross-cultural" and "dialogical" approach: Derrida, Jabes, Levinas, Heidegger, Gadamer, and Mead (ibid., xxiii)! Their use of some of these theories is susceptible (the exception is their emphasis on the structure of question and answer in Socratic dialogue, which depends on Gadamer), as there is no attempt at a theoretical discussion, synthesis, or articulation of what this "cross-cultural dialogical" approach is in such a wide-ranging theoretical context.

11 Abedi and Fischer, *Debating Muslims*, 147.

12 Ibid., 148.

13 Ibid., 1–92.

14 Ibid., xxxii.

15 Ibid.

16 Ibid., 4.

17 While in the first chapter we have seen that Clifford's ethnographer took the position of the native (Cree hunter) in order to legitimize his concept of partial knowledge, we have here the opposite movement of the native becoming the ethnographer.

18 Abedi and Fischer, *Debating Muslims*, 5.

19 Michael M. J. Fischer, *Emergent Forms of Life and the Anthropological Voice* (Durham: Duke University Press, 2003), p. 197.

20 Emile Benveniste, *Problems in General Linguistics*, translated by Mary Elizabeth Meek (Coral Gables, FL: University of Miami Press, 1971).

21 Abedi and Fischer, *Debating Muslims*, 9.

22 Another difficult question might be whether such mirrorings and reflections can always be known, knowable, or under control. Given especially the extensive nature of the anthropological literature and publications, how do we know that

an autobiographical piece is not an unconscious mirroring of an ethnographic or anthropological text?

23 Some of the bracketed passages are only informative, such as the one on the "Anti-Baha'i society" (Abedi and Fischer, *Debating Muslims*, 48–9). A long parenthesis that gives historical information on the figure of Ayatullah Saduqi (ibid., 61) is interestingly interrupted by the autobiographer's ethnographic voice, which is going to tell a story "that can serve as a *symbol* of the situation" (ibid., 66; my emphasis): another shift by which the autobiographical discourse becomes the semantic means (symbol) of a larger etnographic observation about the attitude of Muslim clergy. The autobiographical part of the chapter ends with the "saga of the pain" of the family's move to the United States, left to another writing, and the autobiographer's dream of family reunion (ibid., 91). The last parenthesis is devoted to the brief survey of the relevant anthropological literature on "the cultural psychology of Iranian adjustment to the United states" (ibid.). These examples can be multiplied. The autobiographical is placed within the general anthropological discursive authority.

24 Ibid., 5.

25 Lacoue-Labarthe and Nancy, *The Literary Absolute*, 52–8.

26 Ibid., 52, 53, 54.

27 Ibid., 54.

28 Ibid. The first quote (about genuine *Witz*) is also a quote from Schlegel's fragment 394 (Friedrich Schlegel, *Philosophical Fragments*, translated by Peter Firchow (Minneapolis, MN and Oxford: University of Minnesota Press, 1991), 80).

29 Davis, "(Love is) the Ability of Not Knowing," 147.

30 Lacoue-Labarthe and Nancy, *The Literary Absolute*, 55–6.

31 Abedi and Fischer, *Debating Muslims*, 5. Would my attention be considered obsessional if I remind us that the same word ("sondage") might also be used in the oil industry? An industry that determined Iran's history and put a bloody stamp on the destiny of the Iranian people! The forgotten language of political economy leaves its mark on the graphing of the ethnos.

32 Paul Smith, *Discerning the Subject*, Foreword by John Mowitt (Minneapolis, MN: University of Minnesota Press, 1988), pp. 105–6; my emphasis.

33 There is a straightforwardly moral and ideological aspect of the first autobiographical chapter articulated in statements such as "the freedom of expression" and "the alien openness of Euro-American society" providing the "breeding ground for Islamic fundamentalism and other political activities" including communists, not to mention the descriptions of communists and Islamicists as dogmatic, dangerous, and narrow-minded people (Abedi and Fischer, *Debating Muslims*, 84–90). Is this the authenticity that is supposed to

make people see through the opaqueness of media and politics, by repeating the language of such apparatuses almost word for word? I find this disrespectful to the memories of thousands of young Iranian dissident students abroad during this period, who were closely watched, followed, arrested, tortured, and killed by the Shah's secret police. Anyone who had known one such young Iranian student knows what a difficult and fearful experience they had to endure in the face of genuine danger and threat to their lives. That these movements have unavoidably shared all the characteristics of similar political movements hegemonized by Stalinism or fundamentalism during a certain period of history should not have been abused in a text with such great ethical concerns as touching "the humanity of others." From a methodological point of view, we have no explanation of, not even a single question as to why communism and Islamicism exist among these student groups (for, after all, these are not just worldviews but also *social movements*), except a few facts stating the obvious (the fact that the Shah's regime was repressive, or the fact that Iran is an Islamic country, with a strong clergy who do not like the government, etc.).

34 Abedi and Fischer, *Debating Muslims*, 97–8.
35 Ibid., 102.
36 Ibid., 103.
37 Ibid., 105–6.
38 Abdelkebir Khatibi and Mohammed Sijelmassi, *The Splendor of Islamic Calligraphy* (London: Thames and Hudson, 1996), 18.
39 Ibid.
40 Ibid., 22.
41 Ibid., 42.
42 Ibid., 7.
43 Ibid., 14.
44 Ibid., 91.
45 Derrida, *Of Grammatology*, 167; and Abedi and Fischer, *Debating Muslims*, 112.
46 Derrida, *Of Grammatology*, 70–1.
47 Ibid., 66.
48 Abedi and Fischer, *Debating Muslims*, xxiii.
49 Gadamer's reading of Socratic dialogue evokes an image of partnership in the dialogue, but this remains debatable. In a symptomatic sentence, Gadamer writes: "The maieutic productivity of the Socratic dialogue, the art of using words as a midwife, is certainly *directed toward* the people who are the *partners in the dialogue*, but it is *concerned merely with the opinions they express*, the immanent logic of the subject matter that is unfolded in the dialogue. What emerges in its truth is the logos, which is neither mine nor yours and hence so far transcends the interlocutors' subjective opinions that even the person leading

the conversation knows that he does not know" (Hans-Georg Gadamer, *Truth and Method*, translated by Joel Weinsheimer and Donald G. Marshall (London and New York: Continuum, 2004), 361; my emphasis). It is noticeable that Gadamer's sentence *erases the subject* who directs the maieutic art toward the "partner(s?)." Assuming that the "art of dialogue" is really concerned *only with the opinions the partner expressed*, does the exchange taken as a whole not create *a change in the status of the partner* during and following the demonstration of the truth, especially in comparison with the Socratic subject of docta ignorantia, who obviously needs this partner, directs the art toward her, begins with the knowledge of not-knowing, demonstrates the truth, and thus reaches knowledge (unlike Davis'—and Spivak's—subject whose not-knowing is a refusal of knowledge as appropriation and seeking a different relationship with a partner based on the impossible experience of ethical singularity) (See: Gadamer, *Truth and* Method, 356–62; Davis, "(Love is) the Ability of Not Knowing"; and Spivak, "Ghostwriting.")? The point is precisely that, although the truth may be "neither mine nor yours," and even though it may be partial, it is always *represented* by the one who demonstrates it. Hence the limit of a concept of the ethico-political founded on an epistemological distinction between episteme and doxa.

50 Abedi and Fischer, *Debating Muslims*, 132.

51 Jacques Derrida, *Writing and Difference*, translated by Alan Bass (Chicago, IL: The University of Chicago Press, 1978), 251–77.

52 Abedi and Fischer, *Debating Muslims*, 107–8.

53 Ibid., 108.

54 Ibid., 112.

55 Ibid., 148.

56 Ibid., 102.

57 Ibid.

58 Khatibi and Sijelmassi, *The Splendor of Islamic Calligraphy*, 18.

59 Derrida, *Dissemination*, 26; my emphasis.

60 Derrida, *Of Grammatology*, 65.

61 Derrida also relates the trace with the *absolute past*. In the passive synthesis of time, the trace is that which cannot be summed up in the present, and both retention and protention are traces. But the privileging of protention (or anticipation) would efface the fundamental passivity of the always-already there. The trace thus refers to an absolute past, that is, a past that has never been present (ibid., 66).

62 Ibid., 70.

63 Ibid., 66.

64 Blanchot, *The Infinite Conversation*, 357. Blanchot writes: "to speak poetically is to make possible a non-transitive speech whose task is not to say things (not to

disappear in what it signifies), but to say (itself) in letting (itself) say, yet without taking itself as the new object of this language without object" (ibid.).

65 Derrida, *Positions*, 81.

66 Abedi and Fischer, *Debating Muslims*, 406–19.

67 Ibid., 220–1.

68 Walter Benjamin: *Reflections: Essays, Aphorisms, Autobiographical Writings*, translated by Edmund Jephcott. Edited and with an Introduction by Peter Demetz (New York: Schocken Books, 1978), 146–62 and 239–73

69 See: Benjamin, *Illuminations*, 155–200; Abedi and Fischer, *Debating Muslims*, 157–220.

70 Abedi and Fischer, *Debating Muslims*, 152–3.

71 Ibid., 153.

72 Derrida, *Margins of Philosophy*, 5–6, 21.

73 Abedi and Fischer, *Debating Muslims*, 153.

74 Ali Shariati, *The Hajj*, translated by Ali A. Behzadnia, MD and Najla Denny (Houston, TX: Free Islamic Literatures Inc., 1994).

75 Ali Shariati has two other important texts on women: "Our Expectations of the Muslim Woman" and "Fatima is Fatima." While the former is a programmatic text, which defines the active place of woman in Islamic revolution and society, the latter is a praise of Fatima as a subjective political and moral model for Muslim woman. Shariati certainly intended to produce his own version of emancipated Muslim woman. I thank Jason Bahbak Mohaghegh for drawing my attention to these texts.

76 Deleuze and Guattari, *Anti-Oedipus*, translated Robert Hurley, Mark Seem, and Helen R. Lane (Minneapolis, MN: University of Minnesota Press, 1983), 10.

77 Abedi and Fischer, *Debating Muslims*, 5.

78 Spivak, *A Critique of Postcolonial Reason*, 106.

79 Abedi and Fischer, *Debating Muslims*, 4.

80 Ibid., xix.

81 Ibid., xxiii.

82 Ibid.; my emphasis.

83 Although the authors admit that the concept of dialogue does not exclude relations of power, especially in a pedagogical context (imam-student relationship), obviously they have an investment in the ethical import of this concept, conceived especially as a face-to-face relationship and in terms of its value as speech or word. Interestingly, they never explore Levinas's argument that the teacher's speech is not only a thematization but also "an appeal addressed to my attention" (Emmanuel Levinas, *Totality and Infinity: An Essay on Exteriority*, translated by Alphonso Lingis (Pittsburgh, PA: Duquesen University Press, 1969), 99). For Levinas, there is an internal relationship between ethical transcendence and the transmission of knowledge.

Chapter 3

1 See: Bourdieu, *Outline of a Theory of Practice*; Pierre Bourdieu, *The Logic of Practice*, translated by Richard Nice (Stanford, CA: Stanford University Press, 1990) and "Making the Economic Habitus: Algerian Workers Revisited," *Ethnography* 1.1 (2000): 17–41.

2 Jane E. Goodman and Paul A. Silverstein, eds, *Bourdieu in Algeria: Colonial Politics, Ethnographic Practices, Theoretical Developments* (Lincoln, NE and London. University of Nebraska Press), 2.

3 Pierre Bourdieu, *Sketch for a Self-Analysis*, translated by Richard Nice (Cambridge: Polity 2007), 37–65. This part of Bourdieu's *Sketch for a Self-Analysis* was translated and published before with the title "Algerian Landing" in *Ethnography* (2004). Bourdieu relates numerous instances in which he was obstructed or followed, or his informants were harassed and threatened by the military authority (Bourdieu, *Sketch for a Self-Analysis*, 38, 50, 51–6; and Pierre Bourdieu, "Algerian Landing," translated by Richard Nice and Loïc Wacquant, *Ethnography* 5.4 (2004): 415–43, 416, 426, 427–32). What he fails to articulate is the fact that such attitudes were part of the larger and complex system of colonialism, which also *needed him and placed him there*. To use his own metaphor of "landing," Bourdieu forgets that it was a French plane whose departure and arrival was authorized by the French government that landed him in Algeria. It was sufficient for him to show, when asked by the local military force in the Algerian countryside, his document of permission, signed by the colonial authority. Can one imagine his student and coresearcher Abdelmalek Sayad doing research *on his own* in the same place, which is his own country? Would he be given permission to do research without his French teacher? If forgetting one's national identity is a requirement of scientific objectivity, it seems that Sayad would hardly be able to reach such epistemological heights.

4 Bourdieu, *Outline of a Theory of Practice*, 34–5. It is strange to use this expression for a society that should know no bureaucracy *by Bourdieu's own definition*. This is not only another instance of the discrepancy between theory and example, but also, in isolating the Kabylia as a "closed, traditional society," Bourdieu repeats the same discursive violence as colonialism and erases the actually existing official knowledge inscribed by the colonial government. Of course, the Kabylians and Algerians also experienced Ottoman imperial bureaucracy long before colonialism. Northern Algeria became an Ottoman administrative region following the final conquest in 1529.

5 If, as Bourdieu succinctly argues, practice and representations are endowed with partial systematicity, this is because they are "the product of a small number of generative schemes that are *practically interchangeable*, i.e. capable of producing

equivalent results from the point of view of the 'logical' demands of practice"
(Bourdieu, *Outline of a Theory of Practice*, 113).

6   Ibid., 98.

7   Ibid., 105. Hence the calendar is "synoptic," following Cournot's account of the
formation of linear series in spoken or written discourse (ibid., 97–109, 221).

8   Ibid., 22; and Pierre Bourdieu, *The Logic of Practice*, 106.

9   Bourdieu, *Outline of a Theory of Practice*, 5–6.

10 Ibid., 171.

11 Ibid., 96.

12 Pierre Bourdieu, *In Other Words: Essays Towards a Reflexive Sociology*, translaed by
Richard Nice (Stanford, CA: Stanford University Press, 1990), 188.

13 See Jacques Rancière's astute criticism of Bourdieu's concept of sociology: "The
Ethic of Sociology" (Jacques Rancière, *The Intellectual and His People: Staging the
People, Vol. 2*, translated by David Fernbach (London and New York: Verso, 2012),
144–70). In an earlier piece, Rancière also showed the Platonic aspect of Bourdieu's
concept of doxa: "the right opinion always misses itself" (Jacques Rancière, *The
Philosopher and His Poor*, translated by John Drury, Corinne Oster, and Andrew
Parker (Durham and London: Duke University Press, 2004), 169).

14 Les Back, "Portrayal and Betrayal: Bourdieu, Photography and Sociological Life,"
The Sociological Review, 57.3 (2009): 476–81.

15 Bourdieu, *The Logic of Practice*, 3.

16 Ibid.

17 Goodman and Silverstein, *Bourdieu in Algeria*, 22–3.

18 Jane E. Goodman, "The Proverbial Bourdieu: Habitus and the Politics of
Representation in the Ethnography of Kabylia," in *Bourdieu in Algeria: Colonial
Politics, Ethnographic Practices, Theoretical Developments*, edited by Jane E.
Goodman and Paul A. Silverstein (Lincoln, NE and London: University of
Nebraska Press, 2009), 110–13.

19 See: Starrett, "The Hexis of Interpretation," 953–69; and Bourdieu, *Outline of a
Theory of Practice*, 82, 87, 93–4.

20 For instance "ethos and tastes" are "doubtless sensed in the imperceptible cues of
body *hexis*" (Bourdieu, *Outline of a Theory of Practice*, 82); "Body *hexis* speaks
directly to the motor function, in the form of a pattern of postures that is both
individual and systematic, because linked to a whole system of techniques
involving the body and tools, and charged with a host of social meanings and
values" (ibid., 87); and the much-quoted passage, where the sense of *hexis* is
closest to habitus: "Bodily *hexis* is political mythology realized, *em-bodied*,
turned into a permanent disposition, a durable manner of standing, speaking,
and thereby of *feeling* and *thinking*. The oppositions which mythico-ritual logic
makes between the male and the female and which organize the whole system of

values reappear, for example, in the gestures and movements of the body, in the form of the opposition between the straight and the bent, or between assurance and restraint" (ibid., 93–4). The last quote is followed by the famous Kabylian examples of the manners of walking of men and women.

21 Starrett, "The Hexis of Interpretation," 954; my emphasis.

22 Ibid., 953; my emphasis.

23 Ibid., 954–9.

24 Ibid., 960.

25 Although Starrett makes reference to Foucault's concept of modern discipline, we need to clarify that his approach is completely different than Foucault. Foucault's concept of discourse does not place consciousness or the constitutive subject at the origin of discourse, but sees a discursive formation in terms of a regularity of correlations, positionings, functionings and transformations (Michel Foucault, *Archeology of Knowledge, and the Discourse on Language*, translated by A. M. Sheridan Smith (New York: Pantheon Books, 1972), 38). For Foucault, discourse renders new realities and is related with visibilities, but is never identical to either of these. What Foucault calls the "medical gaze," for instance, is a complex perceptual-linguistic formation that makes the invisible pathological body visible and readable through the employment of a plurality of senses (Michel Foucault, *The Birth of the Clinic. An Archeology of Medical Perception*, translated by A. M. Sheridan (London: Tavistock Publications, 1976)). Similarly, Foucault's concept of power-knowledge would require a different approach to the field of colonial discourse. It seems that Starrett uses vague notions of "discourse" and "discipline" that are attributed to Foucault, as well as the concept of ideology, which Foucault never uses. See also Gilles Deleuze, *Foucault*, translated by Sean Hand (Minneapolis, MN: University of Minnesota Press), 47–69.

26 Starrett, "The Hexis of Interpretation," 963.

27 Ibid., 963; my emphasis.

28 Although Starrett writes on the concept of habitus (rather than specifically on Bourdieu's ethnography of Algeria), he has completely ignored that Bourdieu has produced major empirical research in the field of education and has much to say on the relationship between pedagogy, education, and class. See, for instance, Pierre Bourdieu and Jean-Claude Passeron, *Reproduction in Education, Society and Culture*, translated by Richard Nice (London, Newburry Park, New Delhi: Sage, 1977).

29 Starrett, "The Hexis of Interpretation," 959.

30 Ibid., 953.

31 One is reminded of Homi Bhabha's notions of ambivalence and mimicry. See: *The Location of Culture* (London and New York: Routledge, 1994).

32 Bourdieu, *Outline of a Theory of Practice*, 23–4, 84, 124.

33 Bourdieu's later work, in which he is quite explicit on the role of consciousness and reasoning is perhaps more elaboration than revision or correction of his earlier theory of practice: "One cannot do sociology without accepting what classical philosophers called the 'principle of sufficient reason' and without assuming, among other things, that social agents don't do just anything, that they are not foolish, that they do not act without reason . . . Agents may engage in reasonable forms of behavior without being rational; they may engage in behaviors one can explain, as the classical philosophers would say, with the hypothesis of rationality, without reason as its principle" (Pierre Bourdieu, *Homo Academicus*, translated by Peter Collier (Stanford, CA: Stanford University Press, 1998), 75–6). Starrett (and as we shall see below Mahmood and Hammoudi) pay no attention to such specifications, which delineate a specific level of everyday action.

34 Bourdieu, *Outline of a Theory of Practice*, 76.

35 Ibid.

36 This has been pointed out by more than one critic. See especially Jacques Rancière's devastating criticisms of Bourdieu: *The Philosopher and His Poor*, 165–202; *The Intellectual and His People*, 144–70.

37 See: Mahmood, "Rehearsed Spontaneity," 827–53; Saba Mahmood, "Feminist Theory, Embodiment, and the Docile Agent: Some Reflections on the Egyptian Islamic Revival," *Cultural Anthropology*, 16.2 (2001): 202–36 and *The Politics of Piety: The Islamic Revival and the Feminist Subject* (Princeton, NJ and Oxford: Princeton University Press, 2005).

38 See: Mahmood, *The Politics of Piety*, 17–18, 27–34, 114–15, 120–2, 136–8; Foucault, *The Care of the Self: The History of Sexuality, Volume 3*, translated by Robert Hurley (New York: Pantheon Books, 1986), 37–45. Mahmood agrees with Starrett's criticism of Bourdieu's concept of habitus "as unconscious and ineffable phenomena, learned through imitative practice rather than explicit discourse" (Mahmood, "Rehearsed spontaneity," 836) as well as "Bourdieu's neglect of the role explicit discourse plays in fixing the ideological meaning of embodied practices" (Mahmood, *The Politics of Piety*, 139). She also shares Starrett's view that discourses about body express struggles over contrasting models of society. But she disagrees with the status Starrett accords to the body: "Starrett . . . fails to consider . . . whether the body's potentiality is significant to every ideological system in the same way . . . the body's conceptual relationship with the self and others, and the ways in which it articulates with structures of authority, varies under different discursive regimes of power and truth precisely because the body's ritual practices endow it with different kinds of capabilities" (Mahmood, "Rehearsed spontaneity," 836–7). Given that the body's potential itself ("capabilities" in the plural) is endowed by its ritual practices in the end, it is difficult to see how this is different from Starrett's body as medium. Indeed Mahmood writes that "body is not a medium of signification but the

substance and the necessary *tool* through which the embodied subject is formed" (Mahmood, *The Politics of Piety*, 29; my emphasis).

39 Judith Butler, *Bodies That Matter: On the Discursive Limits of "Sex"* (New York: Routledge, 1993).

40 Mahmood, *The Politics of Piety*, 22.

41 Ibid., 23–4. See also: Claire Colebrook, "Ethics, Positivity and Gender: Foucault, Aristotle and the Care of the Self," *Philosophy Today*, 42.1 (1998): 40–52.

42 Mahmood, *The Politics of Piety*, 28.

43 Mahmood, "Rehearsed spontaneity," 838.

44 Mahmood, *The Politics of Piety*, 136.

45 Ibid., 27.

46 In making this connection, Mahmood follows Colebrook's work on Foucault and Aristotle (Colebrook, "Ethics, Positivity and Gender"). As my stated criticism also implies, however, she does not pay sufficient attention to the important differences that Colebrook draws between Foucault and Aristotle on the one hand (the double register of difference and proximity between the ancient and contemporary worlds), and Foucault and the neo-Aristotelians such as MacIntyre and Taylor on the other, thereby missing Foucault's—and Colebrook's—insistence on *the affirmative openness of ethics*, as opposed to the neo-Aristotelian emphasis on its shared and consensual nature (Colebrook, "Ethics, Positivity and Gender," 43, 45–8).

47 Mahmood, "Rehearsed spontaneity," 839.

48 Ibid., 838.

49 In her Preface to Félix Ravaisson's work *Of Habit*, Catherine Malabou writes that habit has two senses according to this philosopher: "a general and permanent way of being" and "an acquired habit, but habit that is contracted, owing to a change, with respect to the very change that gave birth to it" (Catherine Malabou, "Addiction and Grace: Preface to Felix Ravaisson's *Of Habit*," in *Of Habit*, Felix Ravaisson, translated by Claire Carlisle and Mark Sinclair (London and New York: Continuum, 2008), viii). Malabou reminds us that this is also Deleuze's approach to habit: "habit draws from repetition something new: difference" (Gilles Deleuze, *Difference and Repetition*, translated by Paul Patton (New York: Columbia University Press 1994), 70). I leave aside here the question of the status of Ravaisson's perspective with regard to the deconstruction of habit, which Malabou extensively discusses (Malabou, "Addiction and Grace," xiii–xx).

50 Mahmood, "Rehearsed spontaneity," 843. Both of these have highly specific senses, which dismiss any stereotype of Muslim faith drawing on psychological generalizations such as fear and obedience. Apart from humility, *hushu* also implies a feeling of ease and internal peace, whereas *khashya* signifies a kind of fear mixed with admiration for the greatness of the one who is feared, rather than fear out of one's own weakness.

51 Mahmood, "Rehearsed spontaneity," 843.

52 Ibid., 837.

53 Bourdieu, *The Logic of Practice*, 73; my emphasis.

54 Of course all mimesis is not acquisitive, there is also suggestive mimesis (see especially Mikkel Borch-Jacobsen, *The Emotional Tie: Psychoanalysis, Mimesis, Affect*, translated by Douglas Brick (Stanford, CA: Stanford University Press, 1992), 98–120). Although Bourdieu emphasizes acquisitive mimesis (as a concept of "socialization") and reproduces Plato's restricted concept of mimesis (*The Republic*, translated by Raymond Larson (Arlington Heights, IL: Harlan Davidson, 1979), 376c–403e, 595a–608b), some of his examples imply this more decentered form of mimesis.

55 Mahmood, *The Politics of Piety*, 32.

56 Judith Butler, "Performativity's Social Magic," in *Bourdieu: A Critical Reader*, edited by Richard Schusterman (Oxford: Blackwell, 1999), 115–16.

57 Ibid., 126–7. It is interesting that although Butler refers to Bergson's relevance in a footnote, she does not follow his well-known distinction. This is consistent with her line of criticism, which *cries for a concept of time, or more specifically of absolute past*. Butler argues that, given that the social and linguistic dimensions of performative speech cannot be strictly separated when the body becomes the site of their productivity, what is needed is a thinking of the generative dimension of *habitus* in relation to the efficaciousness of the illocutionary performative speech act (ibid., 115). She also rightly criticizes Bourdieu for confusing "speaking with authority" with "being authorized to speak" and argues for "the *expropriability* of the dominant, 'authorized' discourse that constitutes one potential site of its subversive resignification" (ibid., 123). Interestingly, a certain phrase, "over time," returns in Butler's text: "habitus is formed over time" (ibid., 116); "the girl becomes transitively 'girled' over time" (ibid., 120); and racial and gendered "slurs accumulate over time" (ibid., 125). This phrase refers merely to the passing of time, without actually analyzing the "passing" itself (as I will show, this is the analysis Derrida and Deleuze performed in different ways in relation to Husserl and Bergson). In her example of being "girled," Butler admits a *definite beginning*: "being called a 'girl' *from the inception of existence* is a way in which the girl becomes 'transitively' girled over time" (ibid., 125; my emphasis).

58 Henri Bergson, *Matter and Memory*, translated by Nancy Margaret Paul and W. Scott Palmer (New York: Zone Books, 1991), 79–90.

59 Maurice Merleau-Ponty, *Phenomenology of Perception*, translated by Colin Smith (London and New York. Routledge, 1989), 242. Merleau-Ponty's later writings go further away from the habitual body and begin to include a new dimension of "immemorial time" or "time before time," a past that has never been present but simultaneous with every present (Maurice Merleau-Ponty, *The Visible and the Invisible*, translated by Alphonso Lingis (Evanston, IL: North Western University

Press, 1997), 243–4). For a series of essays that take up the later Merleau-Ponty's "quasi-Bergsonian" reversal of his earlier view and take his thought further in the direction of Bergson, see: Alia Al-Saji, "Merleau-Ponty and Bergson: Bodies of Expression and Temporalities in the Flesh," *Philosophy Today*, 45.5 (2001): 110–23; "The Temporality of Life: Merleau-Ponty, Bergson, and the Immemorial Past," *The Southern Journal of Philosophy*, 45.2 (2007): 177–206; and "'A Past Which Has Never Been Present': Bergsonian Dimensions in Merleau-Ponty's Theory of the Prepersonal," *Research in Phenomenology*, 38 (2008): 41–71. Al-Saji draws our attention to the concepts of flesh, the invisible and pre-personal life in later Merleau-Ponty. For Merleau-Ponty's earlier "misreading" of Bergson in his *Phenomenology*, see Elizabeth Grosz, *Time Travels: Feminism, Nature, Power* (Durham: Duke University Press, 2005), 116–17.

60 Unlike Michel Foucault's agents (*History of Sexuality*, Vol. 1, 31–2). For an excellent reading of this passage in Foucault, see Stephen Jackson, "The Subject of Time in Foucault's Tale of Jouy," *SubStance*, 39.2 (2010): 39–51.

61 Bourdieu, *Outline of a Theory of Practice*, 105; my emphasis.

62 This distinction is almost the same as Bergson's distinction between quantitative (measurable, homogenenous, continuous) and qualitative (immeasurable, heterogeneous, discontinuous) multiplicities (Henri Bergson, *Time and Free Will: An Essay on the Immediate Data of Consciousness*, translated by F. L. Pogson (London: George Allen and Unwin, 1950), 121–3). The kind of relationship (or nonrelationship) between the use of statistical and ethnographic methods in Bourdieu's texts (especially his ethnographies of class taste or education) must be examined from this point of view.

63 Bourdieu, *The Logic of Practice*, 69; my emphasis.

64 See also Bourdieu's interesting discussion of linguistic and "mythical roots" (Bourdieu, *Outline of a Theory of Practice*, 120–1).

65 Pure memory records "all the events of our daily life as they occur in time; it neglects no detail; it leaves to each fact, to each gesture, its place and date. Regardless of utility or of practical application, it stores up the past by the mere necessity of its own nature" (Bergson, *Matter and Memory*, 81). It is "where all the events of our past life are set out in their smallest details" (ibid., 167). That is to say, nothing is ever privileged in the absolute memory.

66 This is why, while literature works analogically, Bourdieu often directly refers to the proverbs as a sociologist interested in practical knowledge. Jane Goodman develops a brilliant criticism of Bourdieu's use of proverbs, his dependence on the notion of a timeless mythopoietic culture, a Herderian oral lore that represented an unmediated native spirit (Goodman, "The Proverbial Bourdieu", 94–132). As she aptly puts it, Bourdieu considers the proverb an "unmediated sign of habitus" without attending to the pragmatics of its use (ibid., 99). But the concept of "miniaturization of language" that Goodman employs to criticize Bourdieu keeps

the same concept of proverb intact. I am reminded here of Walter Benjamin's description of proverb: "a ruin which stands on the site of an old story and in which a moral twines about a happening like ivy around a wall" (Benjamin, *Illuminations*, 108). By defining the proverb as *ruin*, Benjamin refers to the unavoidable loss in the story it tells. The proverb does not miniaturize language, like a plan or representation of a principle (which is how Bourdieu often treats it); it is *produced* where language experiences its limit, that is to say, "the old story" is not "miniaturized" (as if the teller knows what it is), but it is told otherwise, allegorically.

67 In a later work, *Language and Symbolic Power*, Bourdieu makes numerous references to the *heretical* discourse, but his focus immediately turns to the question of its effectivity. It must, for instance, "produce a new common sense and integrate within it the previously tacit or repressed practices within it and experiences of an entire group, investing them with the legitimacy conferred by public expression and collective recognition" (Pierre Bourdieu, *Language and Symbolic Power*, translated by Gino Raymond and Matthew Adamson (Cambridge, MA: Harvard University Press, 1991), 129). In other words, the question of effectivity is not measured in terms of the newness or difference of heretical discourse, but in terms of its capacity to be accepted by its presumed addressees. Furthermore, Bourdieu sees this capacity as an *epistemological* question: "to name the unnamed and to give the beginnings of objectification to pre-verbal and pre-reflexive dispositions and ineffable and unobservable experiences, through words which by their nature make them common and communicable, therefore meaningful and socially sanctioned" (ibid.). It is Bourdieu's unquestioned faith in good, correct epistemology that his critics like Starrett and Mahmood fail to read in him and may therefore be sharing with him. Given the bitter lesson of the twentieth century, the task of a radical, progressive politics must be to keep the so-called pre-verbal and the pre-reflexive as open as possible rather than simply naming it once more.

68 For the circular nature of Bourdieu's concept of misrecognition, see Rancière (Rancière, *The Intellectual and His People*, 161–3). It is not for nothing that Bourdieu refers to his "deep revulsion . . . of the vision of sexuality associated with Georges Bataille and Pierre Klossowski" (Bourdieu, *Sketch for a Self-Analysis*, 2). Bataille's theory of "general economy" focuses on the useless, excess energy as well as loss and destruction, involving not only eroticism, but also religion, mysticism, and poetry (Georges Bataille, *The Accursed Share, Vol. I*, translated by Robert Hurley (New York, Zone Books, 1988), 19–41). For an interesting work that connects Bergson and Bataille, see Suzanne Guerlac: "The Useless Image: Bataille, Bergson, Magritte," *Representations*, 97 (2007): 28–56.

69 Lecture April 4, 1978 (translated by Melissa MacMahon). www.webdeleuze.com/php/sommaire.html

70 See the lecture, March 28, 1978 (translated by Melissa MacMahon). www.
    webdeleuze.com/php/sommaire.html. See also Immanuel Kant, *Critique of
    Judgment*, translated by James Creed Meredith (Oxford: Oxford University
    Press, 2007) §26.

71 Bourdieu, *Outline of a Theory of Practice*, 8. Indeed in a long footnote, Bourdieu
    goes as far as saying that the structure of becoming in the sense of musical theory is
    more appropriate than the concept of linguistic structure to explain any temporally
    structured practice. In practice, musical or poetic structure can be communicated
    only in and through time. But he conceives of time as a "chronologically articulated
    series" that is to say, again in terms of homogeneously divided units (ibid., 198–9).
    Surprisingly, this is the same structure of totalization he warned us about in the
    example of the transformation of time into linear series in the instance of the
    synoptic calendar!

72 Ibid., 105.

73 Lecture April 4, 1978.

74 Rancière, *The Philosopher and His Poor*, 199.

75 Ibid. Although Rancière regards this torsion as the effect of a specific European
    conjuncture (a time when art is freed from authority and before it is reified in the
    notion of autonomy), there is no reason why it should be limited to this particular
    instance. With Gauny the carpenter, we are also reminded of Bourdieu's well-known
    analysis of the Kabyle house (Bourdieu, *The Logic of Practice*, 271–83). Bourdieu has
    forgotten that it is the destructive nature of colonial light that enabled him to give a
    cultural description (an ethno-graphy) of the Kabyle house. He provided us with a
    clear picture and a neatly drawn plan of a *house that was actually in ruins*. Moreover,
    it seems as if this house has never given birth to any daydreamer (but what kind of
    a house was Mouloud Mammeri born into?); its walls, its passages and its corners
    have never been folded into an absolute memory, one that is also underlined by
    Bachelard: "An entire past comes to dwell in a new house . . . And the daydream
    deepens to the point where an immemorial domain opens up for the dreamer of a
    home beyond man's earliest memory. The house, like fire and water, will permit me
    . . . to recall flashes of daydreams that illuminate the synthesis of the immemorial
    and the recollected" (Gaston Bachelard, *The Poetics of Space*, translated by Maria
    Jolas (Boston: Beacon, 1969), 5). In Chapter 7, we will see that women remember a
    different house: one they inhabit but are not allowed to inherit.

76 Fanny Colona, "The Phantom of Dispossession: From *The Uprooting . . . to The
    Weight of the World*," in *Bourdieu in Algeria: Colonial Politics, Ethnographic
    Practices, Theoretical Developments*, edited by Jane E. Goodman and Paul A.
    Silverstein (Lincoln, NE and London: University of Nebraska Press, 2009), 74.
    See also Philip Smith's interesting work, which discusses the presence of Proust in
    Bourdieu's text (Philip Smith, "Marcel Proust as Successor and Precursor to Pierre
    Bourdieu: A Fragment," *Thesis Eleven*, 79 (2004): 105–11). While Smith thinks

that Bourdieu's determinism can be corrected by Proust's notion of remembrance, I think that this requires, first, a general discussion of the role of literary reference in Bourdieu's work; and second, a discussion of the concept of time in Bourdieu as well as a passage from habit to memory and from the anticipatory horizon of forthcoming time to the radical passivity of the absolute past (as I will demonstrate below).

77 This essay is a shortened version of Bourdieu's *Travail et travailleurs en Algerie*, published in 1963.

78 Bourdieu, *Algeria 1960*, 2.

79 In this context, Bourdieu makes a brilliant criticism of Daniel Lerner's sociology of modernization (ibid., 31–2).

80 Ibid., 9.

81 Ibid., 8. In the later theoretical texts such as the *Outline* or *The Logic of Practice*, the "forthcoming reality" is given a positive sense, constitutive of habitus and practice, in opposition to the pure project of negative freedom in Hegel and Sartre (see, for instance, Bourdieu, *The Logic of Practice*, 52–3).

82 It seems that Bourdieu has a similar kind of problem in his research in Béarn (Bourdieu, "The Peasant and His Body," *Ethnography*, 5.4 (2004): 579–99). The conditions of marriage change, but the poor Béarnais men get stuck in their old system and suffer from not being able to find women to marry them! The peasant's practical world is collapsed in confrontation with modernity, and it is this that transforms the living, practical, problem-solving habit into habit in the bad sense of dead automatism, a kind of getting stuck into a world already past. The kind of approach Mahmood and Starrett attribute to Bourdieu might actually be the particular historical condition of the peasant under modernity for Bourdieu. But, even if we follow Bourdieu in forgetting the huge difference between modernity under the colonial condition and modernity in Europe (and even if we forgive Bourdieu's reliance on mainly male informants at the expense of younger women in the Béarnais case, see, for instance, an informative critical reading by Tim Jenkins ("Bourdieu's Béarnais Ethnography," *Theory, Culture & Society*, 23.6 (2006): 45–72)), his thesis is still highly debatable, as we are witness, on the contrary, to the incredible creativity of the peasant under new conditions: the so-called informal sector in the modern cities of the Third World, which Bourdieu calls "sub-proletariat" (and which is indeed a better name for this category), is the mass field of an immense creativity of jobs of all kinds. Bourdieu is never interested in this creativity but only in the already-given sociological problem of *the conditions of rational economic behavior*. Hence he speaks of the "mismatch" between the peasant's world and the modern world, of the "disarray" and "distress" this causes in the peasant, and at best the "conversion" that occurs as a result, or "the collective acquisition of a properly economic habitus." See, for instance, Pierre Bourdieu, "Making the Economic Habitus."

83 Boudieu, *Algeria 1960*, 27.

84 Ibid., 56–62. Bourdieu never takes into account a major feature of this rationalized, planned time: action now with a future reward is an economy of *delay* and *postponement*.

85 Although this is often seen as Bourdieu's criticism of Algerian revolutionary leadership, it is hard to see how different his position is. While Bourdieu criticized revolutionaries for their failure of breaking with the past while maintaining a revolutionary rhetoric, his own position only provides the same rhetoric (the vanguard class of rationalized, modern worker) with a sociological elaboration on opposed conceptions of time.

86 Colona, "The Phantom of Dispossession," 68.

87 Ibid., 70.

88 Ibid., 71–2.

89 Abdellah Hammoudi, "Phenomenology and Ethnography: On Kabyle *Habitus* in the Work of Pierre Bourdieu," in *Bourdieu in Algeria*, 199–254.

90 Ibid., 214.

91 Ibid.

92 See Deleuze, *Difference and Repetition*, 70–9.

93 Hammoudi, "Phenomenology and Ethnography," 219.

94 Ibid., 220; my emphasis.

95 Ibid.

96 Ibid., 224, 225.

97 Ibid., 221; my emphasis.

98 Pierre Bourdieu and Loïc W. D. Wacquant, *An Invitation to Reflexive Sociology* (Chicago, IL: University of Chicago Press, 1992), 40–1. This strange relationship between practice and domination has something to do with the double status of the concept of the "arbitrary" in Bourdieu: a principle is arbitrary because it reproduces a certain domination but also it is arbitrary because it "makes a division in the field of possibilities which is never necessary in itself" (Rancière, *The Intellectual and His People*, 159–60).

99 Merleau-Ponty, *Phenomenology of Perception*, 242.

100 Merleau-Ponty's incomplete work, *The Visible and the Invisible*, includes numerous references to the notion of a pure past: "pure memory" (Merleau-Ponty, *The Visible and the Invisible*, 122); ". . . we find in our experience a movement toward *what could not in any event be present to us in the original and whose irremediable absence would thus count among our originating experiences*" (ibid., 159; my emphasis); an "indestructible" and "intemporal" past, which belongs to a mythical time, *the time before time*, to the prior life, "farther than India and China'" (ibid., 243). By calling it mythical time and by giving it *a place* "farther than India and China," Merleau-Ponty's approach also reaches its limit.

101 Bourdieu, *The Logic of Practice*, 53.

102 Ibid., 56. The same ambiguity is also reflected in the long quote he makes from Durkheim in which the latter talks about, in the same place, "yesterday's man in us," "the past selves" (in plural), "the unconscious part of ourselves," whose demands we tend to ignore while we are vividly aware of the recent acquisitions of civilization "just because they are recent and consequently have not had time to be assimilated into our collective unconscious" (Durkheim quoted in Bourdieu, *The Logic of Practice*, 56). Durkheim shifts from the self to the unconscious, from the individual to the collective, from the recent to the historical, in the same passage.

103 Edmund Husserl, *On the Phenomenology of the Consciousness of Internal Time*, translated by John Barnett Brough (Dordrecht, Boston, MA, and London: Kluwer Academic Publishers, 1991), 21–75.

104 Jacques Derrida, *Speech and Phenomena*, 61–2.

105 Ibid., 67–8.

106 See: Deleuze, *Bergsonism*, 51–72; and *Difference and Repetition*, 79–85.

107 Paola Marrati, *Genesis and Trace: Derrida Reading Husserl and Heidegger* (Stanford, CA: Stanford University Press, 2005), 125; my emphasis.

108 Ibid., 126.

109 Merleau-Ponty, *Phenomenology of Perception*, 110. Merleau-Ponty speaks of "motor project" and "motor intentionality" *but also* "pure stimuli devoid of any practical bearing," "imaginary situations," and "potential movement." He also writes: "Illness, like childhood and 'primitive' mentality, is a complete form of existence and the procedures which it employs to replace normal functions which have been destroyed are equally pathological phenomena. It is impossible to deduce the normal from the pathological, deficiencies from the substitute functions, by a mere change of the sign" (ibid., 107). How to read this methodological advice?

110 Bourdieu, *Practical Reason: On the Theory of Action*, translated by Randall Johnson (Stanford, CA: Stanford University Press, 1998), 80.

111 Bourdieu's privileging of social and practical determination is *not simply a sociological requirement*, which, as a separate discipline, should have no room for philosophical or transcendental reflection. For two reasons: first, Bourdieu's gesture of introducing the question of time into ethnography itself depends on a *philosophical* argument against a static, structural view of the world, independent of the play of time (as he also clearly draws on Husserl); second, Bourdieu's argument, especially in *Distinction*, is often manifestly designed as an *alternative* to the philosophical account of the same subject (taste).

112 Antonio Gramsci, *Selections from Prison Notebooks*, translated by Quintin Hoare and Geoffrey Nowell Smith (London: Lawrence and Wishart, 1971), 324.

113 Bourdieu, *Outline of a Theory of Practice*, 95.

114 Ibid.

115 Bourdieu's understanding of *amor fati* implies an ideological belief in a natural correspondance between who one is and the task assigned to one (a logic tending to produce its own confirmation). The concept of *amor fati* has a completely different sense in Gilles Deleuze: one must embody one's wound; one must welcome the events as they occur rather than denying or resenting them (*The Logic of Sense*, translated by Mark Lester and Charles Stivale (New York: Columbia University Press, 1990), 148–53). Jacques Derrida's emphasis is similar: "the coming of the event is what we cannot and must never prevent, another name for the future itself" (Jacques Derrida and Bernard Stiegler, *Echographies of Television: Filmed Interviews*, translated by Jennifer Bajorek (London: Polity, 2002), 11). This is a horizonless, unanticipable future (ibid., 22).

116 I adopt Paul de Man's concept of crisis (de Man, *Blindness and Insight*, 8), following Gayatri Spivak ("Subaltern Studies: Deconstructing Historiography," in *Selected Subaltern Studies*, edited by Ranajit Guha and Gayatri Chakravorty Spivak (New York and Oxford: Oxford University Press), 4).

117 For "the time out of joint," I refer to Derrida, *Specters of Marx: The State of the Debt, the Work of Mourning and the New International*, translated by Peggy Kamuf (New York and London: Routledge), 1994, 3–48.

118 I am reminded of Frantz Fanon's descriptions of *the change of the corporeal schema* of the colonized under the colonizer's racist gaze: "Below the corporeal schema I had sketched a historico-racial schema. The elements that I used had been provided for me not by 'residual sensations and perceptions primarily of a tactile, vestibular, kinesthetic, and visual character,' but by the other, the white man, who had woven me out of a thousand details, anecdotes, stories. I thought that what I had in hand was to construct a physiological self, to balance space, to localize sensations, and *here I was called on for more*" (*Black Skin White Masks*, translated by Charles Lam Markmann (London: Pluto, 2008), 84; my emphasis).

119 Bourdieu, *The Algerians*, 144–92.

120 Ibid., 146–7.

121 Ibid., 156. Meyda Yeğenoğlu's *Colonial Fantasies* took Fanon's analysis of the veil to a further point and demonstrated how the veil has always been a founding colonial fantasy (*Colonial Fantasies: Towards a Feminist Reading of Orientalism* (Cambridge: Cambridge University Press, 1998), 39–67).

122 Bourdieu, *The Algerians*, 186–7.

123 Ibid., 37–55.

124 Ibid., 54.

125 Bourdieu, *Outline of a Theory of Practice*, 5.

126 Ilana F. Silber, "Bourdieu's Gift to Gift Theory: An Unacknowledged Trajectory," *Sociological Theory*, 27.2 (2009): 175. Silber's perceptive reading follows the

trajectory of Bourdieu's concept of gift in time and demonstrates how his argument oscillates between the emphasis on interest hidden behind the game of time and the disinterested nature of the gift, especially in his last works (ibid., 183–7).

127   Bourdieu, *Outline of a Theory of Practice*, 5–6. Bourdieu's notion of the symbolic is far from being unproblematic, especially when put together with his sometimes hastily employed epistemological distinction between appearance and truth. For instance, in the famous case of the Europeanized mason who was never given any job because he once asked for monetary compensation for a "symbolic meal" he was supposed to be offered but was not by the employer, what does Bourdieu call "symbolic" (ibid., 172–3; 1979, 20–1)? There is an unnoticed double register at work in these uses of the notion of the symbolic, which privileges what is called real over what is called symbolic. Bourdieu surely knows that the symbolic here is no less than a real, warm lunch meal, but he tends to forget that what is offered must have *this real measure* in the eyes of those involved in the exchange (some might get called stingy, another fair, and yet another generous). This is not merely a question of the internal, subjective side of the process of gift, as if the market value is simply the truth of the "symbolic" meal that is by definition unreal and deceptive. What may be disturbing for them may not be the mason's act of unmasking as such but that it is put in terms of market value rather than in the more familiar terms of, say, complaint and gossip, playing the native game of honor and social pressure. While, for Bourdieu, the meaning of practice should be "both their own and alien to them" (Bourdieu, *The Logic of Practice*, 3), he also often erases the ambivalence that should characterize this duality (in favor of a hard epistemological decision) and tends to underestimate seriously the native awareness of it (e.g. paradoxically Bourdieu's concept of "honor" has already assumed those occasions the value of a gift is discussed and measured). Further, as they clearly make a *comparison* with their own system of measuring the value of a meal, the reality of the market exchange is also known well by the people who exclude the mason. Depending on the context, this might even be a form of resistance. We also need to know, for instance, what is said about the employer. Is the employer seen as free to offer a meal or not? Or is his act also registered as a moral failure? Clearly there might be very different social contexts and very different responses, depending on the factors of class, gender, and rural-urban differences, etc.

128   In his *Symbolic Exchange*, Baudrillard offers a radically different interpretation. Seeing power's strategy as gift without counter-gift, he argues that it is the counter-gift that abolishes power. It is the *reversibility* of symbolic exchange that is a threat to power (Jean Baudrillard, *Symbolic Exchange and Death*, translated by Ian Hamilton Grant (Los Angeles, CA and London: Sage, 2011), 43).

129 Marcel Mauss, *The Gift: Forms and Functions of Exchange in Archaic Societies*, translated by Ian Gunnison (New York: Norton & Company, 1967), 15–16.

130 Thierry Kochuyt, "God, Gifts and Poor People: On Charity in Islam," *Social Compass*, 56.1 (2009): 98–116.

131 Ibid., 111.

132 Ibid.

133 Ibid., 112.

134 I need to add that the legal aspect might have further consequences that need to be separately discussed, for the Qur'an also mentions, among the legitimate receivers, "those administered to collect the funds" (9.60), that is, functionaries who collect *zakat*.

135 Bourdieu emphasizes the aspect of obligation: "In Kabylia I collected numerous proverbs which say roughly that a present is a misfortune because in the final analysis it must be reciprocated" (Bourdieu, *Practical Reason*, 94).

136 Jacques Derrida, *Memoirs for Paul de Man* (revised edn), translated by Cecile Lindsay, Jonathan Culler, Eduardo Cadava, and Peggy Kamuf (New York: Columbia University Press, 1989), 149.

137 Bourdieu, *Practical Reason*, 95.

138 Ibid., 74–123.

139 Jacques Derrida, *Given Time I: Counterfeit Money*, translated by Peggy Kamuf (Chicago, IL and London: University of Chicago Press, 1992), 11.

140 Ibid., 12.

141 Ibid., 13.

142 The double bind of the gift is not simply the bind of the subjective and the objective, which is only derivative and which always tends to give priority to a scientific truth in a tendential resolution of the bind (and that is what Bourdieu does twice: first, in declaring that the gift is collective self-deception, hiding interest; and second, in declaring that collective self-deception is socially necessary disinterestedness (Bourdieu, *Practical Reason*, 75–98)).

143 Derrida, *Given Time*, 14; my emphasis).

144 Pheng Cheah, "The Untimely Secret of Democracy," in *Derrida and the Time of the Political*, edited by Pheng Cheah and Suzanne Guerlac (Durham and London: Duke University Press, 2009), 75.

145 Derrida, *Given Time*, 16.

146 Ibid., 17. Derrida refers here to his earlier work, *Cinders*, translated by Ned Lukacher (Lincoln, NE: University of Nebraska Press, 1991).

147 See: www.iranicaonline.org/

148 For instance, *zaman* (time and "times"), *devir* or *devr* (period, age), *müddet* (time, a certain time, duration), *vakit* (time, a specific time, passing time), *an* (now, second, the indivisible, shortest possible time), *lahza* (time at a blink, the shortest

time), *dem* (a passing time, duration or second), *istikbal* (future), *ati* (that time which is ahead of us, future), *mazi* (past), and *saat* (hour).

149 Certainly one needs to discuss the great Sufi tradition here. Ian Almond's learned and challenging work on deconstruction and Sufism continues to be the most important source (*Sufism and Deconstruction: A Comparative Study of Derrida and Ibn 'Arabi* (London and New York: Routledge, 2004)). Although deconstruction speaks to mystic traditions of all religions, it is also a deconstruction of mysticism, as Almond underlines (ibid., 114–15). Almond pays particular attention to the concepts of *al-qidam* and *al-azal* (ibid., 32–3). But I find the concept of the Real he employs (especially as a translation of *al-Haq*) as well as a series of similarities that he finds between the Real and Derrida's concept of differance highly debatable (ibid., 2–37). Further, I am not sure if *al-ghayb al-mutlaq* should be translated as the Absolute Unseen. Although the "unseen" is no doubt a very convenient translation employed by many scholars, *ghayb*, as I have previously mentioned, means "absent." More importantly, what is absent (or unseen) is absent to the human being, *while it is surely present and known (or seen) by God*. It is true that this is in consistency with Ibn-Arabi's emphasis that God can be known only negatively, but again both *al-qidam* and *al-azal* are surely not absent to God, but present to Him. There can be no comparison with differance, or with Derrida's deconstruction of time here. For differance can at best be "pointed to," but no consciousness can ever have access to it. Derrida for instance does not know differance in the way Hegel knows absolute knowledge.

150 Hent De Vries, ed., *Religion: Beyond a Concept* (New York: Fordham University Press, 2008), 70–1.

151 Derrida and Nancy, "Eating Well," 105.

152 Bourdieu and Wacquant, *An Invitation to Reflexive Sociology*, 163; Bourdieu, "Participant Objectivation," translated by Loïc Wacquant, *Journal of Royal Anthropological Society*, 9 (2003): 288–9, 292; and Bourdieu, "Algerian Landing," 433, 435–6, 438.

153 Bourdieu, "Participant Objectivation," 288.

154 Bourdieu, "The Peasant and His Body."

155 Bourdieu and Wacquant, *An Invitation to Reflexive Sociology*, 163.

Chapter 4

1 Lawrence, *Seven Pillars of Wisdom*; Said, *Orientalism*; Gilles Deleuze, "The Shame and the Glory: T. E. Lawrence," *Essays Critical and Clinical*, 115–25.

2 Said, *Orientalism*, 176–7.

3 Vicki Kirby, *Telling Flesh*, 160–1.

4   Said, *Orientalism*, 27.

5   Dennis Porter, "Orientalism and Its Problems," in *The Politics of Theory: Proceedings of the Essex Conference on the Sociology of Literature*, edited by Francis Barker, Peter Hulme, Margaret Iversen, and Diana Loxley (Colchester: University of Essex, 1983), 179–93.

6   Kaja Silverman, *Male Subjectivity at the Margins* (New York and London: Routledge, 1992).

7   Said, *Orientalism*, 188.

8   Ibid., 237.

9   Ibid., 238.

10 Ibid., 240.

11 Ibid., 241.

12 Lawrence, *Seven Pillars of Wisdom*, 657; Said, *Orientalism*, 242.

13 Lawrence, *Seven Pillars of Wisdom*, 547; Said, *Orientalism*, 242.

14 Said, *Orientalism*, 242.

15 Ibid., 244.

16 Said, *Orientalism*, 28; Raymond Williams, *Culture and Society: 1780–1950* (New York and London: Columbia University Press, 1983), 355–6.

17 Said, *Orientalism*, 2.

18 Williams, *Culture and Society*, 305.

19 Interestingly, Williams abandons this notion and uses "dominant" in his later work: *Marxism and Literature* (Oxford and New York: Oxford University Press, 1985), 121–35.

20 Gilles Deleuze, *Masochism: Coldness and Cruelty*, translated by Jean McNeil (New York: Zone Books, 1991).

21 Deleuze, *Essays Critical and Clinical*, 1.

22 Ibid., 5.

23 Deleuze, "The Shame and the Glory," 115; Lawrence, *Seven Pillars of Wisdom*, 23.

24 "The element of this internal genesis seems to us to consist of intensive quantity rather than schema, and to be related to Ideas rather than to concepts of the understanding" (Deleuze, *Difference and Repetition*, 26). For Deleuze's theory of "Ideas," see 168–221. In his *Deleuze on Literature*, Ronald Bogue thinks the notion of genesis is what Deleuze must have in mind in the essay on Lawrence (Ronald Bogue, *Deleuze on Literature* (New York and London: Routledge, 2003), 166–70).

25 Deleuze, "The Shame and the Glory," 115.

26 Ibid., 116.

27 Ibid.

28 Deleuze, *The Logic of Sense*, 1.

29 Bogue, *Deleuze on Literature*, 165–6.

30 Deleuze, "The Shame and the Glory," 118.

31 It might be objected here that for Deleuze (and Guattari) aesthetic figures are not conceptual persona, as they have argued especially in *What is Philosophy?* (Deleuze and Guattari, *What Is Philosophy?*, 177). My question is whether this distinction can be controlled conceptually. Deleuze and Guattari themselves also argue that Mallarmé's mime constructs the concept in extracting an event from a state of affairs (ibid., 160).

32 Deleuze, *The Logic of Sense*, 253–65.

33 Ibid., 258. Here I draw on Daniel W. Smith's introduction to Deleuze's book on Francis Bacon. Smith refers to the work of Erwin Strauss who distinguishes between the sensory and immanent nature of the landscape and the transcendent and abstract nature of geography (Daniel Smith, "Translator's Introduction—Deleuze on Bacon: Three Conceptual Trajectories in *The Logic of Sensation*," in *Francis Bacon: The Logic of Sensation*, translated by Daniel W. Smith (Minneapolis, MN: University of Minnesota Press, 2004), xiv–xv; Erwin Strauss, *The Primary World of Senses: A Vindication of Sensory Experience*, translated by Jacob Needleman (New York: Free Press of Glencoe, 1963), 316–23). Would it not be interesting to read Lawrence's text as a rift between a geographic Lawrence and a simulacral one, a Lawrence who is a master of the desert and another who is lost in the play of light and shadow, one in glory, the other in shame? Gaston Bachelard's notion of "intimate immensity" (forest, desert, sea) is also relevant here (*The Poetics of Space*, 183–210). Bachelard quotes the French Orientalist writer Pierre Loti: "Our eyes turned toward the interior of the country, we questioned the immense horizon of the sand." He immediately adds, not because he has an awareness of Orientalist-colonial worlding but because he is focused on the relationship between imagination and space: "But this immense horizon of sand is a schoolboy's desert, the Sahara found in every school atlas" (ibid., 204).

34 Said, *Orientalism*, 237.

35 Deleuze, "The Shame and the Glory," 117.

36 Angus Calder, "Introduction," in *Seven Pillars of Wisdom*, T. E. Lawrence (London: Wordsworth, 1997), xx–xxi.

37 Deleuze, *The Logic of Sense*, 147–8.

38 Unless we take the rhythm itself as Gestalt, as Jose Gil does in his remarkable book, *Metamorphoses of the Body* (Jose Gil, *Metamorphoses of the Body*, translated by Stephen Muecke (Minneapolis, MN and London: University of Minnesota Press, 1998), 132–3). Deleuze uses the notion of rhythm elsewhere in the essay: Lawrence's gift is to "make entities live passionately in the desert, alongside people and things, in the jerking rhythm of a camel's gait" (Deleuze, "The Shame and the Glory," 119). Gil talks about two different forms, and tends to see Gestalt as a kind of "form of forms" (a paradoxical form, which appears while it cannot appear), whereas Deleuze's concept of vision seems to involve a strong sensual dimension. The issue is too complicated and requires a more extensive discussion.

39 Lawrence, *Seven Pillars of Wisdom*, 558.

40 Deleuze, *The Logic of Sense*, 150.

41 Gilles Deleuze, *Cinema 2: The Time-Image*, translated by Hugh Tomlinson and Robert Galeta (Minneapolis, MN: University of Minnesota Press, 1989), 126–55.

42 Deleuze, "The Shame and the Glory," 118; Deleuze, *Cinema 2*.

43 Deleuze, *Cinema 2*, 128–9.

44 Ibid., 150–3.

45 Deleuze, "The Shame and the Glory," 118.

46 Ibid., 119.

47 Ibid.

48 Ibid., 119–20, 123–4.

49 Lawrence, *Seven Pillars of Wisdom*, 405; Deleuze, "The Shame and the Glory," 120.

50 Deleuze, "The Shame and the Glory," 124.

51 Ibid., 123. The "composite feeling of shame" is also taken up in *What is Philosophy?* 106–8.

52 Deleuze, "The Shame and the Glory," 120–4.

53 Deleuze, *The Logic of Sense*, 301–20. See Vanessa Brito's interesting commentary, "The Desert Island and the Missing People," translated by Justin Clemens, *Parrhesia*, 6 (2009): 10. In the same context, Brito also refers to Deleuze's early text "Desert Islands" (Gilles Deleuze, *Desert Islands and Other Texts: 1953-1974*, edited by David Lapoujade, translated by Michael Taormina (New York: Semiotexte, 2004), 9–14).

54 Deleuze, "The Shame and the Glory," 125.

55 Ibid., 121.

56 Zafer Aracagök, "Decalcomania, Mapping and Mimesis," *Symploke*, 13(1–2) (2005): 283–302.

57 Ibid., 300.

58 Lawrence, *Seven Pillars of Wisdom*, 336.

59 Ibid., 337.

60 Ibid.

61 See especially Books 2 and 3, § 375–407 (Plato, *The Republic*, 46–77).

62 Lawrence also writes: "If I could not assume their character, I could at least conceal my own and pass among them without evident friction, neither a discord nor a critic but an unnoticed influence" (Lawrence, *Seven Pillars of Wisdom*, 13). Shall we call this the dominative mood of a becoming-invisible?

63 Lawrence, *Seven Pillars of Wisdom*, 14–15.

64 "I loved you, so I drew these tides of men into my hands and wrote my will across the sky in stars / To earn you freedom, the seven pillared worthy house, that your eyes might be shining for me When we came" (Lawrence, *Seven Pillars of Wisdom*, 1).

65 Calder, "Introduction," vi.

Chapter 5

1   Christopher L. Miller, "The Postidentitarian Predicament in the Footnotes of
    A Thousand Plateaus: Nomadology, Anthropology, and Authority," *Diacritics*,
    23.3 (1993): 6–35; Miller occasionally went beyond the issue of colonialism and
    expressed a more general discontent in Deleuze and Guattari's engagement with
    binarisms. Miller's essay was later published as a chapter in his *Nationalists and
    Nomads: Essays on Francophone Literature and Culture* (Chicago, IL and London:
    Chicago University Press, 1998), 171–210.

2   Eugene W. Holland, "Representation and Misrepresentation in Postcolonial
    Literature and Theory," *Research in African Literatures*, 34.1 (2003): 159–73; Miller
    has also responded to Holland's criticism: "We Shouldn't Judge Deleuze and
    Guattari: A Response to Eugene Holland," *Research in African Literatures*, 34.3
    (2003): 129–41. For conceptual personae, see Gilles Deleuze and Felix Guattari,
    What is Philosophy? 61–84.

3   Holland, "We Shouldn't Judge Deleuze and Guattari," 165–6.

4   And it is not a given to be anti-imperialist, as we have learned from Bill Warren,
    Imperialism, the Pioneer of Capitalism (London: Verso, 1980).

5   It seems to me that, despite the severity of his criticism, this is what Miller too
    expects from Deleuze and Guattari's text. His essay is written as a criticism of
    the alternative that Deleuze and Guattari offer as a way out of the predicament
    between identitarianism and alterism, and all he demands in the end is "a more
    convincing ethic of flow than the one proposed by Deleuze and Guattari!" (Miller,
    "Postidentitarian Predicament," 33).

6   I cannot think of a better example than Zafer Aracagök's scrupulous deconstruction
    of Deleuze and Guattari's distinction between mapping and tracing. See his
    "Decalcomania, Mapping and Mimesis."

7   Miller, "Postidentitarian Predicament," 11 (my emphasis). This is also the "question
    that haunts the book from the beginning: what if anything does this project of
    nomadology have to do with real and 'actual' nomads?" (ibid., 10).

8   This criticism is limited to Miller's essay on Deleuze and Guttari. I do not herein
    consider Miller's work on French literature and anthropology.

9   Julie Wuthnow, "Deleuze in the Postcolonial: On Nomads and Indigenous Politics,"
    Feminist Theory, 3.2 (2002): 183–200.

10 In the main body of her essay, she focuses on authors known as Deleuzian and
    their articulations of nomadism. Depending almost solely on others, Wuthnow
    seems to respond to a debatable academic construct. Interestingly, Miller's
    opening argument also begins with a reference to Brian Massumi's presentation
    of Deleuze and Guattari's approach, before he turns to a close textual following of
    references.

11 Wuthnow, "Deleuze in the Postcolonial," 186.

12 Gilles Deleuze and Felix Guattari, *A Thousand Plateaus*, translated by Brian Massumi (Minneapolis, MN: University of Minnesota Press, 1987), 381.

13 Deleuze and Guattari, *Anti-Oedipus*, 131.

14 Deleuze and Guattari, *What is Philosophy?* 16.

15 Deleuze and Guattari see the human subject ". . . as the being who is in intimate contact with the profound life of all forms or all types of beings, who is responsible for even the stars and animal life . . ." (*Anti-Oedipus*, 4).

16 Deborah Root, "Misadventures in the Desert" 81–96.

17 Root, "Misadventures," 82.

18 Ibid., 85.

19 Ibid., 90.

20 Isabelle Eberhardt, "Pencilled Notes," in *The Oblivion Seekers*, 68–70.

21 Eberhardt, *The Oblivion Seekers*, 68.

22 Ibid.

23 Ibid., 69.

24 Ibid. (my emphasis).

25 Isabelle Eberhardt, *In the Shadow of Islam*, 17.

26 Eberhardt, *The Oblivion Seekers*, 68.

27 Ibid., 70.

28 Deleuze and Guattari, *A Thousand Plateaus*, 380; Eberhardt, *In the Shadow of Islam*, 17. For other discussions of nomadism and colonialism in Eberhardt's work see Laura Rice, "Nomad Thought," 151–76; Hedi Abdel-Jaouad, "Isabelle Eberhardt: Portrait of the Artist as a Young Nomad," *Yale French Studies*, 2.83 (1993): 93–117.

29 Deleuze and Guattari, *A Thousand Plateaus*, 381.

30 According to Rice, in making an alliance with Lyautey, "Eberhardt bridged what Deleuze has termed the 'nomadic unit' and the 'despotic unit'" ("Nomad Thought," 164–5).

31 Unlike T. E. Lawrence, the only rationale for this mimicry of cross-dressing seems to be the desire for travel, to "pass" the gender line so as to be able to gain freedom of observation: "Of course, there's nothing remarkable about me. I am able to pass everywhere completely unobserved, an excellent position to be in for observing. If women are not good at this, it is because their costume attracts attention. Women have always been made to be looked at, and they aren't yet much bothered by the fact. This attitude, I think, gives far too much advantage to men" (*In the Shadow of Islam*, 38).

32 Especially in her second return, Eberhardt took financial help from a French lady who wanted her to investigate the mysterious murder of her husband in Algeria. Although she only used this opportunity to finance her excursions and writing and

made no investigation of the murder, her purported intention was sufficient for the disturbed local officers to observe her with suspicion and distrust (Bowles in Eberhardt, *The Oblivion Seekers*, 10).

33 Laura Rice offers a rich and reasonable account of the incident and the trial, see her "Nomad Thought," 168–70.

34 Rice, "Nomad Thought," 173–5.

35 Eberhardt, *The Oblivion Seekers*, 23–30, 44–50.

36 Eberhardt, *In the Shadow of Islam*, 45–6. *Ksar* means "castle" in Maghrebi Arabic. *Zawiya* is a religious school or monastery.

37 Eberhardt, *In the Shadow of Islam*, 46.

38 Ibid.

39 Ibid.

40 Ibid., 48.

41 Ibid., 47.

42 Ibid.

43 Ibid.

44 Freed from its temporalization, that is, freed from the "chronos" in which past and future are but forms of the present, such freedom is the time of the event, the mobile instant of "counter-actualization" divided between past and future. Ba Mahmadou's unique way of performing servitude can be interpreted as a form of "counter-actualization" rather than "actualization" in Deleuze's terms (*The Logic of Sense*, 150–1). This might be what the philosopher means by the difference between accepting a state of affairs and affirming the event. If we push the reading in this direction, we must say that Ba Mahmadou does *not accept servitude* as a mere state of affairs in the present (in which case he would be actualizing it), but *affirms it* as the event of his life, his wound, and embodies it: No complaints, no evasion, he is not servile to servility. Instead he continually withdraws something from the present moment of the actualization of servitude: that which is *in* the event of servitude but not reducible to its actualization, the "aternal" or the "untimely" ("becoming young again and aging in it") (Deleuze and Guattari, *What is Philosophy?* 111–12). That is *his difference*. He "disengages from [the servitude] an abstract line, and keeps from the event only its contour and its splendor, becoming thereby the actor of one's own events—a *counter-actualization*" (Deleuze, *The Logic of Sense*, 150). His performance is a staging of servitude, which marks its constitutive difference rather than subordinating it to the present. As an intelligent observer, Eberhardt immediately recognizes this difference and calls it "nobility." The implication is that it would be difficult to crush this man. In this way, this, to her mind, unusual black man's performance re-marks and sets off *the event in her* beyond the state of affairs: "I should first have to be cured of my prejudices about superior races, and my superstitions about inferior ones" (Eberhardt, *In the Shadow of Islam*, 47).

45 Eberhardt, *In the Shadow of Islam*, 39.

46 "Monotonous immensity of the high plateau . . . I feel myself lost in the forest"; "the sky opens, infinite, profound with the great transparency of a tranquil ocean"; "the starry skies . . . religious in their vastness"; "immense and glowing horizon . . . a zone of pure sand"; "the same monotony of immense curving lines"; "immense beaches of the night"; "the vast, the divine solitude of all my being" (Eberhardt, *In the Shadow of Islam*, 15, 23, 25, 31, 40, 70, 80).

47 Eberhardt, *In the Shadow of Islam*, 31. For "intimate immensity" see Bachelard, *The Poetics of Space*, 183–210.

48 Bachelard, *The Poetics of Space*, 184, 204.

49 Ibid., 204–5.

50 Eberhardt, *In the Shadow of Islam*, 25.

51 Ibid., 79.

52 Ibid., 116.

53 Ibid., 76.

54 For music and dance, see Eberhardt, *In the Shadow of Islam*, 76–80; for the experience of hashish, see Eberhardt, *The Oblivion Seekers*, 70–4.

55 Eberhardt, *In the Shadow of Islam*, 77 (my emphasis).

56 Ibid., 114.

57 Ibid., 111.

58 Georges Bataille, *Theory of Religion*, translated by Robert Hurley (New York: Zone Books, 1992). In what follows, I will focus on Bataille's argument in the first part. I am not discussing all the intricacies of Bataille's theory, but only emphasize the aspects of immanence and intimacy.

59 Georges Bataille, *The Accursed Share*, Volumes II and III, translated by Robert Hurley (New York: Zone Books, 1993), 199.

60 When Eberhardt writes, "see in all creatures a motive for rejoicing, in homage to the Creator," this is what she means (*In the Shadow of Islam*, 117).

61 I take here Bataille's description of poetry as sacrifice of words as a metaphor for literary language in general. Bataille also writes that "poetry leads from the known to the unknown" (Georges Bataille, *Inner Experience*, translated by Leslie Ann Boldt (New York: SUNY Press, 1988), 135–6.

62 See for instance Maurice Blanchot, *The Unavowable Community*, translated by Pierre Joris (Barrytown, Station Hill, 1988), 3–4, 15–19: Benjamin Noys, *Georges Bataille: A Critical Introduction* (London: Pluto, 2000), 66. I need to underline once more that I refer to a productive tension in these works.

63 Georges Bataille, *Erotism: Death and Sensuality*, translated by Mary Dalwood (San Francisco, CA: City Lights, 1986), 17–18, 197–220.

64 Eberhardt, *The Oblivion Seekers*, 31–6, 51–5 and *In the Shadow of Islam*, 61–2, 74–6.

65 Assia Djebar, *Women of Algiers in Their Apartments*, translated by Marjolijn de Jager (Charlottesvilles, VA and London: University Press of Virginia/Caraf

Books, 1992), 133–52. Eberhardt is often upset with what she regards to be an unquestioning acceptance and surrender on the part of women, and their refusal of her: "Women cannot understand me, they see me as a freak. I am much too simple for their taste, which is obsessed with the superficial and the artifice . . . When woman becomes the comrade of man, when she ceases to be a plaything, she will begin another existence. But for now, they only know how to breathe in time and to the theme of waltz" (*In the Shadow of Islam*, 69). People point to the possibility of change with the new generation, but she is not hopeful at all: "I don't believe it at all; or else this is just another trick of education which will never stand up to the pressure of the salons . . . Woman herself will be everything desired, but I've seen no sign that men desire her to change except within the limits of fashion. A slave or an idol, this is what they can love—never an equal" (ibid., 70). She must have in mind women of her own cultural and social environment, as she finds the dangerous South better than the artificial Europe: ". . . I relapse into my feeling of exile, wishing to bury myself even deeper in this hostile south, without any desire for the Paris I have known, where the newspapers' lip service to feminism was even more repugnant to me than the Parisian coquettes" (ibid., 71).

66 Eberhardt, *In the Shadow of Islam*, 91–2, 97–9.
67 Spivak, *A Critique of Postcolonial Reason*, 113.
68 Eberhardt, *In the Shadow of Islam*, 114–17.
69 Ibid., 116.
70 Ibid.
71 Ibid., 117.
72 "Seeing in all creatures a motive for rejoicing, in homage to the Creator" is an Islamic perspective.

Chapter 6

1 Fethi Benslama, *Psychoanalysis and the Challenge of Islam*, 6 (my emphasis).
2 Ibid.
3 Ibid., 5.
4 Ibid., 7 (my emphasis).
5 Throughout the text, Benslama constantly reminds us that there is of course variety and variation. But the fact that he has to repeat this is itself symptomatic of the strong reductionist tendency in his argument. See Joseph Massad's excellent criticism of Benslama, "Psychoanalysis, Islam and the Other of Liberalism," *Umbr(a): A Journal of the Unconscious: Islam* (2009), 43–68.
6 Benslama, *Psychoanalysis and the Challenge of Islam*, 4.
7 Ibid., 2 (my emphasis).

8 Ibid., 5.

9 Ibid., 9.

10 Ibid., 10.

11 Ibid., 27.

12 Benslama makes a distinction between "fundamentalism" whose only reference is religion and "Islamism" that involves "science" and the concept of "people" (then fundamentalism becomes really a fringe tendency). But this becomes misleading, for he actually continues to treat "Islamism" as a form of fundamentalism.

13 Ali Bulaç, "Medine Vesikası Hakkında Genel Bilgiler," *Birikim*, 38–9 (1992), 102–11. The Charter of Madina was drafted by the prophet Muhammad, probably shortly after the *hijra*, his migration and exile in Madina in 622. It is a formal agreement between Muslims, Jews, Christians, and pagans living in Madina and is considered by some to be the first instance of an Islamic state. Successfully bringing to an end communal and tribal conflicts, the charter instituted a number of rights and responsibilities for various religious communities of Madina by bringing them within the fold of a single community. Ali Bulaç is not a member of the Islamic party in government and he is sometimes associated with a minority Islamic group known as "Emek ve Adalet Platformu" (Platform for Labor and Justice).

14 It is not that I regard this document as an ideal (nor the Turkish variation of political Islam, obviously!), but I offer this as only one instance of a complex field that Benslama unfairly reduces to a simple formulation, and which finds its echo in the images of hegemonic Western media.

15 Benslama, *Psychoanalysis and the Challenge of Islam*, 59–60.

16 Ibid., 60.

17 Ibid.

18 Ibid., 62.

19 The scandal that led to Bourguiba's removal from power by his own men (his insistence on the execution of a group of Islamists) is an instance of this authoritarianism, which is a characteristic feature of nationalist elites in the Muslim periphery. So much for Benslama's relative exception!

20 Benslama, *Psychoanalysis and the Challenge of Islam*, 61.

21 Ibid., 8–9.

22 It is hard to disagree with Joseph Massad's harsh description of "a deep narcissistic injury" given this insistence to isolate Islam from its recent history (Massad, "Psychoanalysis, Islam, and the Other of Liberalism," 46).

23 Deleuze and Guattari, *Anti-Oedipus*, 222–61.

24 Kierkegaard defines this particular instance of despair as "defiance": despair is conscious of itself as an activity, it arises from within the self. But this is the infinite or most abstract form of the self. The self is in fact severed from any relation to the power that established it. It is by means of this infinite, abstract form that the

self wants in despair to rule over himself. His concrete self has limits, but he wants to refashion a self such as he wants by means of the abstract, infinite form (Søren Kierkegaard, *The Sickness unto Death*, translated by Alastair Hannay (London and New York: Penguin, 1989), 80–3). This fits the image of the Islamist at first glance, and one can see what Benslama means. When it is taken as a kind of essence and when considered in the overall context, however, it may turn out to be a reduced portrayal of Islamism. Kierkegaard's formulation is picked by Benslama probably because it constructs a dramatic opposition with the "desire to be an other"; otherwise, Nietzsche's concept of "*ressentiment*" would do the job, especially for the fundamentalist version of political Islam. We should note, though, something that Benslama overlooks: if "desire to be an other" is not directly involved in Kierkegaard's analysis of despair, it is not alien to it (ibid., 17–19).

25   I am referring to Partha Chatterjee's well-known analysis of nationalism as the synthesis of Enlightenment Reason and national culture (Partha Chatterjee, *Nationalist Thought and the Colonial World: A Derivative Discourse* (Minneapolis, MN: University of Minnesota Press, 1993), 3). Of course, the Islamic synthesis is quite different. Among the various examples of the contemporary Islamic concept of science, the founder of the Nur movement Said-i Nursi's metaphor of universe is certainly the most striking. See: Şerif Mardin, *Religion and Social Change in Turkey* (New York: SUNY Press, 1989), 203–16. This openness to science includes psychoanalysis too (Massad, "Psychoanalysis, Islam, and the Other of Liberalism," 58).

26   Benslama, *Psychoanalysis and the Challenge of Islam*, 30–2.

27   Ibid., 37.

28   Michel Foucault, *The Care of the Self* (*The History of Sexuality*, Vol. 3), 42–3.

29   See, for instance, Alberto Toscano's interesting analysis of Hezbollah's politics (Alberto Toscano, "Dual Power Revisited: From Civil War to Biopolitical Islam," *Soft Targets*, 2.1 (2007), www.softtargetsjournal.com/v21/alberto_toscano.php). A different example is the Turkish Islamic government, which applies liberal and neoliberal policies that can be described as instances of biopower and biopolitics. This is an emergent, varied, and complex field of struggles; Hezbollah and Turkish Islam are not examples of the same invariable core.

30   Benslama, *Psychoanalysis and the Challenge of Islam*, 36–43.

31   Ibid., 221.

32   In this context, see Meyda Yeğenoğlu's stimulating study of European attitude toward Muslim migrants (Meyda Yeğenoğlu, *Islam, Migrancy and Hospitality in Europe* (Palgrave-Macmillan: New York, 2012)).

33   J. Hillis Miller, "Derrida's Politics of Autoimmunity," *Discourse*, 30:1–2 (2008): 223. Psychoanalysis is surely close to deconstruction, but Benslama's maximalization of this closeness is problematic: "Freud radically conceptualized theory as a form

of deconstruction" (Benslama, *Psychoanalysis and the Challenge of Islam*, ix). Psychoanalysis certainly challenges given norms, but it does not want this to be a radical challenge. Moreover, when Benslama refers to the "impossible kernel around which language forms an imaginary shell" (ibid.), it is important to underline that, while Lacanian psychoanalysis understands this impossible kernel in terms of the Real (that which cannot be symbolized), deconstruction emphasizes that the shell and the kernel are *in touch*, and the impossible can perhaps be described as the movement or experience of this relationship. See Derrida's foreword to Abraham and Torok: "*Fors*: The Anglish Words of Nicholas Abraham and Maria Torok," translated by Barbara Johnson in Abraham and Torok, *The Wolf Man's Magic Word*, xi–xlviii.

34 I put aside the peculiar yet familiar opposition between mimesis and imitation that Benslama makes. It is not difficult to understand what he means by this. But it is striking to use such a problematic opposition for a psychoanalyst whose text is full of references to Derrida and Lacoue-Labarthe!

35 Another *ayat* was sent for confirmation: "Never did We send a messenger or a prophet before thee, but, when he framed a desire, Satan threw some (vanity) into his desire: but Allah will cancel anything (vain) that Satan throws in, and Allah will confirm (and establish) His Signs: for Allah is full of knowledge and wisdom" (22.52).

36 Benslama, *Psychoanalysis and the Challenge of Islam*, 12.

37 Ibid., 13.

38 Ibid.

39 Ibid., 14.

40 If Benslama's analysis is correct, this should actually put the relationship with the Qur'an, especially the relationship established with it in reading or recitation, at the center of Islamic subjectivity, rather than being a simple reference to the origin as the Mother Book. To put it briefly, if the cut has a priority, why and how does Benslama take the order "read" as if what is in question is a simple repetition? I will go back to this question in the next chapter through Abdelkebir Khatibi's very different psychoanalytic interpretation.

41 Ibid., 17–18.

42 Ibid., 18–19.

43 Ibid., 19 (my emphasis).

44 Ibid.

45 Ibid.

46 Ibid., 20 (my emphasis).

47 Ibid.

48 Ibid.

49 Ibid., 21 (my emphasis).

50 Philippe Lacoue-Labarthe, *The Subject of Philosophy*, translated by Thomas
     Tresize, Hugh J. Silverman, Gary M. Cole, Timothy D. Bent, Karen McPherson,
     and Claudette Sartiliot (Minneapolis, MN and London: University of Minnesota
     Press, 1993).

51 Ibid., 1.

52 Friedrich Nietzsche, *The Will to Power*, translated by Walter Kaufmann and
     R. J. Hollingdale (New York: Vintage Books, 1968), § 538; Lacoue-Labarthe,
     The Subject of Philosophy, 3.

53 Benslama, *Psychoanalysis and the Challenge of Islam*, 21.

54 Ibid. From this, Benslama will move on to a reading of Freud's concept of religious
     "illusion" as an effect of the *truth* of religion, *which is the force of desire*, and which
     originates in the despair of abandonment and "in the desire to protect ourselves
     from it by inventing a tutelary power comparable to the one we attribute to the
     father" (ibid., 22).

55 Salman Rushdie, *The Satanic Verses* (New York: Viking, 1989), 123.

56 Ibid., 272.

57 Lacoue-Labarthe, *The Subject of Philosophy*, 4. This is the last of the four necessary
     conditions in order to speak the language that Nietzsche wanted to speak, a
     language "other by virtue of an alterity that is itself other than dialectical alterity"
     (ibid.).

58 Ibid., 5.

59 Friedrich Nietzsche, *Twilight of the Idols & the Anti-Christ*, translated by
     R. J. Hollingdale (Harmondsworth: Penguin, 1978), 41.

60 Lacoue-Labarthe, *The Subject of Philosophy*, 5.

61 Ibid., 7.

62 Ibid., 8.

63 Ibid. (my emphasis).

64 Ibid.

65 Ibid., 12.

66 This passage (from the restricted to the generalized writing) is the whole question
     Lacoue-Labarthe discusses, when he refers to the "unapparent difference" of
     Nietzsche's leap (ibid., 7–8), or "coming to the text," and not being able to come to it
     at the same time, "for the text is precisely without a shore" (ibid., 11, 12).

67 Ibid., 13.

68 Ibid., 16.

69 Lacoue-Labarthe, *The Subject of Philosophy*, 12.

70 There is clearly an affinity between "dispossession" and "ex-appropriation"
     (Derrida) in the first chapter, and "unworking" (Blanchot) in the second chapter:
     "we write: we are dispossessed, something is constantly fleeing outside us, slowly
     deteriorating" (ibid., 12).

71 Gayatri Chakravorty Spivak, "Reading *The Satanic Verses*," *Third Text*, 11 (1990): 49.

72 Ibid., 48–9.

73 Ibid., 49.

74 In his recent television appearences and speeches Salman Rushdie has taken a position fraught with sweeping, monolithic statements about Islam.

75 Benslama, *Psychoanalysis and the Challenge of Islam*, 69.

76 Ibid., 71.

77 Ibid., 74–5.

78 Ibid., 79.

79 Ibid., 81. Benslama further underlines Hagar's special power of vision: she sees the fountain in the desert, and the farthest regions of heaven as the depths of the earth.

80 Ibid., 82.

81 Ibid., 84.

82 Ibid., 86–7.

83 Ibid., 87.

84 Ibid.

85 "Say: He is Allah, the One and Only; Allah, the Eternal, Absolute; He begetteth not, nor is He begotten; And there is none like unto Him" (The Holy Qur'an, 112).

86 Benslama, *Psychoanalysis and the Challenge of Islam*, 87.

87 Ibid., 92.

88 Ibid., 87.

89 Jacques Derrida, *Given Time*, 7.

90 Benslama, *Psychoanalysis and the Challenge of Islam*, 88.

91 Ibid.

92 Derrida, *Given Time*, 7.

93 Ibid., 16.

94 Ibid. (my emphasis).

95 Contrary to Benslama's "there is a there-is-not," Derrida speaks of the intersection of a certain "there is there" with the giving of the gift in his *Cinders* (Derrida, *Cinders*, 57, 60; Derrida, *Given Time*, 17).

96 Derrida writes that "in order for there to be a gift event . . . something must come about or happen . . . in a time without time, in such a way that the forgetting forgets, that it forgets *itself*, but also in such a way that this forgetting, without something being present, presentable, determinable, sensible or meaningful, is not nothing" (Derrida, *Given Time*, 17). If forgetting is a condition of the gift (not in the sense of a cause but in the sense we mean when we say the "human condition"), the gift is also a condition of forgetting; their conditions are in each other (ibid., 17–18).

97 Benslama, *Psychoanalysis and the Challenge of Islam*, 81; Gen. 16.13.

98 Ibid., 81.

99   Jacques Derrida, "Geschlecht: Sexual Difference, Ontological Difference," *Research in Phenomenology*, 13 (1983): 72 (my emphasis).

100 Benslama, *Psychoanalysis and the Challenge of Islam*, 103.

101 Ibid., 102.

102 Benslama has also forgotten that the practice of veiling is not specific to Islam. For an interesting discussion of its justification by St. Paul, see Badiou (Alain Badiou, *St. Paul: The Foundation of Universalism*, translated by Ray Brassier (Stanford, CA: Stanford University Press, 2003), 105).

103 Benslama, *Psychoanalysis and the Challenge of Islam*, 140.

104 Ibid., 126.

105 Ibid., 140.

106 Ibid., 141.

107 Ibid.

108 Pheng Cheah, "Posit(ion)ing Human Rights in the Current Global Conjuncture," *Public Culture*, 9.2 (1997): 242.

109 It is this force that philosophers such as Gilles Deleuze and Jacques Derrida refer to in their respective approaches: the force of justice and singularity. Deleuze emphasizes, for instance, that "rights aren't created by codes and pronouncements but by jurisprudence. Jurisprudence is the philosophy of law, and deals with singularities, it advances by working out from singularities" (Gilles Deleuze, *Negotiations 1972–1990*, translated by Martin Joughin (New York: Columbia University Press, 1990), 153). In the "Force of Law" (Jacques Derrida, *Acts of Religion*, edited and introduction by Gil Anidjar (New York and London: Routledge, 2002), 230–98), Derrida distinguishes between law and justice. Justice is impossible, in a sense closer to the impossibility of the gift, and undeconstructible. But I cannot but desire it. This is the force that makes deconstruction of the law possible. While the rule or the code is always there, it cannot solely govern the scene of judgment, as justice is always a singular response to the singularity of the "case," of the other. Deleuze's "jurisprudence" can be considered in terms of the creative practice of this deconstructive force of justice within the text of the law.

110 Benslama, *Psychoanalysis and the Challenge of Islam*, 142.

Chapter 7

1   See for instance Slavoj Žižek, *The Fragile Absolute: Why is the Christian Legacy Worth Fighting for?* (New York and London: Verso, 2001); and *The Puppet and the Dwarf: The Perverse Core of Christianity* (Boston, MA: MIT Press, 2003). As expected, Žižek is in complete agreement with Fethi Benslama's account: "A Glance into the Archives of Islam." Available at www.lacan.com/zizarchives.htm

2   Alain Badiou, *The Rebirth of History: Times of Riots and Uprisings*, translated by Gregory Elliott (New York and London: Verso, 2012), 77.

3   Alain Badiou, *St. Paul: The Foundation of Universalism*, translated by Ray Brassier (Stanford, CA: Stanford University Press, 2003), 99.

4   Ibid., 110.

5   This was also partly because of the need to avoid argument and conflict (ibid., 100). But then, might the Muslim Brothers have followed a similar tactic during the long period of resistance at Tahrir Square?

6   Michel de Certeau, *The Practice of Everyday Life*, translated by Steven Rendall (Berkeley, CA: University of California Press, 1984), 35–6.

7   Edward Said, *Orientalism*, 6.

8   Benslama, *Psychoanalysis and the Challenge of Islam*, 13.

9   Ibid., 12–13.

10 Ibid., 14.

11 *The Holy Qur'an*, translated by Abdullah Yusuf Ali (Wordsworth: Hertforshire, 2000), Surah, 96, Verse 1.

12 Orientalist Catholic thinker Louis Massignon was strongly influenced by Islam's acceptance of the whole Abrahamic tradition and wanted to convince both Christianity and Islam to reconsider themselves in a new Abrahamic narrative, in his writings as well as in his well-known project of *Badaliya*. Massignon was an administrator of French colonialism in the Middle East and later a supporter of Algerian national liberation. See Louis Massignon, *Testimonies and Reflections: Essays of Louis Massignon*, edited by Herbert Mason (Notre Dame: Notre Dame University Press, 1989).

13 Emmanuel Levinas, *Totality and Infinity*, 48–52.

14 Emmanuel Levinas, *God, Death, and Time*, translated by. Bettina Bergo (Stanford, CA: Stanford University Press, 1993), 121–224.

15 Jean-François Lyotard, *The Differend: Phrases in Dispute*, translated by Georges Van Den Abbeele (Minneapolis, MN: University of Minnesota Press, 1988), 110–18.

16 Emmanuel Levinas, *Existence and Existents*, translated by Alphonso Lingis (Dordrecht: Kluwert Academic Publishers, 1988), 21.

17 Emmanuel Levinas, *Time and the Other*, translated by Richard A. Cohen (Pittsburgh: Duquesne University Press, 1987), 46.

18 Levinas, *Existence and Existents*, 59.

19 Emmanuel Levinas, *Ethics and Infinity: Conversations with Philippe Nemo*, translated by Richard A. Cohen (Pittsburgh, PA: Duquesne University Press, 1985) 48, 49.

20 For instance, in his interview with Philippe Nemo, Levinas says that this tendency was already in his early work: "I distrust the compromised word 'love,' but the responsibility for the Other, being-for-the-other, seemed to me, as early

as that time, to stop the anonymous and senseless rumbling of being. It is in the form of such a relation that the deliverance from the 'there is' appeared to me. Since that compelled my recognition and was clarified in my mind, I have hardly spoken again in my books of the 'there is' for itself. But the shadow of the 'there is,' and of non-sense still appeared to me necessary for the test of dis-interestedness" (ibid., 52). It is not clear, however, how the shadow of the "there is" and of nonsense are necessary for the test of the social relationship. It is precisely this kind of question that I am posing here.

21 Emmanuel Levinas, *Totality and Infinity*, 50.

22 Emmanuel Levinas, *God, Death, and Time*, 137.

23 Ibid., 142.

24 Ibid., 211.

25 Ibid., 203.

26 Philippe Lacoue-Labarthe, "Talks," *Diacritics*, 14.3 (1984): 30.

27 Louis Althusser, "The Only Materialist Tradition, Part I: Spinoza" in *The New Spinoza*, edited by Walter Montag and Ted Stolze (Minneapolis, MN: University of Minnesota Press, 1998), 10.

28 Massignon, *Testimonies and Reflections*, 74–5.

29 See also Edward Said's insightful reading of Freud's relationship to the non-European: Edward Said, *Freud and the Non-European* (London and New York: Verso, 2003).

30 Abdelkebir Khatibi, "Frontiers: Between Psychoanalysis and Islam," translated by Burcu Yalım, *Third Text*, 23.6 (2009), 692. When Massignon referred to the third wife Aisha's account in the above citation, he was actually referring to Aisha as the later narrator, the verbal chronicler of Islam. Khatibi refers to Khadija as one of the first witnesses.

31 Abraham and Torok, *The Wolf Man's Magic Word*.

32 Gayatri Chakravorty Spivak, "Psychoanalysis in Left Field and Fieldworking," *Speculations after Freud: Psychoanalysis, Philosophy and Culture*, edited by Sonu Shamdasani and Michael Munchow (London and New York: Routledge, 1994), 54–5.

33 Ibid., 55.

34 Khatibi, "Frontiers: Between Psychoanalysis and Islam," 692.

35 The Holy Qur'an, Surah 75, Verses 16–18.

36 Jacques Derrida, *Positions*, translated by Alan Bass (Chicago, IL: University of Chicago Press, 1981), 139.

37 Philippe Lacoue-Labarthe, *Typography: Mimesis, Philosophy, Politics*, edited by Christopher Fynsk (Stanford, CA: Stanford University Press, 1989), 59.

38 Jacques Derrida, *Of Grammatology*, 167.

39 Lacoue-Labarthe, *Typography*, 160.

40 Gilles Deleuze and Felix Guattari, *Kafka: Toward a Minor Literature*, translated by Dana Polan (Minneapolis, MN: University of Minnesota Press, 1989), 21.

41 Deleuze, *The Logic of Sense*, 3.

42 Derrida, *Specters of Marx*, 62–3.

43 Assia Djebar. *Far From Madina*, translated by Dorothy S. Blair (London: Quartet Books, 1995).

44 Walter Benjamin, *Illuminations*, 336.

45 Gayatri Chakravorty Spivak, "Echo," in *The Spivak Reader: Selected Works of Gayatri Chakravorty Spivak*, edited by Donna Landry and Gerald MacLean (New York: Routledge, 1996), 175–202.

46 Spivak, "Ghostwriting," 79.

47 Djebar, *Far From Madina*, 67–8.

48 Spivak, "Ghostwriting," 81.

49 Djebar, *Far From Madina*, 49.

50 Ibid.

51 Spivak, "Ghostwriting," 81.

52 Ibid., 82.

53 A continental equivalent is Leibniz's notion of the "incompossible," which is extensively discussed in the works of Gilles Deleuze (Deleuze, *Cinema 2*, 130; *The Logic of Sense*, 169–80; *The Fold: Leibniz and the Baroque*, translated by Tom Conley (Minneapolis, MN and London: University of Minnesota Press, 1993), 59–75; and *Difference and Repetition*, 47–8). The concept of the incompossible signifies a world, which is in contradiction with the compossible or existing world, but not contradictory in itself. Hence "an Adam who did not sin" (or "a Fatima who resisted") is perfectly possible but it is not possible at the same time with "an Adam who sinned" (or "a Fatima who did not resist"); hence it is an incompossible. Deleuze emphasizes the possibility of a narrative in which incompossibles can exist together. In our reading, this would have to be a narrative that works discontinuously, by interrupting itself.

54 David Lewis's pioneering analysis of counterfactuals based on possible world semantics is regarded as the most important contribution (David Lewis, *Counterfactuals* (Oxford: Blackwell, 1973)).

55 Djebar, *Far From Madina*, 3.

56 Spivak, "Ghostwriting," 79.

57 Khatibi, "Frontiers," 692.

58 Ibid., 691.

59 Lacoue-Labarthe, "Talks," 32 (the first emphasis is mine).

60 Djebar, *Far From Madina*, 273–9.

61 Ibid., 278.

Conclusion

1   I would like to warn the reader that these observations were written before the recent events of mass resistance in Turkey and the mass protest and the following coup in Egypt in the June of 2013.

2   Jacques Derrida, *Acts of Religion*, edited by Gil Anidjar (London: Routledge, 2002), 42–101.

3   Ibid., 79.

4   Ibid., 82.

5   Ibid., 43.

6   Ibid., 80.

7   Ibid., 45.

8   Ibid., 27–8.

9   Carl Schmitt and later Derrida have argued that all sovereignty is political. Carl Schmitt, *Political Theology: Four Chapters on the Concept of Sovereignty*, translated by George Schwab (Cambridge, MA, and London, England: MIT Press, 1985) and Jacques Derrida, *Politics of Friendship*, translated by George Collins (London and New York: Verson, 1997).

10 For Anatolian tigers, see Evren Hoşgör, "Islamic Capital/Anatolian Tigers: Past and Present," *Middle Eastern Studies*, 47.2 (2011): 343–60.

11 In his third term in government, the Turkish moderate Islamist Prime Minister Recep Tayyip Erdoğan has been employing neoliberal policies for over ten years now. Recently there is an emerging socialist Muslim group, which, harshly critical of the government's capitalist policies, joined the left rather than Islamist trade unions last May Day in Turkey.

12 I am reminded of Derrida's cautious remark here: "*Islam, or a certain Islam*, would . . . be the only religious or theocratic culture that can still, in fact or in principle, inspire and declare any resistance to democracy" (Jacques Derrida, *Rogues: Two Essays on Reason*, translated by Pascale-Anne. Brault and Michael Naas (Stanford, CA: Stanford University Press, 2005), 29; emphasis is mine). Is this falsified now? Not at all, it is simply wrong to think that Islam is the only religion to declare resistance to democracy.

13 For a powerful analysis that perceives in this development the end of the postcolonial period and its ideologies, see Hamid Dabashi, *The Arab Spring: The End of Postcolonialism* (London: Zed Books, 2012).

14 Cesare Casarino and Antonio Negri, *in Praise of the Common: A Conversation on Philosophy and Politics* (Minnesota, MN and London: University of Minnesota Press, 2008).

15 The criticisms that I have directed at Alain Badiou's seamless and totalizing approach in the previous chapter must be read in this sense (*The Rebirth of History*,

2012). There are no classes and no ideologies, and all contexts are the same in Badiou's approach; there is only an abstract "capitalism" that people resist (in different stages theorized by Badiou). The problem with this analysis is that it is rather too obviously true. It is not "universality" but its failure.

16 See also Samir Amin's political economy of the Arab Spring: "The Arab Revolutions: A Year After," *Interface: A Journal for and about Social Movements*, 4.1 (May 2012), 33–42. Was the most interesting Turkish case a prelude to these developments rather than a model (as is now suggested)? I cannot discuss this here.

17 Spivak, *Outside in the Teaching Machine*, 194. Spivak's reading reminds us of this point, which is overlooked in Foucault scholarship. Indeed Foucault carefully underlines that individualism, the positive valuation of private life, and the intensity of the relations to self are interconnected, "but these connections are neither constant nor necessary" and "there are societies or groups in which the relation to self is intensified and developed without this resulting, as if by necessity, in a strengthening of the values of individualism or of private life" (Michel Foucault, *The Care of the Self* (*The History of Sexuality Volume 3*), translation by Robert Hurley (New York: Vintage, 1980), 42, 43).

18 Foucault, *The Care of the Self*, 43.

19 Spivak in Gayatri Chakravorty Spivak, Sara Danius, and Stefan Jonsson, "An Interview with Gayatri Spivak," *boundary 2*, 20.2 (1993): 48.

20 Gayatri Chakravorty Spivak, "From Haverstock Hill Flat to US. Classroom, What's Left of Theory?" in *What's Left of Theory? New Work on the Politics of Literary Theory*, edited by Judith Butler, John Guillory, and Kendall Thomas (New York: Routledge, 2000), 17.

21 She warns for instance that "[t]he structural outlines of responsibility-based cultural practices begin to atrophy into residual scaffolding as industrial capitalist imperialisms impose the dominant structures, whose motor is rights-based" and further "as soon as a culture systematizes responsibility, the contingency of 'responsibility' begins to atrophy even without the intervention of an 'alien dominant.'" ("From Haverstock Hill," 12). See also Mark Sanders' illuminating comments in his *Gayatri Chakravorty Spivak: Live Theory* (New York and London: Continuum, 2006), 69–70.

22 Saba Mahmood's research on the mosque women's movement was a contemporary instance of problematization by means of which a female self is cultivated in protection from the vicissitudes of modernity. These women have identified a problem of *taqwa* under modern conditions—we should keep the implicit reference to the sense of selfhood in mind here. Their search for *taqwa* cannot be reduced to a simple question of following Islamic prohibition, as it is deeply related with a question of subjectivity for these women. But, at the same time, it cannot but turn into a matter of identity.

23   The root is *h-r-m*, and other words from the same root would be: *harem* (the part
     of a house occupied by the women) and *haram* (illicit, forbidden). Depending
     on the context, there might be a serious shift of meaning in translation. When
     Nilüfer Göle's well-acclaimed study is titled *The Forbidden Modern* in English,
     the immediate reference is the concept of law as prohibition, and that which is
     disallowed is the modern. But in the original title, *Modern Mahrem*, the Turkish
     reader reads something else: the sense that the concept of privacy or intimacy
     obtains in modernity! (And this should not be difficult to understand for the
     English-speaking reader.) The idea that the private and the intimate are forbidden
     to other people is certainly not specific to Turkish or Islamic cultures, though it
     might be differently accented in these cultures than in the metropolitan English-
     speaking cultures. The labor of translation goes well beyond technical difficulty;
     it already assumes the cultural work, which the translated word is supposed to
     account for. Nilüfer Göle, *Modern Mahrem: Medeniyet ve Örtünme* (İstanbul: Metis,
     1991); *The Forbidden Modern: Civilization and Veiling* (Michigan: University of
     Michigan Press, 1997).

24   Especially in the first chapter of *The Use of Pleasure* (*The History of Sexuality
     Volume 2*), translated by Robert Hurley (New York: Vintage Books, 1986), 3–13. In
     the history of Islam, one can find numerous instances of moral problematization,
     especially in various Sufi sects. See for instance Ahmet T. Karamustafa's interesting
     study of dervishes: *God's Unruly Friends: Dervish Groups in the Islamic Middle
     Period 1200–1550* (Salt Lake City: University of Utah Press, 1994).

25   Michel Foucault, *The Birth of Biopolitics: Lectures at the College de France
     1978–1979*, translated by Graham Burchell (New York: Picador/Palgrave
     MacMillan, 2008). About Hamas, see Alberto Toscano, "Dual Power Revisited."
     This is not a homogeneous field at all. As consumerism is perhaps the most
     problematic area for Islam, it is certain that issues of health such as obesity,
     drinking, and smoking are areas of biopolitical intervention for a rising Islamic
     governmentality. A typically neoliberal biopolitical concern can be found in
     the Turkish moderate Islamist government's carefully designed public media
     campaigns against smoking and obesity identified as major health issues that
     affect the population, as well as its campaigns that encourage daily exercise and
     running. A recently prepared draft law that would restrict where alcoholic drinks
     are sold and consumed has created a great deal of controversy. Although the
     government argues that the bill seeks to protect society, particularly children,
     from the harmful effects of alcohol, it is seen as a hidden effort of Islamization of
     private life. Interestingly there is no manifest religious reference in the messages.
     People are interpellated or addressed as individuals who must take care of
     their own bodies (hence the call for personal responsibility and self-care), on
     the one hand; there is a visible emphasis on the family (hence responsibility to
     others, that is, children), on the other. These and similar practices are typically

liberal and neoliberal in that their aim is to effect the individuals at the level of their everyday conduct and create new forms of moral problematization and subjectivation. These various secular and medical figures of pure health are now already within Islam without making it any less religious.

26 For messianicity without messiah, see Derrida, *Specters of Marx*, 33. For the distinction between justice and law, see: "Force of Law: The 'Mystical Foundation of Authority,'" in *Acts of Religion*, 242–3; and for promise, see "Faith and Knowledge," 98–9.

27 I am certainly not saying that this is the argument that will solve all the problems of the reform process. Nor am I saying that Islam might provide a new collective identity for Turks and Kurds—this will hardly work. Indeed, I am not even providing an analysis of this process. I am only trying to understand the way in which political Islam thinks and acts. It is simply unethical not to support the peace and reform process, and the above are meant to be critical remarks rather than a dismissal. To these criticisms of Turkish Islamism, I should also add the Kurdish leadership's striking failure to produce a specifically anti-racist discourse, which is originated in their drastically schematic analysis of the Turkish nation-state and Turkish nationalism.

28 Since they are now part of the parliamentary political field (which involves the media apparatus of representation, staging, and information as a constitutive element), it is indeed very hard to employ the religious text for ethical problematization. Maintaining itself as mere faith or dogma, the religious text becomes a means of pure identity politics: less alcohol licensing to the premises, more mosque constructions.

29 Spivak, "Terror," 87. Once the Islamist government is in a process of peace and negotiation with the Kurdish leadership, it would be impossible and unfair to say that they completely fail to listen to the other. The negotiation here should not be seen a merely liberal application; it is also a very old positive tradition between societies. My criticism begins where the whole process is reduced to *a political conduct governed by solely cognitive measures and manipulation*. I do hope that my careful reader understands all these reservations and explanations that I have made in the last three footnotes.

30 Spivak, "Terror," 108.

31 Immanuel Kant, *Religion within the Boundaries of Mere Reason and Other Writings*, translated by Allen Wood and George Di Giovanni (Cambridge: Cambridge University Press, 1998), 72–3.

32 Spivak, "Terror." 102.

33 Ibid., 107–9, passim.

34 Runions' fascinating article is one of the best discussions of Spivak's work: "Detranscendentalizing Decisionism: Political Theology after Gayatri Spivak," *Journal of Feminist Studies in Religion*, 25.2 (2009): 67–85.

35 Spivak, "Translator's Preface" (1995); Davis, "(Love is) the Ability of Not Knowing" (2002).

36 Sanders, *Gayatri Chakravorty Spivak*, 22. As Sanders explains, "speaking otherwise" is Spivak's rendering of allegory: *allos* (other) + *agoreuein* (public speech). See also, Paul de Man, *Allegories of Reading: Figural Language in Rousseau, Nietzsche, Rilke, and Proust* (New Haven, CT: Yale University Press, 1979), especially 300–1.

37 Sanders, *Gayatri Chakravorty Spivak*, 17–18.

38 Spivak, "Terror," 87, 94, 100 and 108–9.

39 Ibid., 108. Hannah Arendt, *Lectures on Kant's Political Philosophy*, edited with an Interpretive Essay by Ronald Beiner (Chicago, IL: University of Chicago Press, 1982).

40 Spivak, "Terror," 109.

41 Arendt, *Lectures*, 219–25. Arendt explicitly refers to Kant's Third Critique on 223.

42 "Kant's idea of a common ethical life—a *gemeines Wesen* for which the translation 'public sphere' would be altogether inadequate—is based not on the separation of the public and the private but on the fact that all human beings have the same reason and therefore the goal of humanity is collective" (Spivak, "Terror," 108).

43 Jacques Derrida and Bernard Stiegler, *Echographies of Television: Filmed Interviews*, translated by Jennifer Bajorek (Cambridge: Polity, 2002), 3–4.

44 Spivak, "Terror," 87.

45 Derrida, *Echographies of Television*, 11. Badiou's account, which I have discussed in the previous chapter, is, in a way, an almost religious desire to have the event of revolution without the experience of it. How fine everything would be if there were no difference!

Bibliography

Abdel-Jaouad, Hedi. "Isabelle Eberhardt: Portrait of the Artist as a Young Nomad." *Yale French Studies*, Vol. 2, No. 83 (1993), 93–117.

Abedi, Mehdi and Michael M. J. Fischer. *Debating Muslims: Cultural Dialogues in Postmodernity and Tradition*. Madison, WI: University of Wisconsin Press, 1990.

Abraham, Nicolas and Maria Torok. *The Wolf Man's Magic Word: A Cryptonymy*. Minneapolis, MN: University of Minnesota Press, 1986.

—. *The Shell and the Kernel: Renewals of Psychoanalysis*. Chicago, IL and London: University of Chicago Press, 1994.

Abu-Lughod, Lila. *Veiled Sentiments: Honor and Poetry in a Bedouin Society*. Berkeley, CA, Los Angeles, CA and London: University of California Press, 1986.

—. *Writing Women's Worlds: Bedouin Stories*. Berkeley, CA, Los Angeles, CA, and London: University of California Press, 1993.

Ali, Tariq. *The Clash of Fundamentalisms: Crusades, Jihads and Modernity*. London and New York: Verso, 2002.

Almond, Ian. *Sufism and Deconstruction: A Comparative Study of Derrida and Ibn 'Arabi*. London and New York: Routledge, 2004.

Al-Saji, Alia. "Merleau-Ponty and Bergson: Bodies of Expression and Temporalities in the Flesh." *Philosophy Today*, Vol. 45, No. 5 (2001), 110–23.

—. "The Temporality of Life: Merleau-Ponty, Bergson, and the Immemorial Past." *Southern Journal of Philosophy*, Vol. 45, No. 2 (2007), 177–206.

—. "'A Past Which Has Never Been Present': Bergsonian Dimensions in Merleau-Ponty's Theory of the Prepersonal." *Research in Phenomenology*, Vol. 38, No. 1 (2008), 41–71.

Althusser, Louis. *Lenin and Philosophy and Other Essays*. Translated by Ben Brewster. London and New York: Verso, 1977.

—. "The Only Materialist Tradition, Part I: Spinoza." In *The New Spinoza*. Edited by Walter Montag and Ted Stolze. Minneapolis, MN: University of Minnesota Press, 1998, 3–19.

Amin, Samir. "The Arab Revolutions: A Year After." *Interface: A Journal for and about Social Movements*, Vol. 4, No. 1 (May 2012), 33–42.

Aracagök, Zafer. "Decalcomania, Mapping and Mimesis." *Symploke*, Vol. 13, No. 1–2 (2005), 283–302.

—. *Desonance: Desonating (with) Deleuze*. Saarbrücken: VDM Verlag, 2009.

Arendt, Hannah. *Lectures on Kant's Political Philosophy*. Edited with an Interpretive Essay by Ronald Beiner. Chicago, IL: University of Chicago Press, 1982.

Asad, Talal. *Genealogies of Religion*. Baltimore: Johns Hopkins University Press, 1993.

—. *Formations of the Secular*. Stanford: Stanford University Press, 2003.

Back, Les. "Portrayal and Betrayal: Bourdieu, Photography and Sociological Life" *Sociological Review*, Vol. 57, No. 3 (2009), 471–90.

Badiou, Alain. *St. Paul: The Foundation of Universalism*. Translated by Ray Brassier. Stanford: Stanford University Press, 2003.

—. *The Rebirth of History: Times of Riots and Uprisings*. Translated by Gregory Elliott. New York and London: Verso, 2012.

Bachelard, Gaston. *The Poetics of Space*. Translated by Maria Jolas. Boston, MA: Beacon Press, 1969.

Bataille Georges. *Erotism: Death and Sensuality*. Translated by Mary Dalwood. San Francisco, CA: City Lights, 1986.

—. *The Accursed Share, Vol. I*. Translated by Robert Hurley. New York: Zone Books, 1988a.

—. *Inner Experience*. Translated by Leslie Ann Boldt. New York: SUNY Press, 1988b.

—. *Theory of Religion*. Translated by Robert Hurley. New York: Zone Books, 1992.

—. *The Accursed Share, Vols. II and III*. Translated by Robert Hurley. New York, Zone Books, 1993.

Baudrillard, Jean. *Symbolic Exchange and Death*. Translated by Ian Hamilton Grant. Los Angeles, CA and London: Sage, 2011.

Behar, Ruth and Deborah A. Gordon (eds). *Women Writing Culture*. Berkeley, CA and Los Angeles, CA: University of California Press, 1996.

Benjamin, Walter. *Illuminations: Essays and Reflections*. Translated by Harry Zohn. New York: Schocken Books, 1968.

—. *Reflections: Essays, Aphorisms, Autobiographical Writings*. Translated by Edmund Jephcott. Edited and with an Introduction by Peter Demetz. New York: Schocken Books, 1978.

Benveniste, Emile. *Problems in General Linguistics*. Translated by Mary Elizabeth Meek. Coral Gables, FL: University of Miami Press, 1971.

Bergson, Henri. *Time and Free Will: An Essay on the Immediate Data of Consciousness*. Translated by F. L. Pogson. London: George Allen and Unwin, 1950.

—. *Matter and Memory*. Translated by Nancy Margaret Paul and W. Scott Palmer. New York: Zone Books, 1991.

Benslama, Fethi. *Psychoanalysis and the Challenge of Islam*. Translated by Robert Bononno. Minneapolis, MN and London: University of Minnesota Press, 2009.

Bhabha, Homi K. *The Location of Culture*. London and New York: Routledge, 1994.

Blanchot, Maurice. *The Unavowable Community*. Translated by Pierre Joris. Barrytown, Station Hill, 1988.

—. *The Infinite Conversation*. Translated by Susan Hanson. Minneapolis, MN and London: University of Minnesota Press, 1993.

—. *Friendship*. Translated by Elizabeth Rottenberg. Stanford: University of California Press, 1997.

Bogue, Ronald. *Deleuze on Literature*. New York and London: Routledge, 2003.

Borch-Jacobsen, Mikkel. *The Emotional Tie: Psychoanalysis, Mimesis, Affect*. Translated by Douglas Brick. Stanford, CA: Stanford University Press, 1992.

Bourdieu, Pierre. *The Algerians*. Translated by Alan C. M. Ross. Boston, MA: Beacon Press, 1962.

—. *Outline of a Theory of Practice*. Translated by Richard Nice. Cambridge: Cambridge University Press, 1977.

—. *Algeria 1960*. Translated by Richard Nice. Cambridge, London, New York: Cambridge University Press, 1979.

—. *Homo Academicus*. Translated by Peter Collier. Stanford, CA: Stanford University Press, 1988.

—. *The Logic of Practice*. Translated by Richard Nice. Stanford, CA: Stanford University Press, 1990a.

—. *In Other Words: Essays Towards a Reflexive Sociology*. Translated by Richard Nice. Stanford, CA: Stanford University Press, 1990b.

—. *Language and Symbolic Power*. Translated by Gino Raymond and Matthew Adamson. Cambridge, MA: Harvard University Press, 1991.

—. *Practical Reason: On the Theory of Action*. Translated by Randall Johnson. Stanford, CA: Stanford University Press, 1998.

—. *Pascalian Meditations*. Translated by Matthew Adamson. Stanford, CA: Stanford University Press, 2000.

—. "Making the Economic Habitus: Algerian Workers Revisited." *Ethnography*, Vol. 1, No. 1 (2000), 17–41.

—. "Participant Objectivation." *Journal of Royal Anthropological Society*, Vol. 9, No. 2 (2003), 281–94.

—. "Algerian Landing." *Ethnography*, Vol. 5, No. 4 (2004), 415–43.

—. "The Peasant and His Body." *Ethnography*, Vol. 5, No. 4 (2004), 579–99.

—. *Sketch for a Self-Analysis*. Translated by Richard Nice. Cambridge, MA: Polity Press, 2007.

Bourdieu, Pierre and Jean-Claude Passseron. *Reproduction in Education, Society and Culture*. Translated by Richard Nice. London: Newburry Park, New Delhi: Sage, 1977.

Bourdieu, Pierre and Loïc W. D. Wacquant. *An Invitation to Reflexive Sociology*. Chicago, IL: University of Chicago Press, 1992.

Brito, Vanessa. "The Desert Island and the Missing People." *Parrhesia*, No. 6 (2009), 7–13.

Bulaç, Ali. "Medine Vesikası Hakkında Genel Bilgiler." *Birikim*, No. 38–9 (1992), 102–11.

Butler, Judith. *Bodies That Matter: On the Discursive Limits of "Sex."* New York: Routledge, 1993.

—. "Performativity's Social Magic." In *Bourdieu: A Critical Reader*. Edited by Richard Schusterman. Oxford: Blackwell, 1999, 113–28.

Calder, Angus. "Introduction." In *Seven Pillars of Wisdom*. Thomas E. Lawrence. London: Wordsworth, 1997, V–XXV.

Casarino, Cesare and Antonio Negri. *In Praise of the Common: A Conversation on Philosophy and Politics*. Minnesota and London: University of Minnesota Press, 2008.

Chatterjee, Partha. *Nationalist Thought and the Colonial World: A Derivative Discourse*. Minneapolis, MN: University of Minnesota Press, 1993.

Cheah, Pheng. "Posit(ion)ing Human Rights in the Current Global Conjuncture." *Public Culture*, Vol. 9, No. 2 (1997), 233–66.

—. "Given Culture: Rethinking Cosmopolitical Freedom in Transnationalism." In *Cosmopolitics: Thinking and Feeling Beyond the Nation*. Edited by Pheng Cheah and Bruce Robbins. Minneapolis, MN: University of Minnesota Press, 1998, 290–327.

—. "The Untimely Secret of Democracy." In *Derrida and the Time of the Political*. Edited by Pheng Cheah and Suzanne Guerlac. Durham and London: Duke University Press, 2009, 74–96.

Clifford, James. "Introduction: Partial Truths." In *Writing Culture: The Poetics and Politics of Ethnography*. Edited by James Clifford and George E. Marcus. Berkeley, CA, Los Angeles, CA, and London: University of California Press, 1986a, 1–27.

—. "On Ethnographic Allegory." In *Writing Culture: The Poetics and Politics of Ethnography*. Edited by James Clifford and George E. Marcus. Berkeley, CA, Los Angeles, CA, and London: University of California Press, 1986b, 98–121.

—. *The Predicament of Culture: Twentieth Century Ethnography, Literature and Art*. Cambridge, MA and London: Harvard University Press, 1988.

—. *Routes: Travel and Translation in the Late Twentieth Century*. Cambridge, MA: Harvard University Press, 1997.

—. "Mixed Feelings." In *Cosmopolitics: Thinking and Feeling Beyond the Nation*. Edited by Pheng Cheah and Bruce Robbins. Minneapolis, MN: University of Minnesota Press, 1998, 362–70.

—. *On the Edges of Anthropology, Interviews*. Chicago, IL: Prickly Paradigm, 2003.

Clifford, James and George E. Marcus (eds). *Writing Culture: The Poetics and Politics of Ethnography*. Berkeley, CA, Los Angeles, CA, and London: University of California Press, 1986.

Cohen, Sande. *Academia and the Luster of Capital*. Minneapolis, MN and London. University of Minnesota Press, 1993.

Colebrook, Claire. "Ethics, Positivity and Gender: Foucault, Aristotle and the Care of the Self." *Philosophy Today*, Vol. 42, No. 1 (1998), 40–52.

Colona, Fanny. "The Phantom of Dispossession: From *The Uprooting* . . . to *The Weight of the World*." In *Bourdieu in Algeria: Colonial Politics, Ethnographic Practices, Theoretical Developments*. Edited by Jane E. Goodman and Paul A. Silverstein. Lincoln, NE and London: University of Nebraska Press, 2009, 63–93.

Cowan, Jane K. *Dance and the Body Politic in Northern Greece*. Princeton: Prienceton University Press, 1990.

Dabashi, Hamid. *Post-Orientalism: Knowledge and Power in Time of Terror*. New Brunswick and London: Transaction Publishers, 2008.

—. *The Arab Spring: The End of Postcolonialism*. London and New York: Zed Books, 2012.

Davis, Dawn Rae. "(Love is) the Ability of Not Knowing: Feminist Experience of the Impossible in Ethical Singularity." *Hypatia*, Vol. 17, No. 2 (2002), 145–61.

De Certeau, Michel. *The Practice of Everyday Life*. Translated by Steven Rendall. Berkeley, CA: University of California Press, 1984.

Deleuze, Gilles. *Foucault*. Translated by Sean Hand. Minneapolis, MN: University of Minnesota Press, 1988.

—. *Cinema 2: The Time-Image*. Translated by Hugh Tomlinson and Robert Galeta. Minneapolis, MN: University of Minnesota Press, 1989.

—. *The Logic of Sense*. Translated by Mark Lester and Charles Stivale. New York: Columbia University Press, 1990a.

—. *Negotiations 1972–1990*. Translated by Martin Joughin. New York: Columbia University Press, 1990b.

—. *Bergsonism*. Translated by Hugh Tomlinson and Barbara Habberjam. New York: Zone Books, 1991a.

—. *Masochism: Coldness and Cruelty*. Translated by Jean McNeil. New York: Zone Books, 1991b.

—. *The Fold: Leibniz and the Baroque*. Foreword and Translation by Tom Conley. Minneapolis, MN and London: University of Minnesota Press, 1993.

—. *Difference and Repetition*. Translated by Paul Patton. New York: Columbia University Press, 1994.

—. *Essays Critical and Clinical*. Translated by Daniel W. Smith and Michael A. Greco. Minneapolis, MN: University of Minnesota Press, 1997a.

—. "The Shame and the Glory: T. E. Lawrence." In *Essays Critical and Clinical*. Translated by Daniel W. Smith and Michael A. Greco. Minneapolis, MN: University of Minnesota Press, 1997b, 115–25.

—. *Desert Islands and Other Texts: 1953–1974*. Edited by David Lapoujade. Translated by Michael Taormina. New York: Semiotexte, 2004a.

—. *Francis Bacon: The Logic of Sensation*. Translated by Daniel W. Smith. Minneapolis, MN: University of Minnesota Press, 2004b.

Deleuze, Gilles and Felix Guattari. *Anti-Oedipus*. Translated by Robert Hurley, Mark Seem, and Helen R. Lane. Minneapolis, MN: University of Minnesota Press, 1983.

—. *A Thousand Plateaus*. Translated by Brian Massumi. Minneapolis, MN: University of Minnesota Press, 1987.

—. *Kafka: Toward a Minor Literature*. Translated by Dana Polan. Minneapolis, MN and London: University of Minnesota Press, 1989.

—. *What is Philosophy?* Translated by Hugh Tomlinson and Graham Burchell. New York: Columbia University Press, 1994.

De Man, Paul. *Allegories of Reading: Figural Language in Rousseau, Nietzsche, Rilke, and Proust*. New Haven, CT: Yale University Press, 1979.

—. *Blindness and Insight: Essays in the Rhetoric of Contemporary Criticism*. Minneapolis, MN: University of Minnesota Press, 1983.

Derrida, Jacques. *Speech and Phenomena and Other Essays on Husserl's Theory of Signs*. Translated by David Allison. Evanston, IL: Northwestern University Press, 1973.

—. *Of Grammatology*. Translated by Gayatri Chakravorty Spivak. Baltimore, MD and London: Johns Hopkins University Press, 1976.

—. *Writing and Difference*. Translated by Alan Bass. Chicago, IL: University of Chicago Press, 1978.

—. *Dissemination*. Translated by Barbara Johnson. Chicago, IL: University of Chicago Press, 1981.

—. *Positions*. Translated by Alan Bass. Chicago, IL: University of Chicago Press, 1981.

—. *Margins of Philosophy*. Translated by Alan Bass. Chicago, IL: University of Chicago Press, 1982.

—. "Geschlecht: Sexual Difference, Ontological Difference." *Research in Phenomenology*, Vol. 13 (1983), 65–83.

—. "*Fors*: The Anglish Words of Nicholas Abraham and Maria Torok." Translated by Barbara Johnson. Foreword to Abraham, Nicolas and Maria Torok. *The Wolf Man's Magic Word: A Cryptonymy*. Minneapolis, MN: University of Minnesota Press, 1986, xi–xlviii.

—. *The Ear of the Other: Otobiography, Transference, Translation*. Translated by Peggy Kamuf and Avital Ronell. Lincoln, NE and London: University of Nebraska Press, 1988.

—. *Memoirs for Paul de Man* (revised edn). Translated by Cecile Lindsay, Jonathan Culler, Eduardo Cadava, and Peggy Kamuf. New York: Columbia University Press, 1989.

—. *Cinders*. Translated by Ned Lukacher. Lincoln, NE: University of Nebraska Press, 1991.

—. *Given Time I: Counterfeit Money*. Translated by Peggy Kamuf. Chicago, IL and London: University of Chicago Press, 1992.

—. *Aporias*. Translated by T. Dutoit. Stanford, CA: Stanford University Press, 1993.

—. *Specters of Marx: The State of the Debt, the Work of Mourning and the New International*. Translated by Peggy Kamuf. New York and London: Routledge, 1994.

—. *Politics of Friendship*. Translated by George Collins. London and New York: Verson, 1997.

—. *Acts of Religion*. Translated by Gil Anidjar. New York and London: Routledge, 2002.

—. *Rogues: Two Essays on Reason*. Translated by Pascale-Anne Brault and Michael Naas. Stanford, CA: Stanford University Press, 2005.

Derrida, Jacques and Jean-Luc Nancy. "'Eating Well' or the Calculation of the Subject: An interview with Jacques Derrida." In *Who Comes After the Subject?* Edited by

Eduardo Cadava, Peter Connor, and Jean-Luc Nancy. New York and London: Routledge, 1991, 96–119.

Derrida, Jacques and Bernard Stiegler. *Echographies of Television: Filmed Interviews.* Translated by Jennifer Bajorek. London: Polity Press, 2002.

De Vries, Hent (ed.). *Religion: Beyond a Concept.* New York: Fordham University Press, 2008.

Direk, Zeynep. "On the Sources and Structure of Derrida's Radical Notion of Experience." *Tympanum: A Journal of Comparative Literary Studies*, Vol. 4 (2000), www.usc.edu/dept/comp-lit/tympanum/4/direk.html

Djebar, Assia. *Women of Algiers in Their Apartments.* Translated by Marjolijn de Jager. Charlottesville and London: University Press of Virginia/Caraf Books, 1992.

—. *Far From Madina.* Translated by Dorothy S. Blair. London: Quartet Books, 1995.

—. *L'amour, la fantasia.* Paris: Edition Albin Michele, 1996.

—. *Aşk ve Fantazya.* Translated by Ayşegül Sönmezay. Istanbul: Can, 2001.

Doughty, Charles Montagu. *Travels in Arabia Deserta*, Volumes I and II. London: Elibron, 2006.

Eberhardt, Isabelle. *The Oblivion Seekers.* Translated by Paul Bowles. San Francisco, CA: City Lights, 1975.

—. *In the Shadow of Islam.* Translated by Sharon Bangert. London: Peter Owen, 1993.

Fabian, Johannes. *Time and the Other: How Anthropology Makes Its Object.* New York: Columbia University Press, 1983.

—. *Time and the Work of Anthropology: Critical Essays 1971–1991.* Chur, Switzerland and Philadelphia, PA: Harwood Academic, 1991.

Fanon, Frantz. *The Wretched of the Earth.* Translated by Contance Farrington. New York: Grove Weidenfeld, 1963.

—. *Black Skin White Masks.* Translated by Charles Lam Markmann. London: Pluto Press, 2008.

Fischer, Michael M. J. *Emergent Forms of Life and the Anthropological Voice.* Durham, NC: Duke University Press, 2003.

Foucault, Michel. *Archeology of Knowledge, and the Discourse on Language.* Translated by A. M. Sheridan Smith. New York: Pantheon Books, 1972.

—. *The Birth of the Clinic. An Archeology of Medical Perception.* Translated by A. M. Sheridan. London: Tavistock Publications, 1976.

—. *Discipline and Punish: The Birth of the Prison.* Translated by Alan Sheridan. Harmondsworth: Penguin, 1978.

—. *Power/Knowledge: Selected Interviews and Other Writings: 1972–1977.* Edited by Colin Gordon. New York: Pantheon Books, 1980a.

—. *History of Sexuality*, Vol. 1. Translated by Robert Hurley. New York: Vintage, 1980b.

—. *The Use of Pleasure (The History of Sexuality Vol. 2).* Translated by Robert Hurley. New York: Vintage Books, 1985.

—. *The Care of the Self (The History of Sexuality Vol. 3).* Translated by Robert Hurley. New York: Pantheon Books, 1986.

—. *The Birth of Biopolitics: Lectures at the College de France 1978–1979*. Translated by Graham Burchell. New York: Picador/Palgrave MacMillan, 2008.

Gadamer, Hans-Georg. *Truth and Method*. Translated by Joel Weinsheimer and Donald G. Marshall. London and New York: Continuum, 2004.

Geertz, Clifford. *Local Knowledge: Further Essays in Interpretive Anthropology*. New York: Basic Books, 1983.

Gil, Jose. *Metamorphoses of the Body*. Translated by Stephen Muecke. Minneapolis, MN and London: University of Minnesota Press, 1998.

Göle, Nilüfer. *The Forbidden Modern: Civilization and Veiling*. Michigan: University of Michigan Press, 1997.

—. *Modern Mahrem: Medeniyet ve Örtünme*. Istanbul: Metis, 1991.

Goodman, Jane E. "The Proverbial Bourdieu: Habitus and the Politics of Representation in the Ethnography of Kabylia." In *Bourdieu in Algeria: Colonial Politics, Ethnographic Practices, Theoretical Developments*. Edited by Jane E. Goodman and Paul A. Silverstein. Lincoln, NE and London: University of Nebraska Press, 2009, 94–132.

Goodman, Jane E. and Paul A. Silverstein (eds). *Bourdieu in Algeria: Colonial Politics, Ethnographic Practices, Theoretical Developments*. Lincoln, NE and London. University of Nebraska Press, 2009.

Gramsci, Antonio. *Selections from Prison Notebooks*. Translated by Quintin Hoare and Geoffrey Nowell Smith. London: Lawrence and Wishart, 1971.

Grosz, Elizabeth. *Time Travels: Feminism, Nature, Power*. Durham: Duke University Press, 2005.

Guerlac, Suzanne. "The Useless Image: Bataille, Bergson, Magritte." *Representations*, Vol. 97, No. 1 (2007), 28–56.

Hammoudi, Abdellah. "Phenomenology and Ethnography: On Kabyle Habitus in the Work of Pierre Bourdieu." In *Bourdieu in Algeria: Colonial Politics, Ethnographic Practices, Theoretical Developments*. Edited by Jane E. Goodman and Paul A. Silverstein. Lincoln, NE and London: University of Nebraska Press, 2009, 199–254.

Holland, Eugene W. "Representation and Misrepresentation in Postcolonial Literature and Theory." *Research in African Literatures*, Vol. 34, No. 1 (2003), 159–73.

Hoşgör, Evren. "Islamic Capital/Anatolian Tigers: Past and Present." *Middle Eastern Studies*, Vol. 47, No. 2 (2011), 343–60.

Husserl, Edmund. *On the Phenomenology of the Consciousness of Internal Time*. Translated by John Barnett Brough. Dordrecht, Boston, MA, London. Kluwer Academic Publishers, 1991.

Jackson, Stephen. "The Subject of Time in Foucault's Tale of Jouy." *SubStance*, Vol. 39, No. 2 (2010), 39–51.

Jameson, Fredric. *Postmodernism, or the Cultural Logic of Late Capitalism*. Durham, NC: Duke University Press, 1991.

Jenkins, Tim. "Bourdieu's Béarnais Ethnography." *Theory, Culture & Society*, Vol. 23, No. 6 (2006), 45–72.

Kant, Immanuel. *Critique of Pure Reason*. Translated by Paul Guyer and Allen W. Wood. Cambridge: Cambridge University Press, 1998.

—. *Religion within the Boundaries of Mere Reason and Other Writings*. Translated and Edited by Allen W. Wood and George Di Giovanni. Cambridge: Cambridge University Press, 1998.

—. *Critique of Judgment*. Translated by James Creed Meredith. Oxford: Oxford University Press, 2007.

Karamustafa, Ahmet T. *God's Unruly Friends: Dervish Groups in the Islamic Middle Period 1200–1550*. Salt Lake City: University of Utah Press, 1994.

Khatibi, Abdelkebir. "Frontiers: Between Psychoanalysis and Islam." Translated by Burcu Yalım. *Third Text*, Vol. 23, No. 6 (2009), 689–96.

Khatibi, Abdelkebir and Mohammed Sijelmassi. *The Splendor of Islamic Calligraphy*. London: Thames and Hudson, 1976.

Kierkegaard, Søren. *The Sickness unto Death*. Translated by Alastair Hannay. London and New York: Penguin, 1989.

Kirby, Vicki. "Re-writing: Postmodernism and Ethnography." *Mankind*, Vol. 19, No. 1 (1989), 36–45.

—. "Viral Identities: Feminisms and Postmodernisms." In *Australian Women: New Feminist Perspectives*. Edited by Ailsa Burns and Norma Grieve. Oxford: Oxford University Press, 1993, 120–32.

—. *Telling Flesh: The Substance of the Corporeal*. New York and London: Routledge, 1997.

Kochuyt, Thierry. "God, Gifts and Poor People: On Charity in Islam." *Social Compass*, Vol. 56, No. 1 (2009), 98–116.

Lacoue-Labarthe, Philippe. "Talks." *Diacritics*, Vol. 14, No. 3 (1984), 23–37.

—. *Typography: Mimesis, Philosophy, Politics*. Edited by Christopher Fynsk. Stanford, CA: Stanford University Press, 1989.

—. *The Subject of Philosophy*. Edited by Thomas Tresize. Translated by Thomas Tresize, Hugh J. Silverman, Gary M. Cole, Timothy D. Bent, Karen McPherson, and Claudette Sartiliot. Minneapolis, MN and London: University of Minnesota Press, 1993.

Lacoue-Labarthe, Phillipe and Jean-Luc Nancy. *The Literary Absolute: The Theory of Literature in German Romanticism*. Translated by Philip Barnard and Cheryl Lester. Albany, NY: SUNY Press, 1988.

Lavie, Smadar. *The Poetics of Military Occupation: Mzeina Allegories of Bedouin Identity Under Israeli and Egyptian Rule*. Berkeley, CA, Los Angeles, CA, and London: University of California Press, 1990.

Lawrence, Thomas Edward. *Seven Pillars of Wisdom*. London: Wordsworth Classics, 1997.

Leroi-Gourhan, André. *Gesture and Speech*. Translated by Ann Bostock Berger. Cambridge, MA and London: MIT Press, 1993.

Levinas, Emmanuel. *Totality and Infinity: An Essay on Exteriority*. Translated by Alphonso Lingis. Pittsburgh, PA: Duquesen University Press, 1969.

—. *Ethics and Infinity: Conversations with Philippe Nemo.* Translated by Richard A. Cohen. Pittsburgh, PA: Duquesne University Press, 1985.

—. *Time and the Other.* Translated by Richard A. Cohen. Pittsburgh, PA: Duquesne University Press, 1987.

—. *Existence and Existents.* Translated by Alphonso Lingis. Dordrecht: Kluwert Academic Publishers, 1988.

—. *God, Death, and Time.* Translated by Bettina Bergo. Stanford, CA: Stanford University Press, 1993.

Lewis, David. *Counterfactuals.* Oxford: Blackwell, 1973.

Lyotard, Jean-François. *The Postmodern Condition: A Report on Knowledge.* Translated by Geoff Bennington and Brian Massumi. Minneapolis, MN: University of Minnesota Press, 1984.

—. *The Differend: Phrases in Dispute.* Translated by Georges Van Den Abbeele. Minneapolis, MN: University of Minnesota Press, 1988.

Mahmood, Saba. "Rehearsed spontaneity and the conventionality of ritual: Disciplines of *Salat.*" *American Ethnologist*, Vol. 28, No. 4 (2001a), 827–53.

—. "Feminist Theory, Embodiment, and the Docile Agent: Some Reflections on the Egyptian Islamic Revival." *Cultural Anthropology*, Vol. 16, No. 2 (2001b) 202–36.

—. "Ethical Formation and Politics of Individual Autonomy in Contemporary Egypt." *Social Research*, Vol. 70, No. 3 (2003), 837–66.

—. *The Politics of Piety: The Islamic Revival and the Feminist Subject.* Princeton, NJ and Oxford. Princeton University Press, 2005.

Malabou, Catherine. "Addiction and Grace: Preface to Felix Ravaisson's *Of Habit.*" In *Of Habit.* Felix Ravaisson. Translated by Claire Carlisle and Mark Sinclair. Preface by Catherine Malabou. London and New York: Continuum, 2008, VII–XX.

Mamdani, Mahmood. *Good Muslim, Bad Muslim: America, the Cold War, and the Roots of Terror.* New York: Pantheon Books, 2004.

Marcus, George E. *Ethnography through Thick and Thin.* Princeton, NJ: Princeton University Press, 1998.

Marcus, George and Michael M. J. Fischer. *Anthropology as Cultural Critique.* Chicago, IL: University of Chicago Press, 1986.

Mardin, Şerif. *Religion and Social Change in Turkey.* New York: SUNY Press, 1989.

Marrati, Paola. *Genesis and Trace: Derrida Reading Husserl and Heidegger.* Stanford, CA: Stanford University Press, 2005.

Massad, Joseph. "Psychoanalysis, Islam and the Other of Liberalism." *Umbr(a): A Journal of the Unconscious: Special Issue on Islam* (2009), 43–68.

Massignon, Louis. *Testimonies and Reflections: Essays of Louis Massignon.* Edited by Herbert Mason. Notre Dame, IN: Notre Dame University Press, 1989.

Mauss, Marcel. *The Gift: Forms and Functions of Exchange in Archaic Societies.* Translated by Ian Gunnison. New York. Norton & Company, 1967.

Merleau-Ponty, Maurice. *Phenomenology of Perception.* Translated by Colin Smith. London and New York. Routledge, 1989.

—. *The Visible and the Invisible*. Translated by Alphonso Lingis. Evanston, IL: North Western University Press, 1997.

Miller, Christopher L. "The Postidentitarian Predicament in the Footnotes of *A Thousand Plateaus*: Nomadology, Anthropology, and Authority" *Diacritics*, Vol. 23, No. 3 (1993), 6–35.

—. *Nationalists and Nomads: Essays on Francophone Literature and Culture*. Chicago, IL and London: Chicago University Press, 1998.

—. "'We Shouldn't Judge Deleuze and Guattari': A Response to Eugene Holland." *Research in African Literatures*, Vol. 34, No. 3 (2003), 129–41.

Miller, Hillis J. "Derrida's Politics of Autoimmunity" *Discourse*, Vol. 30. No. 1 & 2 (2008), 208–25.

Morey, Peter and Amina Yagin. *Framing Muslims: Stereotyping and Representation After 9/11*. Cambridge, MA: Harvard University Press, 2011.

Nietzsche, Friedrich. *The Will to Power*. Translated by Walter Kaufmann and R. J. Hollingdale. New York: Vintage Books, 1968.

—. *Twilight of the Idols & the Anti-Christ*. Translated by R. J. Hollingdale. Harmondsworth: Penguin, 1978.

Noys, Benjamin. *Georges Bataille: A Critical Introduction*. London: Pluto, 2000.

Plato, *The Republic*. Translated by Raymond Larson. Arlington Heights, IL: Harlan Davidson, 1979.

Porter, Dennis. "Orientalism and Its Problems." In *The Politics of Theory: Proceedings of the Essex Conference on the Sociology of Literature*. Edited by Francis Barker, Peter Hulme, Margaret Iversen, and Diana Loxley. Colchester: University of Essex, 1983, 179–93.

Rancière, Jacques. *The Philosopher and His Poor*. Translated by John Drury, Corinne Oster, and Andrew Parker. Durham and London: Duke University Press, 2004.

—. *Staging the People: The Proletarian and His Double*. Translated by David Fernbach. London and New York: Verso, 2011.

—. *The Intellectual and His People: Staging the People, Vol. 2*. Translated by David Fernbach. London and New York: Verso, 2012.

Ravaisson, Felix. *Of Habit*. Translated by Claire Carlisle and Mark Sinclair. Preface by Catherine Malabou. London and New York: Continuum, 2008.

Rice, Laura. "'Nomad Thought': Isabelle Eberhardt and the Colonial Project." *Cultural Critique*, No. 17 (1990–1), 151–76.

Root, Deborah. "Misadventures in the Desert: *The Sheltering Sky* as Colonialist Nightmare." *Inscriptions*, No. 6 (1992), 81–96; http://culturalstudies.ucsc.edu/PUBS/Inscriptions/vol_6/Root.html

Rosaldo, Renato. *Culture and Truth: The Remaking of Social Analysis*. Boston, MA: Beacon Press, 1993.

Runions, Erin. "Detranscendentalizing Decisionism: Political Theology after Gayatri Spivak." *Journal of Feminist Studies in Religion*, Vol. 25, No. 2 (Fall 2009), 67–85.

Rushdie, Salman. *Imaginary Homelands: Essays and Criticism 1981–1991*. London: Granta, 1991.

—. *The Satanic Verses*. New York: Viking, 1989.

Said, Edward W. *Orientalism*. Harmondworth: Penguin, 1978.

—. *Covering Islam: How the Media and the Experts Determine How We See the Rest of the World*. New York: Pantheon Books, 1981.

—. *Freud and the Non-European*. London and New York: Verso, 2003.

Sanders, Mark. *Gayatri Chakravorty Spivak: Live Theory*. New York and London: Continuum, 2006.

Schlegel, Friedrich. *Philosophical Fragments*. Translated by Peter Firchow. Foreword by Rodolphe Gasché. Minneapolis, MN and Oxford: University of Minnesota Press, 1991.

Schmitt, Carl. *Political Theology: Four Chapters on the Concept of Sovereignty*. Translated by George Schwab. Cambridge, MA and London, England: MIT Press, 1985.

Shariati, Ali. *The Hajj*. Translated by Ali A. Behzadnia, MD and Najla Denny. Houston, TX: Free Islamic Literatures Inc., 1994.

Shariati, Ali. "Our Expectations of the Muslim Woman." Available at www.iranchamber. com/personalities/ashariati/works/expectations_of_muslim_woman.php

—. *Fatima is Fatima*. Translated by Laleh Bakhtiar. Tehran: The Shariati Foundation and Hamdami Publishers, 1980. Available at www.al-islam.org/fatimaisfatima/

Shostak, Marjorie. *Nisa: The Life and Words of a !Kung Woman*. New York: Vintage Books, 1983.

Silber, Ilana F. "Bourdieu's Gift to Gift Theory: An Unacknowledged Trajectory." *Sociological Theory*, Vol. 27, No. 2 (2009), 173–90.

Silverman, Kaja. *Male Subjectivity at the Margins*. New York and London: Routledge, 1992.

Smith, Daniel W. "Translator's Introduction. Deleuze on Bacon: Three Conceptual Trajectories in *The Logic of Sensation*." In *Francis Bacon: The Logic of Sensation*. Gilles Deleuze. Translated by Daniel W. Smith. Afterword by Tom Conley. Minneapolis, MN: University of Minnesota Press, 2004, vii–xxxiii.

Smith, Paul. *Discerning the Subject*. Foreword by John Mowitt. Minneapolis, MN: University of Minnesota Press, 1988.

Smith, Philip. "Marcel Proust as Successor and Precursor to Pierre Bourdieu: A Fragment." *Thesis Eleven*, Vol. 79, No. 1 (2004), 105–11.

Spivak, Gayatri Chakravorty. *In Other Worlds*. New York and London: Routledge, 1988a.

—. "Subaltern Studies: Deconstructing Historiography." In *Selected Subaltern Studies*. Edited by Ranajit Guha and Gayatri Chakravorty Spivak. New York and Oxford: Oxford University Press, 1988b, 3–32.

—. *The Postcolonial Critic*. Edited by Sarah Harasym. New York and London: Routledge, 1990a.

—. "Reading *The Satanic Verses*." *Third Text*, Vol. 4, No. 11 (1990b), 41–60.

—. *Outside in the Teaching Machine*. New York and London: Routledge, 1993

—. "Psychoanalysis in left field and fieldworking: examples to fit the title." In *Speculations after Freud: Psychoanalysis, Philosophy and Culture*. Edited by Sonu Shamdasani and Michael Munchow. London and New York: Routledge, 1994, 41–76.

—. "Translator's Preface." In *Imaginary Maps*. Mahasweta Devi. Translated by Gayatri Chakravorty Spivak. New York and London: Routledge, 1995a, xxiii–xxx.

—. "Ghostwriting." *Diacritics*, Vol. 25, No. 2 (1995b), 65–84.

—. "Echo." In *The Spivak Reader: Selected Works of Gayatri Chakravorty Spivak*. Edited by Donna Landry and Gerald MacLean. New York: Routledge, 1996.

—. *A Critique of Postcolonial Reason*. Cambridge, MA: Harvard University Press, 1999.

—. "From Haverstock Hill Flat to US. Classroom, What's Left of Theory?" In *What's Left of Theory? New Work on the Politics of Literary Theory*. Edited by Judith Butler, John Guillory, and Kendall Thomas. New York: Routledge, 2000.

—. "Terror: A Speech After 9/11." *boundary 2*, Vol. 31, No. 2 (2004), 81–111.

Spivak, Gayatri Chakravorty, Sara Danius, and Stefan Jonsson. "An Interview with Gayatri Spivak." *Boundary 2*, Vol. 20, No. 2 (Summer 1993), 24–50.

Starrett, Gregory. "The Hexis of Interpretation: Islam and the Body in the Egyptian Popular School." *American Ethnologist*, Vol. 22, No. 4 (1995), 953–69.

Strauss, Erwin. *The Primary World of Senses: A Vindication of Sensory Experience*. Translated by Jacob Needleman. New York: Free Press of Glencoe, 1963.

Taylor, Mark (ed.). *Deconstruction in Context: Literature and Philosophy*. Chicago, IL: University of Chicago Press, 1986.

Terranova, Tiziana. "Futurepublic: On Information Warfare, Bio-racism and Hegemony as Noopolitics." *Theory, Culture and Society*, Vol. 24, No. 3 (2007), 125–45.

The Holy Qur'an. Translated by Abdullah Yusuf Ali. Wordsworth: Hertforshire, 2000.

Toscano, Alberto. "Dual Power Revisited: From Civil War to Biopolitical Islam." *Soft Targets*, Vol. 2, No. 1 (2007). Available at www.softtargetsjournal.com/v21/alberto_toscano.php.

Tyler, Stephen. "The Vision Quest in the West or What the Mind's Eye Sees." *Journal of Anthropological Research*, Vol. 40, No. 1 (1984), 23–40.

—. *The Unspeakable: Discourse, Dialogue and Rhetoric in the Postmodern World*. Madison, WI: University of Wisconsin Press, 1988.

Warren, Bill. *Imperialism, the Pioneer of Capitalism*. London: Verso, 1980.

Visweswaran, Kamala. *Fictions of Feminist Ethnography*. Minneapolis, MN: University of Minnesota Press, 1994.

Wuthnow, Julie: "Deleuze in the Postcolonial: On Nomads and Indigenous Politics." *Feminist Theory*, Vol. 3, No. 2 (2002), 183–200.

Williams, Raymond. *Culture and Society: 1780–1950*. New York and London: Columbia University Press, 1983.

—. *Marxism and Literature*. Oxford and New York: Oxford University Press, 1985.

Yeğenoğlu, Meyda. *Colonial Fantasies: Towards a Feminist Reading of Orientalism*. Cambridge: Cambridge University Press, 1998.

—. *Islam, Migrancy and Hospitality in Europe*. Palgrave-Macmillan: New York, 2012.

Žižek, Slavoj. *The Fragile Absolute: Why is the Christian Legacy Worth Fighting for?* New York and London: Verso, 2001.

—. *The Puppet and the Dwarf: The Perverse Core of Christianity*. Boston, MA: MIT Press, 2003.

—. "A Glance into the Archives of Islam." Available at www.lacan.com/zizarchives.htm

Index